The Waterworks Of London: Together With A Series Of Articles On Various Other Waterworks

Zerah Colburn, William Henry Maw

J. H. Cooper
Jan 20 '68
Philada.

THE

WATERWORKS OF LONDON,

TOGETHER WITH

A SERIES OF ARTICLES

ON

VARIOUS OTHER WATERWORKS.

BY

ZERAH COLBURN AND WILLIAM H. MAW.

(Reprinted from "ENGINEERING.")

PHILADELPHIA:

HENRY CAREY BAIRD,

INDUSTRIAL PUBLISHER,

406 WALNUT STREET.

1868.

CONTENTS.

PART I.

THE WATERWORKS OF LONDON.

PART II.

PROPOSED SCHEMES FOR SUPPLYING WATER TO THE METROPOLIS.

PART III.

MISCELLANEOUS ARTICLES ON WATERWORKS AND WATER SUPPLY.

THE WATERWORKS OF LONDON.

PART I.

At a time when the importance of an unfailing supply of absolutely pure water to the metropolis is becoming so generally recognised, and when it is considered likely that the existing private companies may yet be pensioned off upon their present yearly dividends, and their works superseded by a single and great metropolitan aqueduct from Wales or Westmoreland, it will be convenient to take a general view of these works, and especially of their mode of collecting, raising, and delivering water to consumers.

The metropolis, now numbering upwards of three millions of inhabitants, and covering about 130 square miles, is supplied with water by eight private companies. The present supply averages about 33 gallons per head daily, or about 105 million gallons in all. Of this supply, nearly one-half is drawn from the River Lea and from chalk-springs near Ware, nearly one-half from the Thames, and the rest from the Ravensbourne and from chalk-springs in the valley of that river. The New River and the East London Companies, supplying water from the valley of the Lea, deliver nearly as much daily as the other six companies together. Not, of course, that the Lea is capable of supplying anything like the amount of water to be obtained from the Thames. The Lea, as gauged by Mr. Beardmore at Feilde's Weir, twenty miles from the Thames at Blackwall, and five and a half miles below Ware Mill, discharged a mean overflow of 11,800 cubic feet per minute in 1851 (exclusive of the water abstracted by the New River), 17,892 cubic feet in 1852, and 10,915 cubic feet in 1856. This was from a drainage area of 444 square miles, lying from 80 ft. to 500 ft. above the sea. The length of the main stream above Feilde's Weir is 31 miles, and of its tributaries 92 miles. Now, the Thames, above Staines (below Windsor, and only a few miles above London), has a drainage area of 3086 square miles, and its mean annual discharge is 100,000 cubic feet per minute, or 900,000,000 imperial gallons per day—a quantity eight times beyond the present utmost requirements of the whole metropolis.

The mean summer flow of rivers is, of course, much less than their annual mean, and that of the Lea at Feilde's Weir may be set down at from 6000 to 8000 cubic feet per minute, varying with the season. So great, indeed, is this variation, that Mr. Beardmore has gauged 106,975 cubic feet per minute at one time (November, 1852), and only 4119 cubic feet at another. In addition, however, to these gaugings at Feilde's, there is the whole quantity abstracted above that point by the New River, partly from the Lea and partly from deep springs which would otherwise flow into that river. This additional quantity is now about 2700 or 2800 cubic feet per minute, on the average.

As for the water of the Lea, we may quote here the observations of Mr. Beardmore, the well-known hydraulic engineer, and the author of the valuable "Manual of Hydrology." He says: "The Lea and branches take their rise among hills of gentle inclination, with flat summits about 250 ft. to 350 ft. above the sea. The total area, above its junction with the Thames at Blackwall, is 700 square miles, but its more important feeders cease at 16 miles from the Thames, where the basin is about 500 square miles, and 100 ft. above the sea. Below this point there are clay lands on one side of the valley, and faults, which cut off the chalk beds, occur on the opposite side, so that in dry periods there is but little additional visible feed to the valley. This small river is well known for its pure sources in the tertiary sands and chalk hills of Hertfordshire; hence it has always been a favourite water for the supply of London, and it is owing to the Thames having a similar source, for a large proportion of its volume, that it bears such a high character as a pure potable water. One of the branches of the Lea has such great beds of sand and perennial springs, that the heaviest rains will not produce a flood in the strict sense. It is not uncommon for many months to pass without a sensible discoloration of the Lea water by floods."

The "purity" of the Lea and Thames waters, even at their original sources, is only relative, inasmuch as they contain more than ten times the solid matter per gallon to be found in the waters of the mountain lakes. But in traversing large and thickly inhabited districts they necessarily become contaminated to some extent with sewage and the earthy and organic matters of surface drainage. The grosser particles may be, and are, separated by subsidence and filtration; but, after all, really pure water, unless it be *aqua pura*, as distilled by the chemists, is unknown in London.

We shall divide our account of the water supply of the metropolis into notices of the works of the several companies, and of these the oldest and largest is the

NEW RIVER COMPANY.

The New River, begun in May, 1609, and opened in 1613, by Hugh Myddelton, who was knighted on its completion, has its source in the Chadwell spring, near Ware, at a distance of about 20 miles in a direct line from London. As originally constructed, its length was 38¾ miles; but many of the bends—some of them about Enfield, and between Southgate and Hornsey, being of great extent— have been superseded by direct cuts, and the present length is 28 miles. The original uniform inclination of the river was said to be 3 in. per mile, and as the New River " Head," as the London receiving basin is still called, is 81.8 ft. above Trinity high-water mark, or 94.3 ft. above Ordnance datum (approximate mean tide at Liverpool), the real head or source of the " river " would thus have an elevation of about 91¼ ft. and 103¾ ft. above the respective data. We believe, however, that the inclination of the river was greater, since the level of the Stoke Newington reservoirs is 5.7 ft. above that of New River Head, being 87.5 ft. and 100 ft. above the respective data. With the exception of the source at Chadwell, we give these and other levels as measured above Trinity high water, from the valuable topographical and contour map of the metropolis prepared by R. W. Mylne, C.E., and published for him by Stanford, in 1856. The Chadwell spring was reported to the Board of Health, in 1856, to have a mean discharge of 500 cubic feet per minute, equal to 4,500,000 gallons per day. A little lower down, the Amwell well gives 196 cubic feet by pumping on a 30 ft. lift; the Amwell Hill well gives 285 cubic feet, on a 50 ft. lift. At Cheshunt, nearly half way to London, is a well giving 50 cubic feet per minute, on a lift of 105 ft. These springs and wells do not, however, furnish one-fourth of the present supply, the remainder being drawn from the Lea, near Hertford, the sewage of which town is intercepted from the river. The proportion now drawn from the Lea is 85 per cent. of the entire supply. In 1856, the total quantity drawn directly from the Lea was 1340 cubic feet per minute, the powers of the company permit- ting them to take, if required, 2500 cubic feet. The total present supply from all sources is upwards of 2800 cubic feet per minute, or above 25,000,000 gallons daily; and during the present summer (1866) the company has supplied 180 million gallons weekly. This quantity has been distributed over seventeen square miles of the metropolis, to a po- pulation of upwards of half a million inhabitants, the number of houses supplied in July last being 112,245. This, of course, is exclusive of the

19,000,000 gallons drawn daily from the Lea, near Tottenham, by the East London Company.

The "river," or artificial channel, is of varying width and depth, at places 28 ft. wide, while in many parts it is hardly half that width. The "river," indeed, so far as we can learn, has never been accurately described, the officers of the company having, we believe, always refused particulars of their works for publication. At any rate, they have repeatedly declined to contribute a paper upon them to the Institution of Civil Engineers, and, beyond a few details scattered in various tracts and reports, the library of that body has absolutely no account of this, the principal undertaking for the supply of water to London. A popular account, with statistical details of the reservoirs, &c., appeared a few years since in a weekly paper; and Mr. Burnell, in his "Visits to the London Waterworks," published ten years ago, in the *Journal of Gas Lighting*, gave a few particulars not to be found elsewhere; but, imperfect as it is, our own account will be found by far the most complete of any yet published of the New River works. Mr. Smiles obtained some little information from the engineer to the company for his "Life of Sir Hugh Myddelton," but he gives the delivery of water by the New River as equal to 42 square feet of section at *two* miles an hour, equal, as will be seen by calculation, to 7392 cubic feet per minute, which is much more than twice its present total flow. In describing the works of the other companies, we shall, with a single exception (and this is not a Thames company), have the advantage of the kind co-operation of their engineers, and shall be able to give drawings of some of the engines, and various plans of value to the profession.

The bed of the New River has been estimated to contain 117 million gallons. At Cheshunt are two subsiding reservoirs, of 18 acres 2 roods, and of an estimated capacity of 75,549,375 gallons. At Hornsey is an open reservoir of 39 million gallons; at Stoke Newington, $4\frac{1}{2}$ miles from Charing-cross, are two subsiding reservoirs of a collective area of 42 acres 2 roods, and a capacity of 130 million gallons; while the New River Head, in Clerkenwell, has an area of 5 acres, and a capacity of 2,162,500 gallons. Besides these are the Hampstead and Highgate ponds, containing a supply of unfiltered water for streets. These are, however, much above the level of the "river," the elevation of the Hampstead ponds above Trinity high water being respectively, the "donkey pond" 420 ft. (about), the pond at the hotel 333.9 ft., and the four below it 234.8 ft., 233.4 ft., 219.4 ft., and 196.3 ft.; while the elevations of the Highgate ponds are two at 300 ft., and one each 240.5 ft., 224.3 ft., 223.5 ft., 210.8 ft., and 197.9 ft.

The company has eight or nine pumping stations in all, and at Amwell, Cheshunt, and Tottenham the engines raise water to the " river." The first place on its course where water is pumped from it to a higher level is at Hornsey, perhaps a couple of miles from Stoke Newington and six or seven miles from Charing-cross. Here there are filter-beds for storing 1,440,000 gallons, and the water is pumped to the covered reservoir near Highgate Archway, the elevation of the surface of the water there, when the reservoir is full, being 313.6 ft. above Trinity high water (326.1 ft. O. D.). The " river" at Hornsey being, say, 88 ft. and $100\frac{1}{2}$ ft. above the respective data, the lift is therefore 225.6 ft., exclusive of friction. The engine, made at St. Austell in Cornwall, and formerly, we believe, set up at the artesian well of the Kentish-town waterworks —a well 1300 ft. deep, which never gave water—is of the usual Cornish pattern. It has a 44 in. cylinder, the stroke of piston being 10 ft., while the pole, 15 in. in diameter, has a stroke of 9 ft., the beam of the engine being unequally divided. We were informed that the load on the pump-pole, in addition to its own weight of 1 ton, was $11\frac{1}{2}$ tons; but as this would be equal to 159 lb. per square inch, or $365\frac{3}{4}$ ft. of water, we presume the weight was somewhat overstated, as the friction would, we should suppose, hardly amount to the difference between 225 ft. and 366 ft. From Highgate the water is pumped by an old marine engine to a covered reservoir on Hampstead-heath, the elevation of the surface of the water being 433.6 ft. above Trinity high water, and the lift from Highgate, consequently, 120 ft.; exclusive of friction. The capacity of the Highgate covered reservoir is given as 1,180,000 gallons, and of that on Hampstead-heath as 617,000 gallons. A straight line from Hornsey to the Highgate reservoir at the Archway is about $1\frac{1}{4}$ miles, while the direct-line distance from the Highgate to the Hampstead reservoir is nearly two miles. The lines of mains are, no doubt, much longer, for on a straight line between the two last-named reservoirs, the ground falls 200 ft. below the Hampstead reservoir.

Although a considerable quantity of water flows on to the New River Head, and is distributed thence at a lower level, the chief work of distribution begins at Stoke Newington, which is the principal pumping station of the company, and where are six rotative engines of 1000 nominal horse power collectively. In the Lordship-road, which separates the two large subsiding reservoirs here, there are, besides, two old engines—one a Cornish, the other a marine engine. In the absence of any information, we cannot say whether these engines are now worked, nor, if so, to where they pump. Rather more than $2\frac{1}{4}$ miles from them is the open Camden-square reservoir, near the Cattle Market, for unfiltered water, and the surface of which is at an elevation of 160.1 ft. above Trinity high water. The old engines would no doubt be available for keeping this full, although, as the water here is not permitted to be used for drinking, the reservoir could as well be filled from the lower Highgate pond, supposing the supply to be sufficient.

The water at Stoke Newington first passes from the large subsiding reservoirs into five filter-beds of a total area of 6¼ acres, and at a level of 1 ft. below the reservoirs. As we shall describe the filter-beds of some of the other companies in a further article, we shall not attempt a description of these, which are upon the usual plan, and worked in the usual manner. The water stands 5 ft. deep on the filtering material, which is 4 ft. thick. The top sand, not long since, was from the coast, at Harwich, and the next below is from the neighbourhood of the works. These beds are generally cleaned once every six weeks in winter and every third week in summer. We may note that the large reservoirs, which were constructed nearly thirty-five years ago, under an Act obtained in 1830, were said to have accumulated but 10 in. of deposit when cleaned out and deepened about fifteen years ago—a fact which shows the comparative purity of the New River water, which is now the best supplied to London, so far as chemical analyses show. The total quantity of solid matter contained in it when filtered, during the month of July last (1866), was twenty grains to the gallon, the organic impurity being hardly more than half a grain.

When filtered, the water is pumped partly to the covered reservoir on Claremont-square, just north of the New River Head, and partly to the covered reservoirs in Maiden-lane, or York-road, between Kentish New Town and Upper Holloway, and a quarter of a mile south of Highgate Cemetery. The Claremont-square reservoir is, at the surface of the water when full, 126 ft. and 138½ ft. above the respective Trinity and Ordnance data, the lift from the filter-beds at Stoke Newington being 39 ft. 6 in. Originally the water was pumped into it direct from New River Head, close by, and a few houses were thus supplied under constant service. The engines, three in number, at the Head are still retained, and are sometimes worked, although they are of old construction. The Claremont-square reservoir is said by Mr. Burnell to be 176 ft. by 180 ft., and 22 ft. deep. Its covering of brick arches was estimated, in 1856, at the enormous sum of 21,000l., which estimate is to be found in the report made to the Board of Health. Its capacity is 3,679,000 gallons. The Maiden-lane reservoirs, two in number, are both 219 ft. and 231.5 ft. above the respective Trinity and Ordnance data, the lift from the Stoke Newington filter-beds being 132.5 ft., exclusive of friction. The main is rather more than two miles long, and is 36 in. in diameter, and the friction at the usual rate of supply is equal to about 33 ft. additional lift. These reservoirs, as Mr. Mylne's contour map shows, are well placed upon a promontory of the 200 ft. level jutting out below Highgate. They are each 273 ft. long by 208 ft. wide, and 22 ft. deep, each presenting 56,784 square feet of surface (covered, of course), and they together contain 14,520,000 gallons. They are covered by 9 in. arches of brickwork, of 15 ft. span, sprung from longitudinal walls 14 in. thick. The cost of these reservoirs was estimated, in 1856, as 61,000l.

From the Maiden-lane and Claremont-square reservoirs, and from the New River Head, the water is distributed over the company's district. This district extends to the west of Northumberland House, in the Strand, and is bounded by the north side of Cockspur-street, the east side of the Haymarket, and by Windmill and Poland-streets to Oxford-street, thence along the east side of Tottenham-court-road to Hampstead-road, and along that road to Camden Town. Thence the boundary extends, viâ St. Pancras workhouse, to Highgate, Hampstead being also included. On the east, the district extends to the east side of St. Katharine's Docks, thence, viâ Petticoat-lane, to Bishopsgate-street, along the west side of which, and Shoreditch, it extends to the Drapers' Almshouses, thence to the bridge in the Dalston-road, along the west side of Hackney Brook, and thence to Stoke Newington and Edmonton.

Having now given a general sketch of the sources, in transitu basins, and general distribution of the New River water, it remains to give a more extended account of the pumping engines at Stoke Newington. Many of our readers would regard these as entitled to the first place in our description; but, important as they are, they are intermediate only in an extensive system.

It was long after Mr. Wicksteed had made a position for the Cornish engine in the pumping of water for towns, before the New River engineers even recognised it, so far as recognition amounts to adoption. They now have a few engines on the Cornish principle, the largest being the 66 in. Bull engine at Tottenham, besides one at Hornsey (purchased second-hand a few years ago, and now expanding from half-stroke only), one in the Lordship-road, Stoke Newington, &c. The old engines, two of them at 150 nominal horse power each, at the New River Head, are single-acting, but upon Watt's and not upon the Cornish principle. The modern double-acting engines at Stoke Newington represent the later preferences of the company's engineers, and these have cranks and fly-wheels.

There are six of these engines, which are coupled in three pairs. One pair of engines are by Messrs. James Watt and Co., and the other two pairs are by Messrs. Simpson and Co., of the Grosvenor Works, Pimlico. The Watt engines pump to Claremont-square, and the Simpson engines to Maiden-lane (York-road). The Watt engines have each a single cylinder, while the Simpson engines have high and low pressure cylinders. All the engines have bucket and plunger pumps, as introduced by Messrs. Simpson in the engines for the Richmond and the Bristol Waterworks in 1848. The lift of the Watt pumps is 39 ft. 6 in., and that of the Simpson pumps 132 ft. 6 in., as already stated.

The Watt engines, named the "Lion" and "Lioness," have each a 60 in. cylinder, steam-jacketed and well cased, with a stroke of piston of 8 ft. Near the opposite end of each beam are attached the rods (shrouded or trussed with stiffening rods) of two pumps, the inner one having a bucket of 43¼ in. diameter, a plunger of 30¼ in. diameter, and a stroke of 4 ft. 9 in., the outer one a bucket of 31¼ in., a plunger of 22 in., and a stroke of 7 ft. The end of the beam works a connecting-rod coupled to a crank on the fly-wheel shaft, and the wheel is 25 ft. in diameter, its rim being 2 ft. broad on its side and 17 in. on edge, the whole weight of the fly-wheel and shaft being given as 60 tons. The valves are of the double-beat pattern, worked directly by cams on a shaft at the back of the steam cylinder, which shaft is driven by two pairs of bevel wheels and a cross shaft from the crank-shaft. The inlet to the pumps is 35 ft. below the engine-room floor, and the total height of the pumps, including inlet-pipe, is about 24 ft. The beam, we may add, is 28 ft. long, and nearly 6 ft. deep at the centre.

In the discussion upon Mr. E. A. Cowper's paper, at the Institution of Mechanical Engineers in 1858, the lift of these pumps, *including friction*, was stated by Mr. Garland to be from 80 ft. to 83 ft., although this must, we think, be in excess of the total resistance from Stoke Newington to Claremont-square. Mr. Garland said, furthermore, that these engines had given a duty exceeding by 8 to 10 millions of foot-pounds per hundred-weight of coal that of the best Cornish engines, and by 11 millions that of the Simpson engines working in the same house. In Mr. Bourne's treatise on the steam engine are given diagrams from these engines, not when at their regular work, but in the first grade of expansion, and cutting off, apparently, at about one-fourteenth of the stroke. Much, indeed, has been claimed for these engines, not only above the performance of the best Cornish engines, but, as was to have been expected, a certain partisanship has been maintained as between them and Simpson's engines. Mr. Garland stated, furthermore, that with 30 lb. steam in the cylinder, they cut off regularly at one-fifth stroke, and could cut off at one-tenth. When we saw them, however, in March, 1862, Mr. Bowman, the engineer in charge, informed us that they were cutting off at two-sevenths of the stroke, and that their average duty per cwt. of Duffryn screenings was hardly 70 millions. They made from 10 to 14 revolutions per minute, according to the work to be done, and were thumping, as well as pumping, in fine style. The whole pumpwork of these engines had already been taken out, and many parts renewed and improved, the original design having been most defective. The journals of the 60-ton fly-wheel and shaft were but 15 in. in diameter and 20 in. long; the plummer blocks had given out, and new ones had been put in, held down by 4½ in. bolts, 36 ft. long. Even then, if the plummer blocks were tight, the journals were constantly heating, and to prevent this they were left slack and allowed to thump. The two pumps of each engine originally discharged into the same pipe, but the cross streams burst the pipe, and new outlets had to be provided, while separate air-vessels had to be fitted to each of the four pumps. The delivery valves had also to be taken out, and much larger valves substituted. It must, indeed, have been with the old delivery valves that Mr. Garland observed the total resistance equal to 80 ft. or 83 ft. of water. The workmanship, or mechanical finish, of these engines is very good, but there is a want of proportion in other parts besides in the original pumps and connexions. The flanges of the beams are very light in proportion to the web or flitch, and are in strong contrast with Harvey's beams, as exemplified in his larger Cornish engines. When we called, last week (August, 1866), at Stoke Newington, we were informed that the engines could not be seen, as everything was in confusion, one of them having broken off the piston from the piston-rod. Altogether, we should conclude that they had proved the most unsatisfactory of all the large pumping engines set up in or near London.

We may note here that the engine-house, a large castellated and buttressed building, is very badly lighted, and most inconvenient in its interior arrangement. By a curious "dodge" in the design, the fly-wheels are made to work into deep recesses in the buttresses, which were not, of course, employed for strength, but only for external effect.

The four Simpson engines are, with the exception of the diameters of the buckets and plungers of the pumps, almost, if not quite, identical with those erected by the same makers at the works of the Lambeth and Chelsea companies, near Kingston, or, as the precise localities are termed, Thames Ditton and Seething Wells. We shall shortly publish drawings and descriptive details of these engines, so that we need not describe them at great length here, but we must,

nevertheless, supply a few particulars. The engines were, indeed,
very fully described in Mr. David Thomson's paper, read at the London
meeting of the Institution of Mechanical Engineers, in 1862. Like the
Watt engines, they are double-acting rotative beam engines, each pair
coupled by cranks, at right angles to each other, to a fly-wheel shaft.
They have, however, high-pressure and low-pressure cylinders, the pistons being connected to different points on the same end of the beam,
and thus moving in the same direction. The high-pressure cylinder
stands nearest to the beam centres, and its piston has the shorter
stroke. This cylinder is 28 in. in diameter, and the stroke of the piston
is 5 ft. 6⅜ in. The outer cylinder is 46 in. in diameter, and its piston
has an 8 ft. stroke. The pump, one to each engine, and nearly under
the connecting-rod end of the beam, has a 20 in. plunger and a 27 in.
bucket, with a stroke of 6 ft. 11⅜ in., the connecting-rod pin, a little
further out, moving through 8 ft. and turning a 4 ft. crank, the fly-
wheel being of moderate diameter. In the Thames Ditton engines, the
lift being considerably greater, the plunger of the pump is 16¼ in. and
the bucket 23⅜ in. in diameter, this being almost the only difference
between them and the Stoke Newington engines. In these engines
the connecting-rod is made of plate and angle iron, riveted up in the
box form, all the rivet holes having been carefully drilled. The pump-
rods, in pairs, are similarly made of plate and angle iron, riveted up
to an I section. The steam valves are pistons, 14 in. in diameter,
driven by cams, worked through bevel gearing and a cross shaft from
the crank-shaft. Each piston valve, or rather the assemblage of
valves upon the same spindle, admits the steam to and exhausts it
from both cylinders. The large cylinder has very nearly four times
the capacity of the small cylinder, and the steam is cut off in the latter
at from one-fourth to two-fifths stroke, thus giving a large total expansion, while the mean force upon both pistons is much more nearly
uniform than when expanding to the same total extent in a single
cylinder. It is thus that these engines work steadily, and without
excessive strain, with fly-wheels of but moderate weight. We are
not pronouncing any sweeping opinion in favour of compound engines,
but in the case of water-pumping engines, where the resistance is
unvarying and, so to speak, rigidly opposed to any sudden alteration
of the speed of the forcing parts, there can be no doubt that high and
economical expansion is better attained in a pair of cylinders than in a
single one, unless, of course, the Cornish principle be employed. We
believe the compound engines at Stoke Newington have worked well
ever since they were started, late in 1855, and while they were reported

to have attained a duty, on a trial of seven or eight hours only, of 113 millions, we believe they regularly perform 70 millions.

The six engines are supplied with steam from eighteen boilers, fired with the wetted screenings from smokeless coal. To prevent the formation of scale in these boilers, Mr. Bowman has, for the last five or six years, placed oak chips, billets, &c., within them, and he has found that while the vegetable acid has no effect upon the iron, it entirely prevents the formation of scale of sulphate of lime, this impurity settling as a loose powder, or rather as mud, to the bottom of the boiler.

The engine-house is raised upon a sort of mound, and its chimney is 190 ft. high. A repair-shop, close by, is driven by a turbine, worked with water from the hot wells of the condensers, this water having a head of about 14 ft. Once the heat of the water expanded the parts of the turbine so as to bind the bucket-wheel against the ring, and thus prevented its moving.

The whole of the New River works are reported to have cost 1,421,717*l.* prior to the enforcement of the Act of 1852, and 1,100,000*l.* since, or 2,521,717*l.* in all. They have upwards of 630 miles of mains and branches, 66 acres of subsiding reservoirs, 9 acres of filter-beds, and 3¾ acres of covered reservoirs for filtered water. The gross income is now nearly 200,000*l.* per annum, and the net profits are understood to be about 75,000*l.*, a sum which gives but a very moderate return upon the total capital invested. The company are now (September, 1866) advertising for loans of money at periods of three, five, and seven years.

THE EAST LONDON WATER COMPANY.

The eastern portion of the metropolis, north of the Thames, is supplied by the East London Water Company, drawing its supply from the River Lea, at Tottenham Mills, hardly seven miles, in a direct line, from the outlet of the Lea into the Thames at Blackwall. The drainage area at this point is about 500 square miles, and the annual flow varies according to the season from 12,000 to 20,000 cubic feet per minute, the minimum being about 5000 cubic feet per minute, or 45,000,000 gallons daily. Of this quantity the works under notice abstract at least one-third, while Mr. Bateman estimates the company's intake at 19 million gallons daily. The number of inhabitants supplied in August is given by the Registrar-General as 471,109. The company's engineer gives a much higher number—about 700,000.

The Lea, like the Thames, brings down in solution the sewage of the towns above. The New River Company engage to first deodorise by lime, and then to filter, the sewage of the town of Hertford, before it is discharged into the Lea. The sewage of Ware, however, a little lower down, and below the intake of the New River, flows direct into the Lea, as does that of the smaller towns below Ware, as far as Enfield. The sewage of Enfield, Edmonton, Hornsey, Tottenham, Clapton, and Hackney is intercepted by drains discharging into the Lea below Tottenham Mills, and thus below the intake of the East London water. This water is first led into 70 acres of subsiding reservoirs, on the east or Walthamstow side of the Lea, and is thence conducted by a straight open canal to Lea-bridge, 2¾ miles below. Here are the company's filter-beds, thirteen in number, 19.7 ft. above Ordnance datum, and well above the tidal locks of the Lea, and covering an area of 12 acres. These beds are in two groups, on opposite sides of the Lea, which even here is a very narrow stream—say 60 ft. or 70 ft. wide —the two groups of filters being connected by pipes beneath its bed. The process of filtration is carried out here with as much care as at any waterworks about London, and, so far as chemical analyses show, the water of the East London Company is fully equal to any other supplied to London, with the exception, perhaps, of the New River water, which possesses, however, but a very slight superiority.

These filter-beds rest upon 12 in. of clay puddle, over which is a flooring of concrete 12 in. thick. Upon this are 12 in. of coarse gravel, through which the channels for drawing off the water are laid. Over the gravel is 6 in. of a mixed gravelly sand, known as "hogging," over this 12 in. of sand from the neighbourhood of London, and finally, at the top, 12 in. of fine sea sand. The whole depth of the filtering material is thus 3 ft. 6 in., and over this the water stands 5 ft. deep, and 1 ft. below the edge of the brick curb. The beds are arranged as circular segments around a central well, from which the pumping engine draws. In the lower gravel of each bed a semicircular arched culvert is laid in brickwork from the centre radially out along the axis of the bed, and one or more branch culverts of the same form extend laterally towards the corners of the bed most distant from the well. From the sides of these culverts, narrow channels are formed throughout the bed of gravel, by parallel lines of bricks set on edge, with spaces between their ends, and covered over by bricks laid flat along the top. By these means the water is drawn down very uniformly over the whole surface of the filtering material. In a future article upon the Thames companies, we shall give a plan and section of a filter-bed of the best construction, which will illustrate the subject more clearly.

From the filter-beds the water is pumped, in part, direct over the north-eastern portion of the metropolis, while a further large quantity flows in an iron main to Old Ford, more than two miles below. Here it is received in covered reservoirs, 2½ acres in extent, and 10 ft. 6 in. deep, and pumped thence over the eastern end of London.

The chief interest of the East London works centres in the Cornish pumping-engines, and it was here that the Cornish engine was first applied by Mr. Wicksteed, less than a quarter of a century ago, to the pumping of water for the supply of towns. The rotative engines put down at Old Ford by Messrs. Boulton and Watt, in 1807, are still in working order, but they have long stood unused.

The Cornish engines at Old Ford are, one of 72 in. cylinder, working to an average stroke of 9 ft. 7½ in., one of 80 in. cylinder with a stroke of 9 ft. 9 in., and one of 90 in. cylinder with an average stroke of 10 ft. 7 in. The larger and newer engine at Lea-bridge has a 100 in. cylinder and 11 ft. stroke. We believe that the company has lately put down some additional engine power, but the engines already mentioned will alone require description. They were designed, as we need hardly say, to work with the utmost practicable economy, and the 90 in. cylinder or "Wicksteed" engine is reported to have attained a duty of 93 million pounds lifted one foot by the consumption of 112 lb. of Welsh coal, while the average of all the engines is given by the engineer as 84 millions. There is a large extent of boiler-room, and the rate of combustion is very slow. The steam cylinders are jacketed, and the jacket is furthermore surrounded by a covering 12 in. in thickness of fine ashes. The boilers have 3 ft. of ashes over them, and the steam-pipe is protected by thick lagging. The steam is cut off at about one-fourth stroke, and expanded down to about 8½ lb. below the atmosphere. With all these advantages, the working friction of the engines being also, from their construction, very moderate, and with the best coal, a duty corresponding to even less than 2¼ lb. of coal per indicated or, say, 2¾ lb. per effective horse power, is not now remarkable, although, between twenty and thirty years ago, Mr. Wicksteed found but few who would agree with him even so far as that such a result was possible.

The boilers carry from 30 lb. to 35 lb. steam, and this pressure, corresponding to a temperature of from 275° to 281°, is maintained in the steam jacket, from which the condensed steam, amounting to about $\frac{1}{16}$th part, or nearly 4 per cent., of that used in the cylinder, flows back by gravitation into the boilers, which are set below the level of the engine. Not much more than 20 lb., however, reaches the piston, and the velocity of the latter is so great on the steam stroke, that the pressure falls off as rapidly as in a diagram from a locomotive cylinder when the engine is at full speed, and the cylinder pressure, at the point of cutting off, is but from 10 lb. to 14 lb. above the atmosphere. The whole load upon the piston varies, in the different engines under notice, from 14½ lb. to 16½ lb. per square inch.

The boilers, of the ordinary single-flue Cornish pattern, employed in working the 80 in., 90 in., and 100 in. engines, are as follows, and there is, in addition, one spare boiler to each engine :

Engine Cylinder.	No. of Boiler.	Diameter.		Size of Flue.		Length.		Total Firegrate.
in.		ft.	in.	ft.	in.	ft.	in.	sq. ft.
80	3	6	5½	3	10½	27	9	62½
90	3	6	6	4	0	34	0	74¼
100	4	5	9	3	6	30	0	76.8

an additional boiler being sometimes employed with the 100 in. engine ; the grate area then being 116 square feet.

With a consumption of 4½ lb. of Welsh coal or gas coke per square foot of grate per hour, these boilers evaporate 10 lb. of water per pound of fuel. In burning fine slack coal, however, as is now done, the wetting amounting to ¼ lb. of water to 1 lb. of slack, an evaporation of from 8 lb. to 8¼ lb. of water is obtained ; and thus, as is now pretty generally understood among water companies, brewers, and manufacturers, slack is every way preferable to large coal. The grates of the East London boilers have an air space amounting to from ¼th to ⅙th only of their total area. Steam may be maintained in each boiler, when the engine is not working, by an expenditure of 1 cwt. of coal in the twenty-four hours, or, if steam is let into the cylinder jackets, with 2 cwt. of coal. The draught at the base of the chimney is from $\frac{8}{10}$ in. to $\frac{7}{10}$ in. only of water, and the draught in the side flues from $\frac{1}{10}$ in. to $\frac{8}{10}$ in. only. Observations have shown that the temperature in the side flues has varied between 280° and 415°, while that in the chimney, at 10 ft. below its top, varied from 260° to 318° only. The lower temperature noted in the side flue very nearly approaches that of the steam in the boiler.

In the Cornish beam engine—and all those under notice have beams, the direct-acting Cornish variety being known as the Bull engine—the steam is admitted upon the top of the piston, to throw up the loaded pump-pole. The duty of the steam consists in lifting this load, which is so much dead weight, according to the quantity of water and the height to which it is to be forced, and it is the descent of this weight on the return stroke which forces the water from the pump. The steam stroke, in the case of the engines under notice, is performed in from 1 to 1¼ seconds, or at the rate of from 500 ft. to 600 ft. of piston per minute. A vacuum is at the same time maintained upon the lower side of the piston. Upon its first admission, the pressure of the steam is greatly in excess of the resistance of the loaded pump-pole, which is thus thrown up, or shot up, with a sudden movement; but as the pressure of the steam falls, first by wire-drawing, and afterwards by expansion on the closing of the steam-valve, the cylinder pressure becomes much less than the resistance of the pump-pole, which thus finishes its stroke by exhausted momentum, the cylinder being prolonged sufficiently below to permit of considerable variation of the stroke. No conditions, perhaps, could be more favourable to high expansion, yet as high expansion would require a still higher initial pressure of steam, thus giving increased velocity to the pump-pole, and thereby throwing increased work upon the steam piston to maintain the requisite suction of the pump (to say nothing of the increased strain on the engine), not more than a fourfold expansion is attempted.

When the piston finishes its steam stroke, the equilibrium valve is opened, so that the steam remaining in the cylinder is thrown in equilibrium on both sides of the piston, and the piston is again raised as the loaded pole forces the water out of the pump. This stroke occupies, according to the rate of working, from five to fourteen seconds; but the interior of the cylinder, instead of being in communication with the condenser during this time, and thus exposed to a temperature of perhaps 100°, retains in equilibrium on both sides of the piston all the steam which it held at the termination of the steam stroke, and as this steam has a total pressure of 5 lb. or 6 lb., and therefore a temperature of from 162° to 170°, the cooling of the cylinder is somewhat less than it would be by the ordinary mode of exhausting the steam at the end of the stroke.

As the pump-pole goes down in its case, in forcing out the water, the valve gear is adjusted to first close the equilibrium valve, and then to open first the exhaust and then the steam valve just in time to prevent the piston from striking the top cylinder cover, or rather to prevent the bumpers or catch pieces from striking the spring beams. This adjustment requires to be carefully made, both to prevent possible accidents to the engine, on the one hand, and to prevent a waste of steam between the piston and cylinder cover on the other. A range of a very few inches must be allowed, however, as when the engine increases its speed, the greater velocity of the loaded pole carries it further down into the pump before the motion can be arrested by closing the equilibrium valve, and thus cushioning the steam under the top cylinder cover.

We may have occasion to describe the adjustable cataract of the Cornish engine in connexion with drawings which we hope shortly to publish. It is by this that the speed of the engine is regulated by giving a greater or less time for the pumping or " outdoor" stroke. The usual speed is about eight double strokes per minute, but the speed is sometimes as low as four and at others as high as ten double strokes, varying according to the required supply of water.

In the case of the East London engines, the pump-holes have, generally, the same stroke as the steam pistons, and are of exactly, or nearly, one-half the diameter of the pistons, so as to give a pump pressure nearly four times greater than the mean piston-pressure, the resulting pressure of about 60 lb. in the pump, corresponding to the " head" or hydrostatic column of about 140 ft., against which the engines work, this column being that afforded by a stand-pipe erected near the engine.

The " Wicksteed " 90 in. cylinder engine at Old Ford has a 44 in. pump-pole loaded with 36 tons, while the 100 in. engine at Lea-bridge has a 50 in. pole loaded with 45 tons, these weights being those given to us by the engineers; but as these weights correspond to 53 lb. and 51.3 lb. per square inch of the poles respectively, corresponding to heads respectively of 122 and 118 ft., and as we presume that the pumps do not work under any considerable amount of suction, we think the weights must be somewhat understated. In a series of trials by the engineer, he found that of the whole indicated power $9\frac{1}{4}$ per cent. only was absorbed in engine and pump friction, while a further loss of duty amounting to $9\frac{3}{4}$ per cent. takes place in the pumps, so that, of the whole indicated power, 81 per cent. is given out in effective work. Taking an evaporation of 10 lb. of water per pound of Welsh coal (and this rate has, as we have said, been maintained in regular work), the consumption per indicated horse power has been found to be 2.11 lb., and per effective horse power 2.65 lb.

The inlet valves of the larger engines are double-beat valves (Harvey's patent), two stories high; that is, one double-beat valve above another. The lower valve weighs 1 ton, equal to 2 lb. per square inch of lifting area; the upper valve weighs 16 cwt., giving the same load per inch to be overcome by the suction. The valves lift $3\frac{1}{4}$ in., at which they give a total opening equal to twice the sectional area of the pump-hole. With the high velocity at which the steam stroke is made, the pump inlets require to be even larger than they are. It requires too much suction to open the valves, and this throws additional work upon the piston. The delivery valves consist of a conical series of ring valves closing on india-rubber faces.

The cost of working these engines has been publicly given by the company's engineer as 1s. per day of twenty-four hours for each horse power, including repairs and all expenses except interest upon capital. This was with fuel worth about 11s. per ton, but it is doubtful whether the engines worked continuously for the entire twenty-four hours. The first cost of the large Cornish engines is very considerable, that at Lea-bridge, which is, we believe, a counterpart of the one erected by Harvey, of Hayle, at the Great Wheal Vor Mine, in so far, at least, as the indoor end of the engine is concerned, was understood to have cost the East London Company nearly 14,000l. Their engineer has publicly stated that the cost of such an engine, with six boilers, chimney, air-vessel, stand-pipe, and engine-house, the latter a massive and complete structure, would be from 23,000l. to 24,000l., while the effective horse power would be but about 250. Say what we may of the excellent wearing qualities of the Cornish engine and of its economy of fuel, it is a most expensive machine.

The cost of the East London Company's works prior to 1852 was 745,781l., and it is estimated that half a million has been spent since, giving a total cost of, say, 1,250,000l.

As a portion of the district supplied by the East London Company has this year (1866) been ravaged by cholera, a few words may be added as to the circumstances under which the outbreak occurred. A considerable portion of the district was undrained, except by the River Lea, the works for placing it in communication with the main drainage not having been completed, as, indeed, they will not be until some time next year (1867). Some weeks, however, after the appearance of cholera, viz., on the 24th August, 1866, a temporary engine was set to work by the Metropolitan Board, to divert the discharge of sewage from the River Lea and Limehouse Cut into the northern outfall sewer, near Abbey Mills. How far the ravages made by cholera in the early part of August were due to defective drainage cannot, of course, be proved, although it may be conjectured.

The East London water, so far as is shown by chemical tests conducted by chemists who report to the Registrar-General, and who are, of course, independent of the water companies, is, if anything, slightly softer, and contains less organic impurity, than the average of the waters supplied to the metropolis. We are referring here to the filtered water; but unfiltered water can also be sent from Lea-bridge direct to the engine reservoirs at Old Ford. These covered reservoirs are near the tidal mouth of the Lea, and at about the level of high water;

and it has been questioned whether there is not some infiltration from the river, the contents of which are here of the foulest description. There are, too, large open reservoirs at Old Ford, and these are known to have filled by soakage from the river after they had once been emptied. The contents of these reservoirs can also, " in cases of emergency," be placed in direct communicating with the engine wells. The chief question, and it is one which nothing but strict official inquiry could solve, is whether the company has at any time during this summer (1866) pumped foul instead of filtered water through its mains into London. It has the means of pumping in a supply which would be poisonous almost beyond dispute. The Registrar-General's reports have hinted that at least on one occasion this was done, and so far the East London Company have not publicly noticed this suggestion, nor have they offered any explanation of their precautions, if any, for ensuring a supply of filtered water under all circumstances.

THE WEST MIDDLESEX WATER COMPANY.

Having in our previous articles given an account of the two water companies which obtain their supply from the River Lea and from springs in the neighbourhood of its source, we shall now proceed to notice the works of those companies which draw their water from the Thames; these being the West Middlesex, the Southwark and Vauxhall, the Grand Junction, the Chelsea, and the Lambeth Companies. The three companies first mentioned take their water from the Thames at Hampton, whilst the Chelsea and Lambeth Companies obtain theirs at Seething Wells and Thames Ditton respectively. As we stated in a previous article, the drainage area of the Thames above Staines amounts to 3086 square miles, and its mean annual discharge is 100,000 cubic feet per minute, or 900,000,000 gallons per day. In 1852, when, in consequence of the unsatisfactory nature of the supply then obtained, the Thames water companies shifted their points of supply higher up the river, the minimum quantity of water passing Hampton was estimated at 362,000,000 gallons per day, and various Acts were passed authorising the withdrawal altogether of 100,000,000 gallons per day by the water companies.

The first Thames waterworks of which we shall give an account are those of the West Middlesex Water Company. These works were proposed about the commencement of the present century by Mr. Dodd, and, an Act for their construction having been obtained in 1806, the works at Hammersmith were begun in the following year by Mr. Nicholson, who succeeded Mr. Dodd as engineer to the company. In 1852 the company commenced the removal of their source of supply from Barnes to

Hampton, six miles above the influence of the tide, and they now have at the latter place two direct-acting Cornish or Bull engines of 105 horse power each. These engines have each a cylinder 64 in. in diameter, with a stroke of 10 ft., the diameter of the pump plungers being 45 in., and their stroke, of course, being the same as that of the steam cylinders. They pump the water direct to Barnes through a 36 in. main 8¾ miles in length, passing through Twickenham, Richmond, and Mortlake, this main being laid in duplicate where it is taken under the Thames near Richmond-bridge.

At Barnes are situated three subsiding reservoirs, having a combined area of about 20½ acres, and capable of containing about 55,161,768 gallons, these being arranged as shown in the general plan of the Barnes and Hammersmith works, Fig. 1, Plate I. When the supply was obtained from the Thames at Barnes without pumping, a limit was imposed upon the height at which the reservoirs could be constructed, but now that the water is supplied from Hampton and is raised by engine power, the reservoirs can, of course, be placed at a higher level. Advantage has been taken of this in the construction of the new high-level reservoir, which is that furthest from the river, and the sides of which are carried 5 ft. above those of the older reservoirs; and by the use of this reservoir a higher water level can be maintained in the new filter-beds, and consequently a greater head obtained in the main which conducts the water across the river to the pumping station at Hammersmith opposite, this increased head, of course, increasing the conducting power of the main. We give, in Figs. 20 and 21, Plate II, sections of the embankment of the high-level reservoir, which will explain its construction. The first-mentioned section, Fig. 20, shows the manner in which the 36 in. main from Hampton is led into the reservoir, and from it it will be seen that the end of the main is bent upwards and carried above the ordinary water level, the mouth of the pipe being about 12 in. below the level of the top of the sides of the reservoir. This arrangement of the entering main does away with the necessity for a valve at its end, and prevents any water from flowing back from the reservoir in the event of an accident happening to the main. Where the main passes through the bank of the reservoir it is well puddled, and the bottom of the reservoir is protected from disturbance by the water falling over the bent-up end of the main by means of a pavement of 4 in. York landings, covering an area 20 ft. in diameter beneath the mouth of the pipe. The portion of the main which projects into the reservoir is supported by brick piers, that under the end being 3 ft. square.

The bottom and sides of the new reservoir are covered with a layer of concrete 12 in. thick, this concrete being faced with brickwork for a depth of about 2 ft. above and below the usual water line. The inside slope of the banks is $2\frac{1}{2}$ to 1, and the sides are joined to the bottom by a curve of 38 ft. radius. The total depth of the reservoir, measured from the top of the embankments, varies from 14 ft. to 15 ft.; the depth of the water being generally about 2 ft. 6 in. less than the dimensions just given. The tops of the banks are 21 ft. 6 in. above Ordnance datum, or 2 ft. 6 in. above the level of the engine-house floor, so that the latter, which is 19 ft. above Ordnance datum, agrees with the average level of the surface of the water in the new reservoir. Fig. 21 shows a section through one of the embankments of the high-level reservoir on the line of the 36 in. mains connecting it with the old filter-beds. It will be seen that the main from the reservoir is led into a brick shaft 13 ft. 6 in. in diameter, and from this shaft another 36 in. main is led to the filter-beds, both mains being furnished with sluice valves at the shaft ends. The high-level reservoir is also connected with the other reservoirs and filters, and from the lowest point of it is led a 14 in. pipe for the purpose of emptying it. The average water level in the older reservoirs is 5 ft. below that in the high-level reservoir, and consequently the same distance below the level of the engine-house floor, or 14 ft. above Ordnance datum.

Besides the reservoirs, there are at Barnes five filter-beds, these having an area of about eight acres, and affording storage for rather more than 9,501,200 gallons of water. The three older filter-beds are situated side by side at the end of the high-level reservoir, and a section of one of their end walls is given on the left hand side of Fig. 21, the top of the wall being 8 ft. below the level of the engine-house floor, and the top of the filtering material (when the filter-bed is nearly made up) being 12 ft. below that level, or 7 ft. above Ordnance datum. In the triangular filter-bed at the eastern end of the works, the water level is 2 ft. higher than in the old beds, and in the new bed, which has just been constructed by cutting off a portion of one of the old reservoirs by a bank thrown across it, the water level is 1 ft. 6 in. higher.

The filter-beds are all similar, as far as the arrangement of the filtering material is concerned, and it will therefore be only necessary that we should describe one of them, and we shall choose as our example the new bed of which we have just spoken. Of this bed we give an enlarged plan in Fig. 2, Plate I., this plan showing the arrangement of the drain-pipes, as well as that of the inlet and outlet pipes and culverts. As we have already stated, this filter-bed was formed by cutting off a portion of one of the older reservoirs; and we give in Fig. 8 a section of the separating bank, which shows its construction. The bank is 13 ft. high above the concrete bed of the reservoir upon which it is formed, and is 12 ft. wide at the top, the side slopes being 2 to 1 on the side next the filter-bed, and 2½ to 1 on the side next the remaining portion of the reservoir. The bank contains a puddle core, which rests upon the concrete which formerly formed the bed of the reservoir. The height of the puddle core is 11 ft. 6 in., and its thickness at the base 5 ft. 6 in., this thickness being maintained for a height of 2 ft., after which it diminishes to 2 ft. 6 in. at the top of the core. The side slopes are faced with concrete 12 in. thick for a height of 7 ft. 6 in. (measured perpendicularly), after which the facing is formed of rag stone for a height of 5 ft. 6 in., and above this again the concrete is continued to the top of the bank, which is 2 ft. 6 in. below the level of the engine-house floor, or 16 ft. 6 in. above Ordnance datum. The rag stone facing is, like the concrete, about 12 in. thick, and it is placed so that it extends both above and below the average water levels in both the filter-bed and reservoir.

In the bank just described, there is sunk a brick shaft 12 ft. in diameter inside, as shown in the plan, Fig. 2, and section, Fig. 4. This shaft is built of 14 in. brickwork, the puddle wall being continued round it with a thickness of 2 ft.; the bottom is formed by a brick invert 9 in. thick, and with 6 in. camber, resting upon concrete. Into the shaft are led four pipes, viz., a 40 in. main, communicating with the remaining portion of the old reservoir, as shown in Fig. 4; a 30 in. pipe leading to the new filter-bed; a 36 in. pipe which is carried through the new filter-bed, and is connected with another shaft into which the pipes for supplying the eastern filter-bed are led; and, lastly, a pipe which extends under the embankment to the old filter-beds. The two first-mentioned pipes are furnished with sluices at the shaft end, as shown in the figures. The manner in which the pipes are supported where they are carried out into the filter-bed and reservoir is shown by Figs. 5 and 6, from which it will be seen that they are borne by small brick piers 3 ft. 9 in. long, 14 in. thick, and placed at a distance of 9 ft. apart from centre to centre.

Down the centre of the filter-bed is carried longitudinally the double culvert shown in tranverse section in Figs. 3, 12, 13, and 17, in longitudinal section in Figs. 7 and 1, in outside elevation in Fig. 16, and in plan in Figs. 1 and 9. As will be seen from the enlarged part-elevation and transverse section, Figs. 16 and 17, the lower culvert is 2 ft. 6 in. square, the top being formed of 4 in., and the bottom (which rests upon the concrete forming the bottom of the filter-bed) of 3 in. York landing stones. The sides of the lower culvert are formed of 4½ in. brickwork, the five lower courses being laid with open joints, and these side walls are strengthened at intervals of 5 ft. by solidly built piers 9 in. by 9 in., as shown in Fig. 16. The upper culvert is U-shaped, 2 ft. 6 in. wide and 1 ft. 6 in. deep, the bottom being semi-circular. It is constructed of brickwork built upon the York landing stones forming the top of the lower culvert, the width of the brickwork outside being 4 ft., and the thickness below the bottom of the upper culvert 5 in. At the Western end where the upper culvert receives the entering water from the 30 in. pipe already mentioned, the sides of the culvert are gradually raised, by three steps, to a height of 2 ft. 3 in. above the bottom, the arrangement of pipe and culvert at this point being shown at Fig. 8.

From the lower culverts there are led, at intervals of 20 ft., a series of 6 in. pierced drain-pipes, these extending to a ring of similar pipes which extend round the filter-bed at the foot of the slopes of the banks. As the double culvert above mentioned does not extend the whole length of the filter-bed, the drainage of the eastern end is effected by a series of 6 in. pierced drain-pipes leading into a transverse culvert communicating with the main culvert already described. Of this transverse culvert we give a transverse and longitudinal section in Figs. 14 and 15, from which it will be seen that its construction resembles that of the lower part of the double culvert above mentioned. It is, however, of smaller dimensions, the height inside being 2 ft. and the width 1 ft. 9 in. In order to prevent the lodgment of air in the culverts, they are provided with cast-iron air-pipes, as shown in Figs. 8, 12, and 15, those pipes communicating with the main longitudinal culvert being 6 in. and those leading from the ends of the transverse culvert 4 in. in diameter. Where the air-pipes of the lower central culvert pass through the upper culvert, the latter is widened out to a width of 3 ft. 3 in. inside, in order to maintain a clear water-way ; this widening is shown in Figs. 9 and 12. Air-pipes are also connected at various points with the ring of drain-pipes which runs round the filter-bed, and from the eastern ends of the central culverts there is led a 12 in. pipe, which extends to the river. This pipe, which is used for emptying the filter-bed, has branches, furnished with sluices, communicating with both the upper and lower culverts. The air-pipes are in all cases carried up to the level of the top of the banks, and their arrangement, together with that of the drain-pipes and culverts, is shown in the general plan of the filter-bed, Fig. 2.

At the eastern end of the filter-bed the lower central and transverse culverts communicate with a semicircular shaft, situated at the end of a brick tunnel, which formerly contained the outlet-pipes from the reservoir. This tunnel, which is shown in section in Fig. 7, is 8 ft. 6 in.

high by 5 ft. wide, and is furnished with a sluice at each end. Near the outer end of this tunnel has been built a tumbling-bay of V form in plan, and 6 ft. 6 in. high, the top being 2 ft. below the level of the surface of the sand in the filter-bed. The other end of the tunnel communicates with a circular shaft, into which are also led the outlet pipes from the other filter-beds, and from which a 36 in. conduit-pipe is laid under the bed of the River Thames to the pumping station at Hammersmith.

We must now describe the arrangement of the filtering material, which is shown in the sections, Figs. 3, 12, 13, and 14. It consists, first, of a layer of coarse gravel 12 in. thick, laid upon the concrete bed, and above this of four other layers of gravel of gradually increasing fineness, the thickness of the layers being, successively, 6 in., 3 in., 2 in., and 4 in. Above the gravel is laid a layer of Barnes sand 12 in. thick, and above this again a layer of Harwich sand 21 in. in thickness, this forming the upper surface of the bed. The total thickness of filtering material, when the filter-bed is newly dressed, is thus 5 ft., and the upper surface is 10 ft. 6 in. below the level of the engine-house floor, or 8 ft. 6 in. above Ordnance datum. The level just given only refers to the new filter-bed: the surface of the filtering material in the three old filter-beds is 7 ft. and that in the triangular or eastern filter-bed 9 ft. above Ordnance datum. The beds are generally worked with a head of 3 ft. of water above the surface of the filtering material.

From the above description it will be seen that the water is led into the filter-bed down the central conduit, and, welling over the sides, percolates through the sand and gravel, and is collected by the drain-pipes and culverts beneath. As the filtering goes on, the upper surface of the sand becomes clogged by the matters separated, and at intervals varying from four days to a month, according to the season and the state of the water, the latter has to be drained out and the surface of the sand scraped. The scraping is required on the average every week, and the thickness of the layer of sand removed is about $\frac{1}{2}$ in. The scraping is repeated from time to time until the top layer of sand is reduced to about a foot in thickness, when the bed has to be redressed. We may mention here that an abundant supply of sand and gravel suitable for filtering purposes is obtainable on the West Middlesex Company's own property at Barnes, and this has greatly reduced the cost of forming the filter-beds.

The cleansing of the sand which is scraped off the filter-beds is effected by the aid of a very simple washing-machine, which is erected as required by the side of any of the filter-beds. It consists of a wooden frame supporting a platform, upon which the dirty sand is placed and mixed with water, the mixture flowing down a couple of inclined planes formed by flights of shallow steps. By falling over these steps the lumps are broken up and the dirt separated, and, when the mixed water and sand flows from the bottom of the lower flight of steps, the cleaned sand is soon deposited in channels prepared to receive it, the dirt being carried off in suspension by the water. Two depositing channels are formed at the foot of the inclines, the descending current being turned into them alternately, so that whilst the deposited sand is being removed from one, a fresh supply is being deposited in the other, and so on. The water for washing purposes is supplied by pipes leading from a small pumping engine of 6 horse power, situated in an engine-house near the eastern filter-bed, as shown in the general plan, Fig. 2. The gravel for the lower strata of the filter-beds is separated from the sand and sorted into five different degrees of fineness by a sifting machine provided for the purpose.

From the filter-beds at Barnes the water is conveyed direct to the pumping station at Hammersmith, opposite, by means of a 36 in. conduit-pipe laid under the bed of the river, as we have already mentioned. At Hammersmith the company have five Cornish beam engines, of an aggregate nominal power of 900 horses. No. 1 engine has a 54 in. cylinder, with 8 ft. stroke, and works two pumps—one 20 in. in diameter, with 8 ft. stroke; and one 15 in. in diameter, with a stroke of 6 ft. No. 2 engine has also a 54 in. cylinder and 8 ft. stroke, but it works one pump only, that being 20 in. in diameter, with a stroke of 8 ft. Engines Nos. 1 and 2 are placed in one engine-house, and their valve gear is connected and is regulated by one cataract, so that the engines make alternate strokes. Engine No. 3 has a cylinder 64 in. in diameter, with a stroke of 8 ft., and works one pump 23 in. in diameter, with the same stroke as the steam cylinder. The engine is also fitted with another pump, 18 in. in diameter and 6 ft. stroke, but this is not in use at present. Engines Nos. 1, 2, and 3 were all built by Messrs. Boulton and Watt; but they have been fitted with Cornish nozzles and their parts strengthened by Messrs. Harvey and Co., so as to fit them for working with a higher pressure of steam than was at first intended. The average initial pressure of steam is 23 lb., and it is cut off at one-third the stroke, the speed of working being generally about 14 strokes per minute. All the pumps are of the solid piston class, with the inlet and outlet passages communicating with the upper end of the pump cylinders, so that the water is delivered during the up stroke of the pump piston, or the indoor stroke of the engine. The boilers for supplying steam to engines Nos. 1, 2, and 3 are nine in number, seven of them being in regular use. They are Cornish boilers, with single flues, and are each 30 ft. long, some of them being 7 ft. and some 6 ft. 6 in. in diameter. They are worked up to a pressure of 30 lb.

Engines Nos. 4 and 5 were built by Messrs. Harvey and Co., the former being of 220 and the latter of 300 horse power. They have been at work about eighteen months. Engine No. 4 has a cylinder 72 in. in diameter, and works a double-acting pump 23 in. in diameter, the stroke of both the steam and pump pistons being 10 ft. No. 5 engine has an 80 in. cylinder with 10 ft. stroke, and drives a double-acting pump 24½ in. in diameter, with the same stroke as the steam cylinder. As we have just stated, the pumps of both engines are double acting, the pump piston-rods being loaded, so that during the in-door stroke each engine has to raise not only the water due to the up stroke of the pump piston, but the counterbalance also, the descent of the latter during the out-door stroke delivering the water due to the down stroke of the pump piston. As the pump pistons are loaded so as to deliver the water against the greatest head with which the engines can be loaded, it would sometimes happen that, when the engines are working against a less head, they would perform the out-door stroke too quickly if means were not adopted to prevent it. To avoid this, the engines are both fitted with throttle valves in the equilibrium pipes, so that by partially closing these the transfer of the steam from the upper to the lower end of the cylinders can be checked, and the speed of the out-door strokes regulated. The suction valves of the pumps are four-beat, and the delivery valves, double-beat valves, and the air-vessels on the delivery valves are of wrought iron. Engines Nos. 4 and 5 are alike in their general arrangement, and it will therefore be sufficient that we should describe the latter engine. We may mention, however, that the beam of No. 4 engine is cast in an open-lattice form, and some months ago one flitch of it cracked through just above the main centre. The damage was repaired by the engineer to the West Middlesex Company, Mr. W. B. Hack, by applying a pair of cast-iron struts to the top of the centre of the beam, and carrying wrought-iron truss rods from end to end over these, thus making a very strong job. The struts and tie rods add about 11 tons to the weight of the beam, and it has been found that since they have been applied a better duty has been obtained from the engine.

The general arrangement and details of engine " No. 5 " are shown by the engravings Plates III. and IV., and the following are the leading particulars : This engine is the one most recently erected, and it is, as we have said, a Cornish engine, constructed by Messrs. Harvey and Co., of Hayle, working a double-acting pump. The steam cylinder is

80 in. and the pump cylinder 24¼ in. in diameter, the average stroke of
both the steam and pump pistons being 10 ft. The beam is 32 ft. 6 in.
long between end centres, and is composed of two flitches 6 ft. 3 in. deep
at the centres and 2 ft. 1½ in. at the ends. The web of each flitch is
3 in. thick, and the top and bottom flanges are 6⅛ in. thick by 5⅜ in.
wide. At the points where the centres of the plug-rod, back links, air
and feed pumps pass through the beam, bosses, 6 in. thick and 9 in. in
diameter at the smallest part, are formed on the web. The bosses
through which the main centre passes are 12 in. thick and 2 ft. 6 in. in
diameter at the smallest part, and the bosses for the piston-rod and
pump-rod centres are 8¾ in. thick and 16½ in. in diameter, the web of
the beam around them being also increased in thickness ·to 6 in. for a
diameter of 2 ft. 1½ in. The diameter of the piston and pump rod
centres where they pass through the beam is 8¼ in., whilst that of the
air-pump rod centre is 4 in., and that of the feed-pump rod, plug-rod,
and back link centres 3⅝ in. at the same part. The flitches of the beam
are placed at a distance of 2 ft. 4½ in. apart, and are tied together at
points 3 ft. 6 in. within each end centre by 1¾ in. bolts passing through
the flitches and cast-iron distance pieces. The main centre is 16½ in.
in diameter where it passes through the beam, and 15 in. in diameter
between the flitches; it is secured in its place by two keys in each
flitch, the holes for its reception being accurately bored out, and the
main centre turned to fit them tightly. The bearings of the main centre
are 13 in. in diameter and 1 ft. 5 in. long, and are situated at a distance
apart of 7 ft. from centre to centre. The positions of the various points
of attachment on the beam are given by the following dimensions :
Between main and feed-pump rod centres, 4 ft. 6 in; between main and
plug-rod centres, each 8 ft. 8 in.; and between main and piston-rod
centres and main and pump-rod centres, each 16 ft. 3 in.

The plummer blocks of the main centre are supported by a cast-iron
entablature, and not by a wall as shown in our engraving. The ends
of this entablature, which is 8 ft. 9 in. deep, are built into the walls of
the engine-house, whilst the intermediate portion is supported by four
cast-iron Doric columns placed in pairs—one pair under each plummer
block. Besides these, there are also four half-columns placed against
the walls under the ends of the entablature. The length of the castings
forming the entablature is 20 ft., and the length of the latter between
walls is 17 ft. The height of the main centre above the top of the entablature is 4 ft. 6 in., and its height above the engine-room floor 27 ft.
9 in., the clear height under the entablature being 19 ft. 6 in. The
supporting columns are hollow, their diameter at the top being 18 in.

and at the bottom 22 in., and the bolts holding the bases of the main centre plummer blocks passing down through them. The columns are fluted on the outside, and the least thickness of their metal is about 1¼ in. ; at their lower ends they are fitted into a cast-iron base-plate bedded 6 in. below the floor of the engine-house on a substantial wall.

In Fig. 2, Plate IV., we give a vertical section of the steam cylinder and piston. The diameter is, as we have already stated, 80 in., and the clear distance between covers is, at the sides, 11 ft. 4½ in., the distance in the centre being 3¾ in. more, owing to the dished form of the lower cover. The barrel of the cylinder is formed of metal 1⅜ in. thick, and it is surrounded by a steam jacket 85¼ in. in diameter inside, the thickness of the jacket being also 1⅜ in., and it being strengthened by four annular ribs on the outside. The manner in which the jacket is connected to the cylinder is shown on the engraving, from which it will be seen that the lower end of the jacket fits upon a conical joint face formed on the outside of the cylinder, whilst at the upper end the cylinder has cast on it a flange which is bolted to a corresponding flange cast on the jacket. The thickness of the jacket and cylinder flanges is 2 in. The steam passage leading to the top of the cylinder is 1 ft. 9 in. wide by 8 in. high, and that leading to the bottom of the cylinder 2 ft. 1 in. wide and 10 in. high. The position of the passages is shown in Fig. 2.

The base of the cylinder, which also forms the bottom cover, is 1 ft. 6 in. deep, and that part of it which actually forms the bottom of the cylinder is 1¼ in. thick, and is strengthened by feathers in the under side. The flange of the base to which the steam jacket is bolted is 2 in. thick and the bottom flange 2¼ in. thick, the latter being strengthened by feathers and bosses where the holding-down bolts pass through it. The holding-down bolts are four in number, and are 3¼ in. in diameter at the screwed part, the part below the screws being reduced to 3 in. The top cover of the cylinder is 2 in. thick, and is strengthened by feathers on the upper side. It enters 7½ in. into the cylinder barrel, and is held by thirty-two 1⅜ in. bolts, the flange through which the bolts pass being 2¼ in. thick. The piston-rod stuffing box is 1 ft. 6 in. long and 9¼ in. in diameter inside, the diameter of the rod itself being 7½ in. The gland, which is held by four 1½ in. bolts, is of cast iron lined with gun-metal, and the packing ring is also of gun-metal. The stuffing box is fitted with a lantern brass, which is supplied with steam from the steam jacket by a pipe as shown in Fig. 2. The horizontal distance of the centre line of the steam cylinder from a vertical line drawn through the main centre is 15 ft. 10¼ in., and there is also the same distance between the vertical line just mentioned and the centre line of the pump cylinder.

The steam piston is shown in section in Fig. 2. It is of cast iron, and is 1 ft. 3 in. deep at the centre and 12 in. at the sides, the thickness of the metal being 2 in., and the disc being strengthened by feathers on the under side. The piston-rod, which is 7½ in. in diameter for the main part of its length, is increased in size to 8¼ in. and 10¾ in. in diameter at the part within the boss of the piston, the latter enlargement forming a collar by which the downward pull of the piston is received. The rod is secured in its place by a cotter, placed in a recess formed in the upper side of the piston. The piston packing consists of a cast-iron ring 5 in. deep and 1 in. thick, except near the lower edge, where its thickness is increased by a flange to 1½ in. This ring is packed behind with hemp, the latter being tightened by a junk ring kept in its place by twelve 1½ in. screws, which take into brass nuts let into suitable recesses in the piston.

The steam, equilibrium, and exhaust valves are of the double-beat kind, and are 11 in., 15 in., and 18 in. in diameter respectively; they are arranged in the usual nozzles. The equilibrium pipe between the bottom and top of the cylinder is 15 in. in diameter inside, and is fitted with a throttle valve, the use of this valve being, as we have already explained, to check the rush of the steam from the top to the bottom of the cylinder, and thus to prevent racing during the out-door stroke, in case the head against which the engine is working should be less than that to which the pump-rod is loaded. The lower end of the equilibrium pipe fits into a stuffing box formed on the lower nozzle, this arrangement allowing for the expansion or contraction of the pipe and cylinder. The eduction pipe from the lower nozzle to the condenser is 19 in. in diameter inside. The valves are worked by an arrangement of gear shown in end elevation, in the general view, Plate III., and which is similar to that usually employed on Cornish engines.

The condenser is 2 ft. 9 in. in diameter inside at its largest part, and is about 6 ft. high above the bottom of the passage leading to the air-pump. This passage is 9 in. high by 1 ft. 7 in. wide, and contains the foot valve, which is a cast-iron flap valve hinged at the top and hung perpendicularly. The air-pump is 2 ft. 9 in. in diameter, and the bucket has a stroke of 5 ft. 4 in. The bucket is of cast iron with a gun-metal packing ring, packed behind with hemp in the same manner as the piston ring, and the bucket valve is of india-rubber working on a gun-metal grid. The delivery valve is also of india-rubber, with a gun-metal grid. The air-pump rod is 3½ in. in diameter. The air-pump and condenser are contained in a tank into which the injection water is pumped, the tank being 7 ft. long by 6 ft. 3 in. wide by 7 ft. 10½ in. deep, and being formed of cast-iron plates. The bottom of the tank is 13 ft. 3 in. below the floor of the engine-house. The feed and air-charging pumps are fixed upon the top of the eduction pipe, just over the condenser. They are both plunger pumps, the plunger of the feed pump being 6 in. and that of the air-charging pump 3½ in. in diameter. They both have a stroke of 2 ft. 9 in. The cold-water pump is situated close to the main pump, and is worked by a rod attached to a bracket fixed to the balance box, as shown in the general arrangement.

We now come to the main pump, which is shown in section in Fig. 4. As we have already stated, it is a double-acting pump, with a barrel 24½ in. in diameter and a stroke of 10 ft. The pump piston is of cast iron, and is packed in the same manner as the steam piston. The rod, which is attached to the pump piston, is 6 in. in diameter, and is enlarged and tapered in the pump piston and secured by a cotter, as shown. The upper end of this rod is cottered into a socket formed on the lower end of another rod 7¼ in. in diameter, which passes up through the balance box, and carries the cap to which the pump-rod links are attached. The balance box is a cast-iron box of the shape shown in the general arrangement, the lower part being 7 ft. and the upper part 3 ft. in diameter. The balance box is loaded, so that sufficient pressure is put upon the pump piston to deliver the water during the down stroke against the greatest head against which the engine has to work, the pressure of the steam on the steam piston during the indoor stroke of the engine having to raise the weight of the balance box and its appendages in addition to delivering the water due to the up stroke of the pump. The suction pipe leading to the lower end of the pump barrel is 27 in., and that leading to the upper end 25½ in. in diameter, whilst the passages leading from the ends of the pump barrel to the delivery valves are 26 in. in diameter. The lower suction pipe is made larger than the other, on account of the up stroke of the pump being performed more quickly than the down stroke.

One of the suction valves is shown separately in Fig. 3, from which it will be seen that they are Husband's patent four-beat valves. The dimensions are as follows : Outside diameter of top beat, 10½ in.; inside diameter of 2nd beat, 1 ft. 3 in.; outside diameter of 3rd beat, 2 ft.; inside diameter of 4th beat, 2 ft. 3 in.; height of valve over all, 2 ft. 4½ in. These valves are of gun-metal, and the ribs connecting the upper and lower rings are canted, so that the action of the water on them turns the valves partly round at each stroke of the pump; the seats are also of gun-metal. The upward blow of each valve is received

by a cushion of vulcanised india-rubber, which is secured to the underside of the cast-iron cross at the top of the valve by means of copper
rivets. The delivery valves are ordinary double-beat valves, striking
on hard wood seats. The outside diameter of the top beat is 2 ft. 1¾ in.,
and the inside diameter of the bottom beat 2 ft. 4 in., whilst the height
over all is 1 ft. 10¾ in. The pipe connecting the upper and lower de-
livery-valve boxes is 27 in. in diameter at the top and 26 in. in diameter
at the bottom, and the branch leading to the main is 27 in. in diameter
and is fitted with a sluice-valve. On the delivery pipe is placed a large
wrought-iron air-vessel, the diameter of this vessel at the largest part
being 5 ft. 3 in., and the height at the top of it above the centre of the
delivery pipe being about 21 ft.

In the engine which we have been describing, the steam, which is
supplied from the boilers at a pressure of about 40 lb., is generally cut
off at one-third stroke. The pumps work against a maximum dead
head of 183 ft. 6 in., and when working against this head the pressure
against them, including friction, is equal to a head of 200 ft. The
head just mentioned is that against which they work during part of the
day; during the other part the work is lighter, the head against them
being about 40 ft. less. The average speed at which the engine is run
is 10⅓ strokes per minute, the speed varying from 10 to 12 strokes per
minute.

Outside the engine-house, the 36 in. main into which the engines
pump is fitted with one of Mr. Husband's patent balance valves, which
have been adopted at several waterworks with good results. That at
the West Middlesex works at Hammersmith is the largest that is in
use at any of the metropolitan works; it is shown in section in Fig. 1,
Plate III. The object of the arrangement is to prevent racing of the
engines in the event of a main bursting, and this it does by providing
an almost constant head for the engines to pump against, whether the
main is perfect or not. As will be seen from the engraving, it consists of a kind of three-beat valve placed in a suitable valve-box formed
on the line of the main. Two of the beats of the valve are arranged in
the same manner as those of an ordinary double-beat valve, except
that the inside of the bottom is the same size as the outside of the top
beat; but the third, which is smaller in diameter than the others, is
arranged, as shown in the figure, within the upper of the other two
beats. It will thus be seen that the pressure tending to lift the valve
is that exerted by the water over the whole of the surface within the
third beat. To counterbalance this pressure, whether there is a head
in the main or not, the valve is loaded by means of a ram of the same
diameter as the outside of the third beat, this ram, which bears on the

upper side of the valve, being carried through a stuffing box at the top of the valve-box, and furnished with weights at the upper end, as shown in Fig. 1. The weight applied to the valve in this manner is sufficient to load the area enclosed by the third beat to the same extent per unit of surface as it would be loaded by the head of water against which the pump is intended to work; and it thus follows that, if the main bursts, but little alteration is made in the pressure tending to close the valve, the only loss of downward pressure being that due to the cessation of the pressure exercised by the head of water on the difference in the area enclosed by the first and second beats, which difference of area is acted upon by the ascending water when the valve is open.

In the West Middlesex apparatus the valves and seat are of gun metal, and that part of the plunger which passes through the stuffing-box is sheathed with the same material for a thickness of $1\frac{1}{4}$ in. The outside diameter of the lower beat is 35 in., and the inside diameter of the outer top beat 31 in., whilst the inside diameter of the top central beat is 18 in., and its outside diameter 20 in. The breadth of the faces of the beats is in each case 1 in. The plunger is 20 in. in diameter, and the stuffing-box, through which it passes, is packed with an ordinary cupped leather. The plunger, which is secured to the valve by a cotter $4\frac{1}{4}$ in. by $1\frac{3}{4}$ in., is made with a shoulder which rests upon the top of the gun-metal sheathing, and thus confines the latter between it and the valve. Above the shoulder the diameter of the plunger is reduced to 12 in., and it is fitted with movable weights for giving the necessary pressure. The rising of the valve is checked by a volute spring which encircles the upper part of the plunger, and is carried by a nut or collar screwed upon the latter. When the valve rises the top of the volute spring comes in contact with the underside of a wrought-iron cross, which both acts as a check and as a guide for the top of the plunger, this top part of the latter being further reduced to $7\frac{1}{2}$ in. in diameter. The cross has arms $7\frac{1}{2}$ in. by $3\frac{1}{2}$ in. at the central boss, and $7\frac{1}{2}$ in. by 3 in. at the outer ends; and it is supported by four bolts or columns 5 in. in diameter. The lowest of the weights placed upon the plunger is made with eyes, which embrace and slide upon two of the columns just mentioned, and these two columns have screws formed on them near the lower end, the screws being furnished with nuts carrying collars, upon which, by adjusting the nuts, the weight of the plunger and its attachments can be received.

We have said that the head against which the West Middlesex engines pump is a variable one, and in order, therefore, that the apparatus which we have just been describing should be thoroughly efficient, the load upon the plunger should also be capable of variation.

To enable this alteration of the load to be readily and quickly effected, Mr. W. B. Hack, the engineer to the company, has supplemented Mr. Husband's apparatus by a very simple and effective arrangement of his own, which is also shown in Fig. 1. It consists of a short hydraulic press cylinder, made of gun-metal, and supported upon the top of the cross already mentioned. This cylinder, which is 15 in. in diameter, and is closed at the bottom by a cover, is fitted with a piston packed with a cupped leather. On the upper side of this piston are two studs, which carrry a crosshead working on guide-bolts fixed in the top flange of the cylinder, and from the overhanging ends of this crosshead, there depend links, which are attached to the top weight with which the plunger is loaded. The lower end of the cylinder is connected with the main by a pipe of $\frac{3}{4}$ in. bore, and this pipe being furnished with inlet and discharge cocks, the water can be admitted into or released from the cylinder at pleasure. The action of the apparatus is very simple, and scarcely requires any explanation. When it is required to relieve the balance-valve of a portion of its load, the water is admitted from the main to the lower end of the hydraulic cylinder, when it forces up the piston and, of course, raises the top weight off the others, which rest on the plunger, and thus relieves the valve. By simply letting the water out of the cylinder, the weight is restored to its former position. The whole of the apparatus is inclosed in a light casing, as shown in our engraving.

The steam for engines Nos. 4 and 5 is supplied by ten single-flued Cornish boilers, seven of these being worked to supply one engine, or nine to supply the two. If, however, the two engines should have to be kept in full work, more boiler power would be required. Seven of the boilers are each 28 ft. long and 6 ft. 6 in. in diameter; and the other three, which are made of steel, are each 6 ft. 6 in. in diameter and 24 ft. long. They are all worked at a pressure of 40 lb. per square inch, and the engines are, as we have said, driven at the average speed of about $10\frac{1}{4}$ strokes per minute.

The pump wells of the engines are supplied from the Barnes filter-beds by the 36 in. conduit pipe already mentioned, this pipe branching just outside the works, and one branch leading to the well for engines Nos. 1, 2, and 3, and the other to that for engines Nos. 4 and 5. Both branches are furnished with sluices, so that the supply can be shut off from either well at pleasure; and in the engine-house of Nos. 4 and 5 engines there is placed a small donkey-engine, by means of which the well belonging to those engines can be pumped out when required. This engine also drives the shafting in the adjoining work-shops. During the day, engines Nos. 1, 2, 3, and 5 are employed pumping into three mains of 30 in., 21 in., and 14 in. in diameter respectively, the overplus water, if any, passing into the reservoir at Barrow Hill, the mains being fitted with valves opening towards the reservoir. During the night, engines Nos. 2, 3, and 4 are worked: they pump into the Barrow Hill reservoir, and also supply any demands which may be made upon the mains. No stand-pipes are used, the pumps being all furnished with air-vessels on the delivery side.

The covered reservoir on Barrow Hill, near Primrose Hill, is situated 190 ft. above Ordnance datum; it is of about 1¼ acres area, and will hold about 4,750,000 gallons. At Barrow Hill there are also two double-acting engines, one of them being a beam engine with a cylinder 23 in. in diameter and 5 ft. stroke, working a double-acting pump 12 in. in diameter, also with a 5 ft. stroke. The other is a horizontal engine with a cylinder 23 in. in diameter, working a double-acting pump 11 in. in diameter, the stroke of both steam and pump pistons being 5 ft. These engines are supplied with steam by five single-flued Cornish boilers, 5 ft. in diameter and 20 ft. long, and they are employed in pumping water from the Barrow Hill reservoir to the higher districts, such as part of St. John's-wood, the New Finchley road, Hendon, &c., which could not at present be supplied by gravitation. The company are, however, now (September, 1866) constructing a covered reservoir at the back of Kidderpore Hall, near Child's Hill, from which the future supply of the high level district will be distributed. This reservoir, which will be situated 321 ft. 6 in. above Ordnance datum, will contain about 2,500,000 gallons.

Besides the covered reservoir at Barrow Hill, the company have another at Notting Hill; this reservoir, which is 124 ft. 6 in. above Ordnance datum, having an area of about 1¼ acres, and being capable of storing about 3,672,000 gallons. The present total storage capacity of the company's reservoirs and filter-beds is thus about 73,085,000 gallons, and this will be raised, when the reservoir at Kidderpore Hall is completed, to 75,585,000 gallons. The total nominal power of the company's engines is 1201 horse power, this total being made up of 210 horse power at Hampton, 6 at Barnes, 900 at Hammersmith, and 85 at Barrow Hill.

The total length of the company's mains and services is about 230 miles, and water is supplied by them to about 36,000 tenements. The water is supplied every week-day to the whole district, and in some parts twice a day, whilst in nearly the whole of the town portion of the district, including the poorer localities, a supply of water is also furnished on Sundays. In many parts where the water is not laid on to the houses, a supply is furnished to the poor from stand-pipes. A

D

gratuitous supply of water is also furnished by the company to the
hospitals and charitable institutions within their district, as well as for
extinguishing fires.   In the case of the latter, a reward is given by
the company to the first person who calls the turncock, and the supply
is left on as long as it is required.   According to the Registrar-General's
report for July of the present year, 1866, the average daily quantity
of water supplied by the West Middlesex Water Company is 9,090,414
gallons; and it is also stated in the same report that the quantity of
solid matter contained in the water amounted to only 23.62 parts in
100,000, these impurities including 1.16 parts of organic or volatile
matters, and 16.2 parts of carbonate of lime, or its equivalent of
hardening salts.   The total amount expended upon works, &c., by the
West Middlesex Company was, up to Lady-day, 1866, nearly 774,360l.,
and of this sum nearly 268,000l. have been expended since 1852, when
the company obtained the Act which enabled them to shift their source
of supply from Barnes to Hampton.   We cannot conclude this notice
of the works of the West Middlesex Company without acknowledging
the courtesy with which the engineer of the company, Mr. W. B. Hack,
has not only furnished us with all the required information, but has
also placed at our disposal the numerous drawings from which our
illustrations have been prepared.

THE CHELSEA WATERWORKS COMPANY.

The corporation entitled the Chelsea Waterworks Company is one
whose existence dates from the year 1723, and the first Act obtained
by the company was the 8th of George I., cap. 26.   Subsequently,
further powers were given to them by royal charter, 9th George I.,
letters patent, 7th George II., and Act 49th George III., cap. 157;
and finally, in 1852, the establishment of the present works was
authorised by the Act 15th and 16th Victoria, cap. 156.   The works
were originally situated at Chelsea, the water being taken from the
Thames at that place, and it was at these works that, about the year
1839, the first filter-beds employed by any of the metropolitan water
companies were constructed according to the plans of Mr. J. Simpson,
the engineer to the Chelsea Company.   The works at Chelsea were
abandoned, however, in the year 1856, and since that date the water
supply has been obtained from the river Thames at Seething Wells, a
point some miles above tidal influence.

At Seething Wells the company have two subsiding reservoirs and
two filter-beds, these being situated on a strip of ground which is close
to the bank of the river, and which is separated from that on which
the main engine-houses stand by the turnpike-road leading from

Thames Ditton to Kingston. The river face of the works is formed by a strong wall of concrete, this wall being about 2 ft. 6 in. thick at the top, and being built with a batter on the face of 2 in. per foot. It is strengthened at the back by substantial counterforts placed at a distance apart of about 14 ft. between centres. In this wall are formed openings which are guarded by gratings and screens, and which serve to admit the water from the Thames into the two subsiding reservoirs, the supply being regulated by sluices provided for the purpose. The subsiding reservoirs are placed side by side, and are each 248 ft. long by 202 ft. wide, measured on the beds, and 272 ft. long by 226 ft. wide at the top of the banks, these latter being 12 ft. high above the bottoms, and being constructed with inside slopes of 1 to 1. The reservoirs are excavated partly out of a diluvial covering of the London clay, and partly out of the solid blue clay, and the banks were cut into steps to receive the concrete with which they are faced, no puddle being used. The average thickness of the concrete walls thus laid on the banks is 3 ft. (their inner slope being, as already stated, 1 to 1), and they are in their turn faced with brickwork laid dry.

From what has been already stated, it will be seen that the water in the subsiding reservoirs will, when the sluices are open, be at the same level as that in the river, and the height of the water in the latter, therefore, regulates the depth which can be maintained in the reservoirs. Last week (September, 1866), when, by the kind permission of the engineer, Mr. James Simpson, we visited the works at Seething Wells, the depth of water in the subsiding reservoirs was 6 ft.; but this depth is frequently exceeded, and it is indeed below the average. It was, we believe, intended that these subsiding reservoirs should be used alternately, that is to say, that the water was to be allowed to settle in one whilst a supply was being withdrawn from the other to the filter-beds: this system, however, does not seem to be at all times strictly carried out, as, when we saw them, the water was being both admitted to and withdrawn from both of them simultaneously. Each of the subsiding reservoirs is cleared from the matter deposited in it at intervals of about three months.

From that side of each subsiding reservoir which is farthest from the river, there juts out into the reservoir a pair of concentric horizontal arches, these arches being about 2 ft. 6 in. apart, and being built of brickwork laid with open joints. The space between the arches is filled with shingle, and, as the mouths of pipes leading to the filter-beds are enclosed by them, all the water on its way to the latter undergoes a preliminary filtering before leaving the reservoirs. The two filter-beds are arranged side by side at the southern end of the reservoirs, and are of equal size, each having an area of filter surface of about 45,000 square feet. The sides are made, like those of the reservoirs, of concrete walls faced with brickwork, the inner slopes being 1 to 1. In the drawing of the pump-well of the engines at the Chelsea works, the highest level of the water in the filter-beds is marked as being 6 ft. below the average summer water level in the river, and consequently the same distance below average summer level of the water in the subsiding reservoirs; and, moreover, as we are informed that the mean summer level of the Thames at Seething Wells has been taken as 3 ft. above Trinity high water, it follows that the highest level of the water in the filter-beds is 3 ft. below Trinity high water, or 9 ft. 6 in. above Ordnance datum. The water is taken from a short distance above the bottom of the subsiding reservoirs, so as to leave a certain depth for settlement.

The drainage of the filter-beds is effected by means of a central inclined channel or culvert which is in communication with a number of perforated drain pipes laid in transverse rows. These pipes vary in diameter from 6 in. at the sides of the filter-bed to 12 in. where they join the central culvert, and in addition to being perforated with ¾ in. holes, they are laid with slightly open joints between the ends. The pipes are supported by earthenware chairs, and are covered with coarse gravel to a depth of some inches, the depth of the gravel between the pipes being about 2 ft. Over the coarse gravel is laid 4 in. of fine gravel, and over this again a layer of clean cockle, telina, and other shells, about 6 in. thick, the shells being in their turn covered by 6 in. of coarse sand, and then by fine sand, laid, when the filter is made up, to a depth of 2 ft. 6 in. The total depth of the filtering material is thus about 5 ft. 10 in. At periods varying according to the state of the water, but which may be taken to average about a week, the surface of the top layer of sand is scraped to remove the impurities which are deposited by the water, and which would otherwise clog the filter. A film of sand about ⅛ in. thick is removed by each of these scraping operations, and this dirty sand is washed and then set on one side until required for making up the filter. Each filter-bed is made up once in twelve months, and when this operation takes place, the sand which is left after the scrapings which have taken place is thrown up and deposited upon the top of the clean sand which is taken to make up the bed; and by this means it is ensured that the sand which has been longest in the bed will be the first to be removed and cleaned when the bed is brought into work.

The water is led into the filter-beds at the southern end, or that farther from the subsiding reservoirs, and it is supplied to each bed by seven inlet pipes, each furnished with a sluice for regulating the quantity admitted. The pipes jut out for some feet from the southern banks of the beds, just below the surface of the sand, and each of them terminates in a long wooden trough of square section, these troughs being each closed at the outer end, but open at the top, so that they serve to deflect the entering currents of water upwards and prevent them from washing away the surface of the sand. Just beyond the ends of the troughs there is carried across each filter-bed an iron pipe, furnished with vertical branches extending to the surface of the filtering material, each branch being closed by a plug having attached to it a rod projecting above the water level. These pipes are used for draining the filter-beds in case they should become clogged, in which case the plugs are removed by means of the rods, and the water allowed to escape through the pipes into drains, from which it is raised by means of an engine which will be described presently. Each filter-bed is furnished with overflow sluices at each end, these being used not only for preventing the water from rising too high, but also for allowing any scum to flow over. The general practice is, to open those sluices which are on the lee side of the filter-beds, to which side the scum is driven by the action of the wind.

As the filter-beds are situated at a considerable depth below the surrounding ground level, a double hoist has been erected at the southern end of the wall dividing them, by means of which the sand can be easily raised from the beds to the washing-machine, or lowered from the latter to the beds as required. This hoist consists merely of a couple of platforms moving vertically between guides fixed to a strong timber framing, and raised and lowered alternately by means of chains worked by gearing, the latter being driven by shafting extending from the engine which works the pumps for drainage purposes. Close to the hoist, and driven from the same set of shafting, is the sand-washing machine, this differing materially in appearance from that which we described in the preceding article as being used at the West Middlesex Waterworks. The machine at Seething Wells consists of two concentric revolving cylinders formed of coarse wire gauze, these cylinders having their axes inclined slightly from the horizontal. The axis of the cylinders is a perforated pipe, into which water is led by a suitable joint a tthe lower end; and as this water is under pressure, it is distributed from the perforations over the inner surface of the inner cylinder. Other pipes are also placed on each side of the outer cylinder, these being perforated so as to distribute water over the outer surface. The sand to be washed is supplied by a hopper to the interior of the inner cylinder, and, as the cylinders revolve, it is washed out through the meshes, any coarse gravel or other material which may have become mixed with it rolling down the insides of the cylinders until it is discharged from the lower ends.   The mixed sand and water escaping through the meshes of the cylinders is allowed to flow along suitable channels, where the clean sand is deposited, whilst the dirt is carried off by the water.   There are two of these depositing channels, which are used alternately, as in the case of the West Middlesex machine.

The sand-washing machine, hoist and draining pumps, are worked by a pair of 15-horse non-condensing beam-engines, placed in an engine-house not far from the filter-beds.   These engines, which are coupled, have each a cylinder 14 in. in diameter, with a stroke of 24 in., and they are supplied with steam by three single-flued Cornish boilers, which are worked at 30 lb. per square inch.   The draining-pumps are three in number, and are single acting, each being 20 in. in diameter, with a stroke of 3 ft. 6 in.   Their buckets are worked by connecting-rods coupled to cranks on a countershaft, which is driven from the engine-shaft by gearing.

From the filter-beds the water is led through a culvert laid under the Thames Ditton and Kingston road to the engine pump-wells, in which it usually rises to a level but little below that of the suction-valves of the pumps.   The pumping-engines employed at Seething Wells are all of the double-cylinder rotative class working bucket-and-plunger pumps, and were constructed by Messrs. Simpson and Co., of the Grosvenor Works, Pimlico.   At present there are four of these engines at work pumping filtered water at Seething Wells, but the erection of two others is now nearly completed.*   The engine-house in which the new engines are placed has been built of sufficient size to accommodate four engines, and the delivery mains and air-vessels of the pair of engines now erecting are arranged so that the mains of another additional pair of engines can be readily coupled to them.   In the construction of the new boiler-house also, provision has been made for the accommodation of additional boiler power.

The engines above mentioned are all of similar construction and dimensions.   They are beam engines, and of the two cylinders of each engine the high-pressure cylinder is 28 in. in diameter, with a stroke of 5 ft. 6⅜ in., and the low-pressure cylinder 46 in. in diameter, with a stroke of 8 ft.   They are both jacketed at the sides and bottoms.   The piston-rod of the low-pressure cylinder is coupled to one end of the beam, whilst that of the high-pressure cylinder is attached to it at a point nearer the main centre.   The beam is made with equal arms, and

---

* Since the above was written these engines have been set to work.

to the pump end of it a connecting-rod is attached, the lower end of this rod being coupled to a crank-shaft, which carries a flywheel, and serves for a pair of engines, the cranks of the two engines being placed at right angles. Provision is also made for coupling together the shafts of the four engines which are in one engine-house when they are all at work, but either pair can be worked independently, if desired. The pumps are, as we have already stated, of the bucket-and-plunger class, the buckets being 24 in. and the plungers 17½ in. in diameter. The pump-rods are attached to the beams at a short distance within the connecting-rod centres, and they are made double, so that the cranks can work in between them. The stroke of the pumps is 6 ft. 11 in. The suction and bucket valves are gun-metal ring valves, bedding upon seats of white metal, and the delivery valves are ordinary flap valves hung nearly vertically. Both the connecting and pump-rods are built up of wrought-iron plates and angle-irons, the former rods being of a box and the latter of I section. Each pump-well is 23 ft. 1½ in. long by 9 ft. 6 in. wide, and the bottoms of the wells are 54 ft. below the engine-house floors. The delivery pipes from the pumps of all the four engines now at work are united into one main, and, near the point of junction, pipes are led back to the two air-vessels, which serve for all the pumps. The cold water, feed, and air-charging pumps are worked by rods leading from such points in the engine beams that they all have a stroke of 3 ft. ⅞ in. The feed-pumps are 4 in. and the air-charging pumps 5 in. in diameter, and they are arranged to discharge their contents during the up stroke, so that the greatest strain on their rods is a tensional one. The point of each beam from which the pumps just mentioned are driven is situated between the main pump and the main centre, and the air-pump of each engine is driven from a corresponding point on the other side of the main centre, between the latter and the high-pressure piston-rod centre. One of the chief peculiarities of the engines is the arrangement of the steam valves and gear, which is that designed by Mr. David Thomson, formerly the manager of Messrs. Simpson's works at Pimlico, and Professor Pole. The valves, which are worked by cams, are of the piston kind, and the passages for the steam are so arranged as to reduce to a minimum the loss of pressure arising from the transfer of the steam from the high to the low-pressure cylinder. On Plates V. and VI. we give illustrations of the engines of the same class, and—with the exception of the diameters of the pump-plungers and buckets — of identical dimensions, constructed by Messrs. Simpson for the Lambeth Waterworks, and we shall, in the following article, give a full description of the valve-gear and its action, as well as of the other constructive

details of the engines; and, under these circumstances, it will be unnecessary to add, at present, to the above general particulars of the
engines at the works of the Chelsea Company.

The engines at Seething Wells, above mentioned, pump the water
through a 30 in. main to covered reservoirs at Putney Heath, a distance of 6¼ miles, the main being carried across the Thames by an iron
aqueduct of nine spans. Of these spans the centre one is 90 ft., and
has a clear height underneath it of 20 ft. at high water; the remaining
spans are 60 ft. each. The water is delivered into the Putney Heath
reservoirs by a pipe, the mouth of which is at the top-water level, and
the height at which the water is delivered is therefore a constant one.
We are informed by Mr. Simpson that the reservoirs at Putney Heath
are 170 ft. above Trinity high-water mark, and, on the topographical
contour map published for Mr. R. W. Mylne, C.E., in 1856, the water-
level in them is given as 160 ft. above Trinity high water, these dimensions corresponding to 182 ft. 6 in. and 172 ft. 6 in. above Ordnance
datum respectively. The height of the water in the engine-wells of
course varies according to the level in the filter-beds, and is probably
generally somewhat lower than the latter, owing to the loss of the head
necessary to force the water through the filtering material. Generally,
we believe, the dead head against the pumps is about 182 ft., and the
effective head arising from the dead head, the friction of the mains,
&c., varies according to the number of engines which are at work, and
the speed at which they are working. When we were at the works,
the four engines were running at twelve revolutions per minute, and
the effective head against the pumps was 220 ft. Soon after the four
engines were erected a trial of them, which lasted 24 hours, was conducted by Mr. Joshua Field, and during this trial the average speed
was 14.44 revolutions per minute, and the effective head against the
pumps 234¼ ft., this head being the mean determined from observations
taken every half-hour. In this trial the quantity of water delivered
into the reservoirs was 11,287,208 gallons in the 24 hours, and the
quantity of coal consumed 255 cwt., the consumption showing a duty
of 103.9 millions of pounds raised 1 ft. high by the consumption of
112 lb. of coals. After the experiment of 24 hours was ended, one pair
of engines was stopped, and the other pair worked at such a rate as to
raise 7,500,000 gallons into the reservoirs in 24 hours. This pair was
then stopped, and the other pair subjected to a similar trial. During
the summer months the four engines now at work have but little super-
fluous power. The number of hours run by each pair of engines, during
the last week in August of the present year, 1866, averaged 151 hours,
one pair having been stopped 10 hours and the other 24 hours during the

week. The average speed was 12½ revolutions per minute. In winter-time the work is not quite so heavy, the number of hours worked by each pair of engines averaging about 125 per week. The new engines which we have mentioned are intended as relieving engines, and will not be worked in addition to the four now used, or at all events not for the present.

To supply steam to the four engines now in use, thirteen single-flued Cornish boilers are provided, each boiler being 31 ft. 9 in. long by 5 ft. 8 in. in diameter, and the diameter of the flues being 3 ft. 3 in. The effective heating surface of each boiler is 540 square feet, this including one-third of the internal and two-thirds of the external flue surface. The pressure of steam at which the boilers are worked is 40 lb., and they are situated below the level of the engine-house floor, so that the water arising from the condensation of the steam in the steam jackets can drain back into them. Nine boilers are worked to supply steam to the four engines, and seven boilers to supply steam to one pair of engines, the larger proportionate number used in the latter case being employed in order to avoid delay in lighting up a sufficient number of boilers to work the four engines in case they are required. The pair of new engines which Messrs. Simpson are now (September, 1866) putting up are provided with seven boilers similar to those of the older engines; these new boilers being arranged in two groups, four in one and three in the other. All the boilers are completely fitted with the necessary safety valves, feed valves, water gauges, &c.

The coal used is slack, mixed in some cases with a small proportion of Welsh; on the average, about 10 per cent. of the latter is used. The coal is brought to the works by barges, and unloaded by the aid of a hydraulic crane fixed on the river wall, and worked by water supplied from the mains. The iron boxes in which the coal is raised are placed on suitable trucks and run down an inclined railway which passes, through a tunnel carried under the turnpike road, to a point beneath the coal stores. The line just mentioned is a double one, and the trucks are coupled to a wire rope passing over large pulleys at the head of the incline, so that those trucks which are descending with a load haul up the empty ones. On their arrival beneath the coal stores, the boxes of coal are raised by a hydraulic hoist to the top of the stores, and their contents delivered upon the coal heaps, one side of each box being hinged to allow of its being done readily.

In addition to the engines we have already described, there are at Seething Wells another pair of engines which are employed for pumping unfiltered water through a 15 in. main to another reservoir on Putney Heath, this unfiltered water being used for road watering and similar purposes. The engines just mentioned are condensing beam-engines, each of 25 nominal horse power, and they were built by Messrs. Simpson and Co. They were originally employed for supplying water to the fountains at the Great Exhibition of 1851, whilst they were subsequently in use at the works at Thames Bank, for pumping purposes, and it was from this latter place that they were finally removed to their present situation. They have single cylinders 20 in. in diameter, with a stroke of 3 ft., and drive bucket and plunger pumps with 2 ft. stroke, the buckets being 11¼ in. and the plungers 8 in. in diameter. The steam-valves are worked by cams on the crank-shaft, and the engines are driven at twenty-seven and twenty-eight strokes per minute. They are provided with five single-flued Cornish boilers, three of these boilers being generally in steam at one time. The boilers are worked at a pressure of 40 lb. per square inch.

We have said that the filtered water is pumped from Seething Wells to a pair of covered reservoirs at Putney Heath, through a 30 in. main. This main rises and falls to suit the various gradients of the road along which it is laid, and it is provided with air-cocks at the highest points. The air-cocks are placed, when possible, at the horse-troughs of wayside inns, so that the water escaping from them, small as its quantity is, is not wasted. The arrangement employed to ensure the discharge of the air is very simple. The main communicates with a closed iron box containing a ball-cock, the cock being arranged so that it opens and discharges the air from the upper part of the box when the water level in the latter falls. Another smaller cock communicates with the lower part of the box, and this cock is left constantly open, its size being such that it usually discharges the whole of the air, and also allows a small leakage of water. If, however, the air collects more quickly than it can be discharged by the small cock, the water level in the box falls, and the larger cock is brought into action. The whole of the air-cocks on the line of the main are inspected weekly.

The covered reservoirs on Putney Heath are situated on the highest part of the heath, near the west side of the old Portsmouth road, and also close to the west side of the road from Wimbledon to Fulham. They are of similar dimensions, each being 310 ft. long by 160 ft. wide at the top of the banks, and 20 ft. deep. The sides of the reservoirs are formed by concrete walls laid in steps cut in the banks and having an inside slope of 1 to 1, except in the case of the division wall between the two reservoirs, which is 4 ft. thick at the top, and has a slope of 1¼ to 1 on each side. The bottoms of the reservoirs are formed of concrete beds 1 ft. thick. The covering of the reservoirs is formed by a series of brick arches supported by piers, which run the whole length of the reservoirs. There are eight arches to each reservoir, the side arches being of 20 ft. span and the remainder of 18 ft. 8 in. span. The thickness of the arches is 9 in., and they are covered with a layer of puddle, concrete being employed to fill up the haunches. The rise of the arches is 4 ft. 3 in., and each is provided with a couple of openings in the centre, these openings communicating with a line of 12 in. earthen pipes, which is carried through the spandrils, and is connected with perforated iron caps placed in the wall between the two reservoirs, this arrangement being adopted to ensure the ventilation of the reservoirs above the water level. The piers of the arches are 14 in. thick, and are surmounted by skewbacks formed of moulded bricks from which the arches spring. The piers are perforated by openings 17 ft. 6 in. in diameter, formed at a distance apart of 40 ft. from centre to centre, and each of the 22 ft. 6 in. spaces left between these openings is strengthened by a couple of counterforts 14 in. thick, and projecting at right angles to the piers for a distance of about 6 ft. at the base. The distance between the pair of counterforts of each of the 22 ft. 6 in. lengths is about 13 ft., and between each pair of them there is formed through the pier a smaller circular opening 5 ft. 6 in. in diameter. The supply pipe from Seething Wells enters the reservoirs a few inches below the springing of the covering arches, and at the same level an overflow weir is formed to prevent the reservoir from being filled too full.

The open reservoir at Putney Heath, which receives the unfiltered water intended for street-watering purposes and for the supply of the Serpentine, is situated close to the covered reservoirs already described. Its dimensions at the top of the banks are 194 ft. long by 104 ft. wide, and the depth varies from 12 ft. to 13 ft. 6 in., the bottom having a slope of 1 ft. 6 in. The sides are formed by concrete slopes of $1\frac{1}{2}$ to 1, and the highest water level is $6\frac{1}{3}$ ft. above that in the covered reservoirs. The distributing-pipe is led from a circular well sunk 5 ft. below the floor of the reservoir.

From the covered reservoirs on Putney Heath the filtered water is distributed to the district by gravitation, through two 24 in. mains, whilst the unfiltered water is supplied through a single 12 in. main. The total length of pipeage is about 270 miles. According to the Registrar-General's report for July, 1866, the water supplied by the Chelsea Company contained 24.89 parts of solid matter in each 100,000 parts of water; this amount of impurity including 1.29 parts of organic matter, and 17.4 parts of carbonate of lime, or its equivalent of hardening salts. The daily supply furnished by the company during the month mentioned averaged 8,671,600 gallons per day, this quantity, being distributed amongst 26,463 houses. The water rental of the Chelsea Waterworks Company is now (1866) 64,302*l*.

THE LAMBETH WATERWORKS COMPANY.

The Lambeth Waterworks Company, to which Mr. James Simpson is the engineer, and which now draws its supply of water from the river Thames at Thames Ditton, was the first of the Thames water companies to remove its source of supply above the influence of the tide. It was incorporated in 1785, under the Act 25 George III., cap. 89, and obtained additional powers by the Act 4 William IV., cap. 7, whilst the present works were established under the Act 11 Victoria, cap. 7 (1847). The old works were situated in the Belvidere-road, near Waterloo-bridge; but these were abandoned in 1852, in January of which year the supply was commenced from Thames Ditton.

The Thames Ditton works adjoin those of the Chelsea Company at Seething Wells, which we described in the last article, and, as in the case of those works, the piece of ground on which they stand is divided by the road leading from Ditton to Kingston. The river front of the works is protected by a wall in the same manner as the Chelsea works, an opening in this wall, guarded by gratings and provided with sluices, admitting the water from the river direct to the filter-beds. It will thus be seen that no subsiding reservoirs are at present used, and although the construction of two such reservoirs has been commenced, it is probable that they will not be completed in much less than two years' time. The filter-beds are four in number, and they measure about 90 ft. in extreme length and width; they are each provided with a single inlet pipe. They are enclosed by vertical sides of brickwork, and their form in plan is somewhat peculiar. Those sides which are at right angles to the line of the river are straight; but the other two sides each filter-bed are each formed of a pair of horizontal arches with their concave sides next the bed, these arches springing from the ends of the side walls of the bed, and from the ends of a kind of partition wall which partly divides each bed into two parts. The height of this partition wall falls by a series of steps until at the central part of its length its top is below the water level. The bottoms of the beds are formed of slate slabs, laid with the joints ½ in. open, and supported by dwarf walls of brickwork, so that a shallow chamber for the reception of the filtered water is formed beneath them. The arrangement of the filtering material over the slate slabs is similar to that employed in the beds of the Chelsea Company already described. The beds are worked with a head of from 7 ft. to 8 ft. 6 in. of water, and two of them are generally cleaned out weekly. It is intended to double the size of each of the filter-beds, and the necessary works have been commenced.

As, when the beds require cleaning, considerable delay would be caused if they had to be drained empty in the ordinary way, an engine working a centrifugal pump has been provided for emptying them. This engine, which is placed in an engine-house adjoining the beds, is a condensing beam-engine constructed by Boulton and Watt. It has a cylinder 24 in. in diameter and 3 ft. stroke, and is supplied with steam by a pair of single-flued Cornish boilers. The centrifugal pump, which it drives by a strap from the flywheel, is situated in a well formed beneath the engine-house floor.

The method in which the dirty sand from the filter-beds is washed at the Lambeth works differs from that followed at either the Chelsea or West Middlesex Companies' works. No sand-washing machine is employed, the cleansing of the material being effected by the aid of a hose-pipe, in the following manner: Adjoining the filter-beds there are formed on the surface level three shallow chambers, each about 10 ft. long by 5 ft. wide, these chambers having slightly sloping beds, and their sides being formed by brick walls about 2 ft. high at the upper, and 1 ft. at the lower end. At one of the lower corners of each chamber there is formed a small overflow weir, the dirty water passing over these overflows being conducted by a suitable channel into the drains. Rather more than a cubic yard of the sand to be washed is placed at the upper end of one of these chambers, and a jet of water directed on it by means of a hose-pipe connected with the mains. The man in charge of the hose-pipe so directs the jet that the sand is driven backwards and forwards from one side of the chamber to the other, and the impurities with which it is mixed are thus washed out and carried away by the overflowing water. The process is continued until the water comes over the overflow nearly or quite clear, the time occupied in obtaining this result, with a charge of sand of the amount above mentioned, being about twenty minutes. The chambers are used alternately, the cleaned sand being removed from one whilst the washing process is going on in another.

From the filter-beds the water is conducted to the engine pump-wells, in which, as in the case of the Chelsea works, it usually rises to within a short distance of the suction valves of the pumps. The engines, which, with the exception of a few minor points, are similar to those at the Chelsea works, are double-cylinder rotative beam-engines, constructed by Messrs. Simpson and Co., of the Grosvenor Works, Pimlico, to whom we are indebted for the drawings from which the engravings on Plates V.

and VI. have been prepared. At present (September, 1866) there are two pairs of these engines at work, and another pair is in course of erection,* the engine-house in which the new engines are placed being made of sufficient size to accommodate another pair of engines when required. The two pairs of engines now at work are in one engine-house, this being separated from the new engine-house by an intermediate building containing some of the boilers.

In Fig. 5, Plate VI., we have given an outline diagram of the engines, which, combined with the enlarged views of the most important details, will explain their construction. We may mention here that we have preferred giving a general outline diagram and enlarged details, instead of a complete combined view, as the small scale to which the latter would necessarily have had to been drawn would have prevented the various peculiarities of the engines from being distinctly shown. As we have already stated, they are double-cylinder engines, and, as in the case of those at the Chelsea works, the low-pressure cylinders are 46 in. in diameter and 8 ft. stroke, and the high-pressure cylinders 28 in. in diameter with a stroke of 5 ft. 6$\frac{3}{4}$ in. The pumps have also the same stroke as those of the Chelsea engines, viz. 6 ft. 11 in.; but the diameters of the buckets and plungers are rather less, being 23$\frac{3}{4}$ in. and 16$\frac{1}{4}$ in. respectively. The length of the beams between the end centres is 26 ft. 6 in., and the height of the main centre above the engine-house floor 21 ft. 4 in. As the beams have equal arms, and the connecting-rod centres correspond to those of the low pressure piston-rods, the cranks have a throw equal to half the stroke of the low-pressure pistons, or 4 ft. The crank-shaft bearings are 13$\frac{1}{4}$ in. in diameter, and one shaft serves for each pair of engines, the cranks on it being placed at right angles. The flywheels, of which there is one to each pair of engines, are 21 ft. in diameter, and each weighs 13 tons. The beams are 5 ft. deep in the centre, and each is formed of two flitches, the weight of each flitch being 6$\frac{1}{4}$ tons. The engines are each perfectly balanced by both pistons being made solid, and by about 2$\frac{1}{2}$ tons of balance-weights being placed between the flitches of the beam. The distances between the centres of the three motion-pins and the main centre are respectively 5 ft. 1 in., 9 ft. 2 in., and 13 ft. 3 in., and the parallel motion is arranged as shown in the outline diagram, Fig. 5.

In Fig. 2, Plate V., we give a section of the low-pressure cylinder, valve jacket, and air-pump of one of the Lambeth engines; and in Fig. 6, Plate VI., an elevation of the cam gear by which the valves are

---

* Since the above was written these engines have been completed.

worked. As we remarked in the last article, this arrangement of valves and valve gear was designed by Mr. David Thomson, formerly the manager of Messrs. Simpson's works, and Professor Pole, and it forms one of the principal features of the engines. One valve effects the distribution of the steam to both cylinders, this valve consisting of four pistons disposed in two pairs, one pair at the top and one at the bottom, and united by a pipe, the inside of which communicates with the spaces between the pairs of pistons. The steam is supplied to the valve-box between the two inner pistons, and the condenser communicates with the top and bottom of the valve-box by the arrangement of pipes shown in Fig. 2. The same figure also shows the positions of the ports leading to the high and low pressure cylinders, the passages belonging to the former (which are nearer together than those of the latter) being shown broken off just outside the valve box. The ports are rectangular, and those of the large cylinder extend two-thirds round the circumference of the valve, whilst those of the small cylinder extend but half round. They are all provided with bars across them to prevent the packing rings of the valves from catching the edges of the ports, and these bars are inclined so as to avoid grooving the packing. The valves themselves used to be packed with cast-iron rings having springs behind them; but Messrs. Simpson now fit each piston of the valve with a solid cast-iron ring having a steel "Ramsbottom's" ring recessed into it at its upper and lower edges. The diameter of the valve pistons is about 14 in., and that of the connecting-pipe 6 in. inside.

The action of this valve is as follows :—In Fig. 2, Plate V., the engine is supposed to be making an up stroke, and, in the position shown, the valve shuts off the supply of steam from both ends of the small cylinder, and forms a passage between the lower end of the large and the upper end of the small cylinder. This being the case, the steam passes from the upper end of the small cylinder into the space between the two upper pistons of the valve, and thence, through the connecting-pipe, into the corresponding space between the two lower pistons, this latter space being, when the valve is in the position shown, in communication with the lower port of the large cylinder. At the same time the upper port of the large cylinder is uncovered by the upper piston of the valve, and it is thus in communication with the condenser. Near the end of the up stroke the valve receives an upward movement from its cam, this movement bringing the under edge of the lower of the upper pair of valve pistons above the port communicating with the upper end of the small cylinder, and thus admitting steam to that end, whilst at the same time a communication is opened between the lower end of the small and the upper end of the large cylinder through the pipe connecting the upper and lower parts of the valve, and the lower port of the large cylinder is placed in communication with the condenser. When, during its down stroke, the piston of the high-pressure cylinder has reached the point at which the cam is set to cut off the steam, the valve receives a downward movement sufficient to close the upper port of the small cylinder, and still later in the stroke it receives a further downward movement, which opens up the passage between the top of the small and the bottom of the large cylinder, and uncovers the lower port of the small cylinder for the admission of steam and the upper port of the large cylinder for exhaustion into the condenser. The upward stroke of the pistons then commences; and when the point of cut-off in the small cylinder is reached, the valve receives an upward movement which restores it to the position shown in Fig. 2.

From the above explanation it will be seen that during each revolution of the crank-shaft the valve performs one upward and one downward stroke, and that these strokes are not performed by a continuous motion, but that each consists of two distinct movements or impulses. The arrangement by which this required motion is given to the valve is, as we have already stated, shown in elevation by Fig. 6. The shaft upon which the cam is placed runs at right angles to the crank-shaft, and is driven from the latter by means of a pair of bevel wheels of equal size. The whole of the cam gear is arranged below the floor of the engine-house, and there is a separate cam-shaft for each engine, so that by disconnecting the connecting-rod and cam gear of one engine, the other can be driven independently. Each cam consists of three parts, one of these—that by which the cut-off of the steam is effected—being adjustable. This adjustable portion is shaded with a darker tint in Fig. 6. A second portion of the cam is that which causes the second movement of the valve in each stroke, this part being fixed on the cam-shaft, whilst the third portion is merely an intermediate piece which serves to form a convenient connexion between the other two parts. The direction of the motion of the cam-shaft is shown by the arrows in Fig. 6, in which that part of the cam which effects the second movement of the valve during each stroke is represented as just coming under the upper roller. The point of cut-off can be varied from $\frac{1}{8}$ to $\frac{3}{4}$ the stroke.

The two rollers against which each cam works are carried by levers, one end of each of which is keyed upon a short rocking-shaft carried by suitable bearings, as shown in Fig. 6. Each of the levers is made of two plates placed a short distance apart, and accommodating the cam-roller between them; and the lower lever is prolonged, and has its end connected to a crosshead on the valve-spindle by means of short links—the crosshead just mentioned being adjustable on the valve-spindle by means of nuts above and below it. The upper and lower cam levers are connected by means of links having bearings which take hold of the outer ends of the short spindles upon which the rollers work; and the rocking-shaft, upon which the lower lever is fixed, has also keyed upon it another lever provided with a weight by which the whole weight of the valve, rollers, levers, &c., is counterbalanced. The roller levers are placed at such a distance apart, vertically, that the clear distance between the rollers is slightly greater than the greatest diameter of the cam; and it thus happens that during a portion of the revolution of the cam-shaft the valve, with its attachments, is left entirely free, and is only retained in the position in which it has been last placed, by the cam, by the friction of its pistons and spindle stuffing-box. The cams and cam-rollers are of cast iron, and have chilled surfaces.

The system of valves and gear, which we have described, is one which is found to act extremely well. The valves involve no difficulties of construction, and the loss of pressure which the steam undergoes during its passage from the high to the low pressure cylinder is reduced to a minimum, both by the passages through which it travels being made of moderate dimensions, and as direct as possible, and by preventing any communication between the intermediate passage and the condenser, so

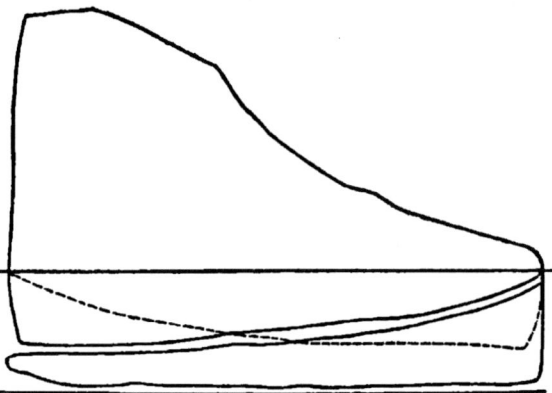

that when the steam enters the passage the latter is already filled with steam of the density which existed in the large cylinder at the termination of the previous stroke. The fact of the pipe connecting the upper and lower parts of the valve passing through the space which is filled with fresh steam from the boiler also causes the steam which is carried through the tube on its way from one cylinder to the other to be slightly reheated during its passage. We give on the previous page an engraving, showing a pair of indicator diagrams taken simultaneously from the top of the small and bottom of the large cylinder when the steam was being cut off in the former at 40 per cent. of the stroke; and it will be seen that the loss of pressure due to the transfer of the steam is really very slight.

In the engines which we are describing, the capacities of the cylinders, passages, &c., are as follows:

	cub. in.	cub. in.
Capacity of small cylinder, 5 ft. 6⅜ in. stroke .		40,870
Clearance at end of small cylinder . . .	308	
Space in port between valve and small cylinder .	805	
Total space between valve and small piston . .		1,113
Capacity of large cylinder, 8 ft. stroke . . .		159,542
Clearance at end of large cylinder . . .	831	
Space in port between valve and large cylinder .	2844	
Total space between valve and large piston . .		3,675
Capacity of all passages in the valve . . .		3,944
Sum of last two capacities		7,619

The expansion of the steam due to these capacities is as follows:

Per-centage of stroke at which the steam is cut off in the small cylinder 25		40
Total expansion at end of stroke in small cylinder, in terms of the bulk before expansion . 3.78		2.41
Amount of expansion on passing from small to large cylinder, in terms of bulk before escaping from small cylinder . . . 1.18		1.18
Total expansion at end of stroke in large cylinder, in terms of original bulk 15.15		9.66
Total amount of efficient expansion in terms of original bulk 12.80		8.19

By the indicator diagrams taken by Mr. Thomson from these engines, it was found that the final pressures in both the small and large cylinders were always in excess of those due to the rates of expansion, and this was the case, notwithstanding that the utmost care was taken to ensure the tightness of the valves. When the steam was cut off at 25 per cent. of the stroke in the small cylinder, the initial pressure being 26 lb. per square inch, it was found in some cases that the final pressure in that cylinder was 2.2 lb. and the final pressure in the large cylinder 0.9 lb. above those theoretically due to the rate of expansion; whilst, when the initial pressure was 35 lb., and the steam was cut off in the small cylinder at 40 per cent. of the stroke, the final pressure in that and the large cylinder were 1 lb. and 1.3 lb. in excess respectively. The actual loss of pressure, as shown by the indicator diagrams, due to the passage of the steam from one cylinder to the other, was in the first of the above-mentioned cases 2.1 lb., and in the second 4.2 lb.

One of the main things gained by the employment of the double cylinder arrangement is the comparatively small variation in the motive force exerted by the two pistons throughout their stroke; thus in the two cases of which we have just given the particulars, if we suppose the pumps to be disconnected, and the whole force exerted by the piston to be transmitted through the connecting-rod, the *mean* pressure on the crank-pin would in the first case amount to 15,240 lb., and in the second case to 22,400 lb., whilst the *maximum* pressures would be 27,838 lb. and 36,058 lb. respectively; and the ratio of maximum to mean pressure would be 1.83 to 1 in the first, and 1.61 to 1 in the second case.

In reality, however, the pressures would be modified by the inertia of the reciprocating parts, which would tend to diminish the effective pressure during the first half and increase it during the latter half of each stroke. The reduction of the initial blow given by the pressure of the steam upon the pistons at the commencement of each stroke, effected by the double cylinder arrangement, of course greatly relieves the strain upon all the working parts, and it thus enables the steam to be safely worked with a higher degree of expansion than it otherwise conveniently could be. A long discussion of the advantages and disadvantages of the single and double cylinder and Cornish and rotative engines would, however, be out of place here, and we must, therefore, return to a description of the engines at the Lambeth Waterworks.

Both cylinders are steam-jacketed at the sides and bottoms; but the top covers are provided with an air space only. Referring to the section of the large cylinder given in Fig. 2, it will be seen that the barrel of the cylinder is bolted to the base by means of an internal flange, whilst the connexion between the base and the steam-jacket is effected by an external flange. At the top the joint between each jacket

E 2

and cylinder is made by a stuffing-box, this arrangement allowing the
cylinder and jacket to expand or contract independently without affecting the tightness of the joint.   Any water arising from the condensation
of the steam in the jacket drains into the bottom jacket of the large
cylinder, and thence back into the boilers, the latter being placed at a
lower level than the engine-house floor.   The pistons are of cast iron,
that of the large cylinder being 12½ in. and that of the small cylinder
20 in. deep.   In the case of the new engines, they are packed with steel
rings on Mr. Ramsbottom's plan.   From Fig. 2 it will also be seen that
stuffing-boxes are introduced for connecting the different parts of the
valve-box and eduction pipe, so that there may be no strains arising
from unequal expansion.   In Messrs. Simpson's new engines the piece
which is shown in Fig. 2, as connecting the upper and lower ends of the
valve-box, is made in two parts united by flanges, and a sufficient in-
terval is left between the upper end of the lower and the lower end of
the upper portions of the valve-box to allow of the two parts of the con-
necting-piece being removed from their places singly, so as to give ready
access to the valve.

The air-pump, which is also shown in section in Fig. 2, is 30 in. in
diameter, and the bucket has a stroke of 3 ft. 0⅜ in.   The valves are of
india-rubber, arranged as shown in the section.   The cold-water pump
and the air-charging and feed pumps are worked by rods coupled to
the beam at a point corresponding to the point of attachment of the
air-pump rod, but on the other side of the main centre, and they also,
therefore, have a stroke of 3 ft. 0⅜ in.   The air-charging and feed pumps
are worked by one rod, and the cold-water pump by another, these
rods being placed side by side, and being coupled to centres on opposite
sides of the beam.   The cold-water pump-rod passes direct to the bucket,
as shown in the section of that pump, Fig. 3, from which it will also be
seen that the valves of the pump are of india-rubber.   The air-charging
pump is placed below the feed pump, but in the same straight line, the
feed pump being inverted, that is to say, the plunger works through the
lower end.   The rod for working these pumps is coupled to a crosshead
above the feed pump, and from this crosshead two rods extend downwards, one on each side of the feed pump, to another crosshead which
extends across between the two pumps.   The two rods and the crossheads just mentioned thus make a sort of vertical frame round the feed
pump, and to the lower of the two crossheads the plunger of the feed
pump and the rod of the air-charging pump are connected.   The feed-
pump plunger is 4 in. in diameter, and the valves are of india-rubber,
1¼ in. thick, working on grids, having openings ¼ in. wide.   The bucket
of the air-charging pump is 5 in. in diameter, and is fitted with india-

rubber valves opening upwards. The delivery valves are also of india-rubber. As the air-charging pump has to work against the full pressure in the mains, the grids upon which the valves work are made with openings only ⅛ in. square, so as to give good support to the india-rubber. The thickness of the latter is ⅞ in. The lower end of the air-charging pump barrel is closed, the air being admitted through a pipe connected with it. This pipe is bent upwards, and is connected to another by which water can be admitted into the pump at pleasure instead of air, it being necessary to do this sometimes to prevent the valves and piston packing from getting too dry and becoming heated. From the above description, it will be seen that both the air-charging and feed pumps, as well as the cold-water pump, deliver their contents during the up stroke, and the chief strain on their rods is therefore a tensional one.

The connecting and pump rods are built up of wrought-iron plates and angle-irons riveted together, all the rivet holes being drilled, and the rivets being turned and put in cold. The connecting-rod, which is 24 ft. long between centres, is of box section, with external angle-irons, whilst the pump rods, of which there are a pair to each engine, are of I section. The connecting-rod is coupled to a bearing between the two flitches of the beam, but the pump-rod bearings are on the outside of each part of the beam, and the two rods are thus placed at a sufficient distance apart to allow the crank and connecting-rod to work in between them. By using this arrangement, the pump rods can be coupled to the beam at a point much nearer to the connecting-rod centre than they otherwise could be, and a longer stroke is thus obtained for the pumps. The lower ends of the pump rods are coupled to a crosshead, which embraces the head of the pump plunger, and is furnished at its ends with guides, which work on suitable guide bars. The arrangement is clearly shown by Figs. 1 and 4.

The main pump is of the combined bucket and plunger class, a description of pump which it is believed was first introduced by Mr. Thomson at the Richmond and Bristol Waterworks in 1848. In the case of the Lambeth engines, the pumps have, as we have already stated, a stroke of 6 ft. 11 in., and the diameter of their buckets is 23¾ in. The plungers are 16¼ in. in diameter; but it must be borne in mind that, in this class of pumps, the pumping power is determined by the length of stroke and diameter of the bucket alone, the size of the plunger merely determining the proportion of the total quantity of water which is delivered during the down stroke; the amounts delivered during the up and down strokes being of course equal, if the plunger has a sectional area equal to half that of the bucket. In Fig. 1, we give a vertical section, and, in Fig. 4, an elevation of one of the pumps. From these views it will be seen that the pump barrel is enlarged at the lower end to join the valve-box containing the suction valves. These valves consist of two annular gun-metal valves of the section shown in Fig. 1, striking on gun-metal seats, and the box containing them, together with the suction pipe, is ordinarily supported partly by the bolts connecting the former with the lower end of the pump barrel, and partly by set screws which bear upon cast-iron girders, carried across the pump well near the level of the suction valves, as shown in Fig. 4. The suction-valve-box is also provided with a wheel or pulley on each side, and by breaking the joint between the valve-box and barrel, and slacking back the set screws just mentioned, the valve-box and suction pipe are lowered until these pulleys rest upon rails cast upon the cast-iron girders to receive them. When the valve-box and its connexions have been then thus made to rest upon the pulleys, it can be readily moved on one side for the purpose of giving access to the suction and bucket valves.

The bucket is furnished with a single annular valve, of the same description as the suction valves, but of slightly different section, as will be seen from Fig. 1. The bucket is connected to the plunger by a short rod keyed into a socket at the lower end of the latter, this rod having a collar formed on it which acts as a check to the bucket valve. The delivery valves are flap valves hung nearly vertically; they are placed in a valve-box connected to a short branch on the pump barrel, the whole arrangement being shown in Fig. 1. As in the case of the engines at the Chelsea Waterworks, the whole of the delivery pipes from the pumps of the four engines which are now at work unite in a 30 in. main, branch pipes from the point of junction communicating with a pair of air-vessels of the shape shown in Figs. 4 and 5. These air-vessels, which are connected at the top and bottom, serve for the four pumps, and the lower part of each of them is 13 ft. 6 in. high, with a diameter of 4 ft. outside, whilst the upper parts are 6 ft. 4 in. high and 2 ft. 6 in. in diameter. A similar arrangement of delivery pipes is being adopted in the new engine now erecting. The pump-well, for each pair of engines, is 23 ft. 1½ in. long, and 9 ft. 6 in wide, and, in the case of the engines now at work, the depth is 49 ft. below the floor of the engine-house. The pump-wells of the new engines, however, are, we believe, being made the same depth as at the Chelsea works, or 54 ft. below the engine-house floor. In the drawing of the pump-well of the engines now working, the engine-house floor is marked as being 8 ft. above the surrounding ground level, and 28 ft. above the mean summer water level; and as this last mentioned level is taken at Thames Ditton as 3 ft. above Trinity high-water mark, the level of the engine-house floor must be 31 ft. above Trinity high-water mark, or 43 ft. 6 in. above Ordnance datum. The lowest level of the water in the filter-beds is also marked on the drawing just referred to as being 38 ft. below the engine-house floor, corresponding to 5 ft. 6 in. above Ordnance datum.

The engines at Thames Ditton pump the water through a 30 in. main, 10¼ miles long, to covered reservoirs at Brixton. The level of the water in these reservoirs is given in the map of the company as 103 ft. above Trinity high-water mark, or 115 ft. 6 in. above Ordnance datum; and the dead head against the pumps, consequently, probably averages about 105 ft. The head actually pumped against is, however, considerably more than this, and it varies greatly at different times of the day. The main leading from Thames Ditton to Brixton has numerous services connected with it, and in the morning, when these are open, the total head against the pumps is only about 165 ft. As the services are closed the head increases to upwards of 200 ft. Soon after the engines were finished, they were tested, by Mr. Joshua Field, by a trial of 24 hours' duration, and during this trial they were worked at 14 revolutions per minute, and the head against the pumps was 210 ft. Under these circumstances it was found by Mr. Field that the actual work done by the engines, as measured by the water delivered by the pumps, amounted to 97,084,894 lb. raised one foot high by the combustion of 112 lb. of Welsh coal. The speed of 14 revolutions per minute is that at which the engines are now usually worked, and the steam is generally cut off at five-eighths of the stroke in the small cylinders. In the summer-time the whole of the engines are kept at work almost continually; but in winter three only are run, one being disconnected. Another 30 in. main is now being put down by the side of that through which the engines at present pump, and near the engine-houses the mains will be fitted with valves, so that either the new or the present engines can be made to pump through either or both mains at pleasure.

The engines are at present supplied with steam by sixteen single-flued Cornish boilers, of the same description as those at the Chelsea works, which we described in the previous article, and three others are now being added. Nine—or, including the three new ones, twelve—of the boilers are situated in the boiler-house between the two engine-houses, and their steam will be available either for the present or the new engines. Twelve boilers are worked to supply steam to the four engines, and the pressure to which the boilers are loaded is 40 lb. per square inch. The coal is unloaded from the barges in the river and brought to the coal stores in the same manner as at the Chelsea Waterworks, of which we have already given an account.

The reservoirs at Brixton have an area of about three acres, and from them the lower parts of Lambeth and the adjoining parishes are supplied by gravitation through two 20 in. and one 10 in. main.   At Brixton, near the reservoirs, there are also three engine-houses, the one containing two engines of 60 horse power each, and the other two each a pair of engines of 30 horse power, all being made by Messrs. Simpson and Co.   The 60 horse engines are beam-engines, on the double-cylinder principle, the low-pressure cylinder of each engine being annular, and surrounding the high-pressure cylinder.   The diameter of the inner cylinder is 16 in., whilst the inner and outer diameters of the annular piston are 25¼ in. and 41 in. respectively.   The stroke of both pistons is 5 ft. 6 in., the two piston-rods of the annular piston and the single piston-rod of the high-pressure piston being coupled to one cross-head.   The distribution of the steam for both cylinders is effected by a single slide-valve of peculiar form, this valve having an expansion valve working at the back of it.   Each valve is driven by an eccentric on the crank-shaft.   The low-pressure cylinder is protected by a steam jacket on the outside, and a steam jacket is also formed between the high and low pressure cylinders.   The arrangement of the pump end of these engines is very similar to that of the engines at Thames Ditton, which we have already fully described.   Each engine drives a bucket and plunger pump, having a bucket 17½ in. and a plunger 12$\frac{7}{16}$ in. in diameter, the stroke being 4 ft. 7¼ in.   These engines are both worked at night, one only being run during the day, and they pump the water between the 100 ft. and 250 ft. contours above the river, supplying Brixton, Dulwich, Beckenham, Penge, Balham, Streatham, Tooting, Selhurst, &c.   At Streatham Hill and Selhurst there are reservoirs which are supplied by these engines, the levels of the reservoirs being respectively 185 ft. and 206 ft. above Trinity high-water mark, or 197 ft. 6 in. and 218 ft. 6 in. above Ordnance datum.   The engines are provided with four single-flued Cornish boilers, of which two are regularly worked.

Of the other engines at Brixton, one pair are ordinarily condensing beam-engines, with cylinders 21½ in. in diameter and 3 ft. stroke. Their connecting-rods are coupled to cranks placed on one crank-shaft at right angles to each other, and they are fitted with bucket and plunger pumps, the arrangement of the pump-rods being the same as in the Thames Ditton engines.   The pump buckets are 12 in. and the plungers 8½ in. in diameter, and the stroke is 2 ft. 7 in.   These engines pump into a reservoir at Rockhills, near the Crystal Palace, through a main from which services are led for the supply of the high districts. The engines can be made to pump either directly into the reservoir or over a stand-pipe at the reservoir, the level at which the water is delivered being in the one case 350 ft. and in the other 400 ft. above Trinity high water, or 362 ft. 6 in. and 412 ft. 6 in. above Ordnance datum. As the Brixton reservoirs, from which these engines draw their water, are 115 ft. 6 in. above Ordnance datum, the dead head against the pump when delivering into the Rockhills reservoir is 247 ft., and when pumping over the stand-pipe 297 ft.; but the actual heads, including friction, are considerably more, being about 375 ft. when pumping into the reservoir, but varying according to the amount of water taken off by the service-pipes. The engines are supplied with steam by three single-flued Cornish boilers worked at 35 lb. per square inch.

The other pair of engines, or, more properly speaking, the other engine, is on the double-cylinder principle, the high and low pressure cylinders being placed at some little distance apart, and their piston-rods being coupled to independent beams, working cranks at right angles to each other. The high-pressure cylinder is 12 in. and the low-pressure cylinder 21¼ in. in diameter, and both have a stroke of 3 ft. The steam from the high-pressure cylinder is exhausted into an intermediate reservoir, where it is reheated by a steam jacket, and is then led into the low-pressure cylinder. The steam is cut off at half-stroke in the high-pressure and at ¼¼ of the stroke in the low-pressure cylinder. The pumps are of the same class as those of the other engines; the buckets are 7⅝ in. and the plungers 5¾ in. in diameter, and the stroke is 31 in. These engines, which have only been erected a few months, work against an actual head (including friction) of 316 ft., and they raise the water into a tank near the Rockhills reservoir. They can also be made to assist the other 30-horse engines, if required. In winter they are run about 7 hours per day, and in summer about 12 or 14 hours per day. They are provided with three single-flued Cornish boilers, of which one only is at present worked. The pressure of the steam is 45 lb. per square inch.

The total length of the pipeage of the Lambeth Waterworks Company is nearly 300 miles, and, in addition to the districts which we have already mentioned, they supply the town of Kingston and its neighbourhood. At Combe Hill they have a reservoir 160 ft. above Trinity high water, or 172 ft. 6 in. above Ordnance datum. Their annual water rental is now 68,248l., and, according to the Registrar-General's report published at the beginning of August, 1866, the average daily supply of water furnished by them was 9,907,400 gallons, this quantity being distributed amongst 36,374 houses. The amount of solid matters contained in 100,000 parts of the water was 25.51 parts, and of this total quantity 1.53 parts consisted of organic matters and 17.2 parts of carbonate of lime or its equivalent, the degree of hardness of the water expressed by Clark's scale being 12.04.

THE GRAND JUNCTION WATERWORKS COMPANY.

The chief works of the Grand Junction Waterworks Company are situated at Kew, and prior to 1852 the company drew its supply of water from the Thames at that place. About the date mentioned, however, the Grand Junction, like the other Thames water companies, moved its source of supply higher up the river, and it now obtains its water from Hampton, where it has works close to those of the South-wark and Vauxhall and West Middlesex Companies. At Hampton the company has two subsiding reservoirs, each covering an area of 45,000 square feet, and from these the water is pumped by two direct-acting Cornish engines of 110 horse power each, through 13,500 yards of 33 in. main to the Kew works. The engines just mentioned have each a cylinder 60 in. in diameter, with 10 ft. stroke, and a pump-pole 42 in. in diameter, the stroke being of course the same as that of the steam cylinder. The main into which the engines pump is provided with a stand-pipe 90 ft. high.

At Kew there are two subsiding reservoirs and three filter-beds, and into one of the former the water is delivered by the main from Hampton. The two subsiding reservoirs, together, cover an area of 245,000 square feet. The three filter-beds, which adjoin these subsiding reservoirs, have a combined area of 225,000 square feet, and, except for a few weeks in the busiest part of the year, two of them only are in use at one time. The water is conducted into each bed by an open culvert which extends transversely from the side of each bed to the centre, where it joins a similar culvert running longitudinally for the greater part of the length of the bed, the two culverts together thus forming a T in plan. The open culverts are constructed of brickwork, and beneath them there are other culverts through which the water is with-drawn from the beds, and, in fact, the arrangement is very similar to that adopted at the West Middlesex works, of which we gave a descrip-tion and illustrations in the early part of this volume. The filtering material of the Kew beds consists of a lower stratum of 1 ft. of coarse gravel, upon which are laid consecutively 9 in. of rough-screened gravel, 9 in. of fine-screened gravel, 12 in. of fine gravel, and from 3 ft. to 4 ft. of Harwich sand. The water is collected from the filtering material and led to the main culverts by a series of small parallel branch drains, the floors of these drains being formed of York landing stones, and the sides and tops of brickwork laid with joints 1 in. open. The collect-ing drains are well packed round with large stones to prevent the finer filtering material from washing into them. The filter-beds are worked with a head of water of about 4 ft., and according to Mr. R. W. Myne's contour map, the level of the water in them is 33.5 ft. above Ordnance datum.

At the Kew works the sand for the filter-beds is washed by placing it in cast-iron vertical cylinders through which an upward current of water is made to flow. These cylinders are each 7 ft. 6 in. in diameter by 3 ft. high, and they have double bottoms between which the water is admitted by means of a pipe connected to the main. The upper bottom of each cylinder is perforated, and upon it is placed the sand to be washed. As the water rises up through it the sand is kept constantly stirred, and the upward current is thus enabled to carry off all the impurities, whilst the sand, being heavier, remains in the vessel. The dirty water flowing over the edge of each vessel is received and conveyed away by suitable drains, these being furnished with a chamber in which any sand which may have been carried over by the water is deposited. When, by the appearance of the overflowing water, it is seen that a charge of sand has been cleaned, the water is turned off, and that remaining in the vessel allowed to escape by means of a cock provided for the purpose. A layer, about 1 in. thick, is then skimmed off the washed sand and set aside to be treated with another charge, and the remainder, which is completely cleansed, is taken out for use in the filter-beds. This mode of washing the sand appears to be a very simple and effective one, and by its use the cost for the labour of sand-washing at the Kew works has been reduced to 4d. per cubic yard.

The pumping power at Kew includes one engine of 300 horse power, one engine of 150 horse power, and three engines of 130 horse power each, these being all Cornish beam-engines, with the exception of the 150-horse engine, which is a direct-acting Cornish engine, constructed by Messrs. Harvey and Co. The 300-horse engine was built by the Perran Foundry Company, and has a cylinder 90 in. in diameter, with 11 ft. stroke, whilst the pump plunger is 33 in. in diameter, and its stroke the same as that of the steam piston. The engine pumps against a dead head of 160 ft. in a stand-pipe close by, this stand-pipe being in communication with the main leading to the low-level districts and the Campden Hill reservoir.

Two of the 130-horse engines also pump into the stand-pipe, these two engines, which are placed in one engine-house, having their valve gear regulated by one cataract, so that they make alternate strokes. The engines have each a cylinder 62 in. in diameter, and a pump plunger 24 in. in diameter, the stroke of both the piston and pump plunger being 8 ft. The other 130-horse engine is of the same dimensions as those forming the pair above mentioned, but it is employed in pumping against a higher lift in order to supply the Ealing district. The water is delivered by it direct into the main for that district, the strain upon the main being relieved by its being connected to the stand-pipe by a pipe which allows a small portion of the water delivered at each stroke of the pump to flow into the latter. The actual head against the pump is 220 ft., and the engine is worked at 10 strokes per minute.

The 150-horse engine is, as we have already stated, a direct-acting or " Bull " engine, constructed by Messrs. Harvey and Co. It has a 70 in. cylinder and 28 in. pump-pole, and its stroke is 10 ft. It is worked at various speeds up to 17 strokes per minute, and is arranged to pump into the stand-pipe. The delivery pipe of this and all the other engines is furnished with an air-vessel. We have said that the 300-horse, the 150-horse, and a pair of the 130-horse engines are arranged to pump into the stand-pipe; but the four engines are not worked at one time, one of them being generally kept standing as a relieving engine. For supplying steam to the 300-horse engine five single-flued Cornish boilers are provided, of which four are regularly worked; and seven similar boilers, of which six are in regular use, are provided for supplying steam to the other four engines. The boilers are worked at a pressure of 45 lb. per square inch.

From the Kew works a main about four and a half miles long extends to the reservoir at Campden Hill, and the engines which we have mentioned as being arranged to pump into this stand-pipe raise a supply of water into this reservoir during the night, whilst during the day they supply the low-level district. The Campden Hill reservoir is a covered one, and has a capacity of about 4,000,000 gallons, whilst its water level is, according to Mr. R. W. Mylne's contour map, to which we have already referred, 133.8 ft. above Ordnance datum. At Campden Hill, also, the Grand Junction Company have two direct-acting Cornish engines which raise the water from the reservoir just mentioned, for the supply of the high-level districts, the engines pumping against a head of 120 ft. in a stand-pipe. The engines were constructed by Messrs. Harvey and Co., and have each a cylinder 70 in. in diameter. The pump plungers are 33 in. in diameter, and the stroke of the engines is 10 ft. They are provided with nine Cornish boilers, of which six are in regular use; these boilers being each 30 ft. long, 6 ft. in diameter, and having each a single flue 3 ft. 8 in. in diameter. The steam, which is supplied at an average pressure of 35 lb. per square inch, is cut off in the engines at one-third the stroke; and the engines are run at a speed of ten strokes per minute. According to the Registrar-General's report for the month of August 1866, the Grand

Junction Waterworks Company were then supplying an average quantity of 9,800,484 gallons daily, this quantity being distributed amongst 25,636 houses. The total quantity of impurities contained in the water amounted to 25 parts in 100,000, 1.09 parts of this quantity being organic impurities and 16.8 parts of carbonate of lime or its equivalent.

THE SOUTHWARK AND VAUXHALL WATERWORKS COMPANY.

The Southwark and Vauxhall Waterworks Company, to whom Mr. Joseph Quick is the engineer, supply at the present time a daily quantity of water exceeding by about 20 per cent. that distributed by any one of the other Thames companies. Their works at Battersea were formed in 1842, and in 1857 they shifted their source of supply to Hampton, where their pumping station adjoins those of the Grand Junction and West Middlesex Companies.

At Hampton the water is admitted direct from the Thames into a subsiding reservoir, having an area of 83,000 square feet, and an average capacity of about 5,000,000 gallons, the depth of the water in the reservoir varying according to the height of the water in the river. From the subsiding reservoir the water is pumped by three direct-acting or " Bull " engines through a 36 in. main, about thirteen miles in length, to the works at Battersea, where the other subsiding reservoirs and the filter-beds are situated. Of the engines at Hampton, two have each a 60 in. cylinder with 10 ft. stroke, the diameter of the pump-pole being in each case 32 in. The other engine has a 70 in. cylinder and 42 in. pump-pole, the stroke being, as in the case of the other engines, 10 ft. The engines all pump into the main against a head of 135 ft. in a stand-pipe.

The water coming through the 36 in. main from Hampton is, at Battersea, delivered over a weir and then conducted into one of the subsiding reservoirs. From this it is led into the second subsiding reservoir, and thence to the filter-beds. The area of one of the subsiding reservoirs is 187,670 square feet, and that of the other 93,000 square feet, the depth being in each case about 10 ft., and the contents being about 12,000,000 and 6,000,000 gallons respectively. The larger reservoir is divided longitudinally by a bank which reaches up to the water level; and, as each part of the reservoir is furnished with the necessary inlet and outlet pipes, either part can be drained and cleaned out whilst the other part is in use. As we have stated, the water from Hampton is usually allowed to flow through both the subsiding reservoirs on its way to the filter-beds, but arrangements are provided for feeding the latter direct from the 36 in. main if it should at any time become necessary to do so.

The filter-beds at Battersea are five in number, and they have a combined area of nine acres. In construction they greatly resemble those of the Grand Junction works at Kew, already described, the water being distributed over the filtering material from a central open culvert, and collected by branch drains communicating with a main receiving drain situated under the distributing culvert. Both the main and branch drains are constructed of bricks laid with open joints. The beds of the filters are each formed of a layer of concrete about 1 ft. thick, laid on puddle, and above this are placed the filtering materials in the following order: first, 12 in. of boulders, then 6 in. of coarse gravel, then 6 in. of fine gravel, then 6 in. of hoggin, and, finally, 3 ft. of Harwich sand. The filters are generally worked with a head of about 4 ft. of water, but this head can be increased if required. One of the filter-beds was originally of a circular form with side slopes of 2 to 1 ; but a portion of this bed has been cut off by a branch of the London, Chatham and Dover Railway, and the remaining portion has been altered—vertical brick side-walls with a concrete backing having been substituted for the inclined ones. By this alteration the filtering capacity of the bed has been very greatly increased, a result which appears to be entirely due to the extension of the drainage area beneath the filtering material. In fact, in general the extent of this drainage area gives a better indication of the filtering power of a bed than the area of the surface of the filtering material. In filters having sides made with a flat slope, the latter is frequently very much greater than the former, and a considerable portion of it—that lying around the edges beyond the line of the drains—is almost ineffective.

The machine for sand-washing employed at the Battersea works consists of a cast-iron vessel with a double bottom. The upper bottom is perforated, and upon it the sand is placed to a depth of about 3 ft. Water is admitted between the bottoms, and this, rising up through the sand, flows over on one side, carrying the impurities and some sand with it. The overflowing water is allowed to run down a wire screen placed in an inclined position, the inclination of the screen being so regulated that whilst a great portion of the water with the impurities in suspension passes over it into the drains, the remainder falls through, carrying the washed sand with it, this sand and water being then made to traverse a channel in which the sand is deposited.

The pumping power at Battersea consists of five beam-engines and one direct-acting or "Bull" engine—all being of the Cornish class. Two of the beam-engines are employed in pumping to the high-level districts in the neighbourhood of Wimbledon, whilst all the rest of the engines pump into the mains for the lower district.   The two engines supplying the Wimbledon district were made by Messrs. Harvey and Co.; they have each a cylinder 55 in. in diameter and 8 ft. stroke, and they each work a double-acting pump, the diameter of the pump-piston being in the case of one engine 15½ in., and in that of the other 14½ in., whilst the stroke is, in both cases, the same as that of the steam-pistons, or 8 ft.   These engines deliver the water against a head of 300 ft., and pump through one of Husband's patent relief valves, of the kind of which we gave an engraving (in connexion with one of the engines of the West Middlesex Waterworks) in an earlier part of the present volume.   They can, however, be made to pump into the same stand-pipe as the other engines, if required.

The Bull engine was also built by Messrs. Harvey and Co.; and it was the first engine of its class erected in London by those makers. It has a cylinder 70 in. and a pump-pole 33 in. in diameter, the stroke being 10 ft.   This engine, like the others, pumping into the low-level mains, delivers its water against an average head of 170 ft. in a stand-pipe.   Generally speaking, this engine is run about 12 hours per day. Next to the Bull engine is a beam-engine—at present under repair— also made by Messrs. Harvey and Co.   This engine has a cylinder 68 in. and pump-pole 33 in. in diameter; the stroke of both the steam piston and pump plunger being 10 ft., and, like the Bull engine, it pumps into the stand-pipe.

The next engine is one built by the Perran Foundry Company.   It has a cylinder 64 in. in diameter and 11 ft. 6 in. stroke; and a pump plunger 33 in. in diameter and 10 ft. stroke, the beam having unequal arms.   The remaining engine, which was constructed by Messrs. Harvey and Co., is the largest, its cylinder being 112 in. and its pump plunger 50 in. in diameter, whilst the stroke is in each case 10 ft.   The bed-plate of the cylinder of this engine is fixed upon the 30-ton block of granite exhibited in the Great Exhibition of 1851, and the steam nozzles are fitted to the cylinder on the side furthest from the main centre, the steam valves being worked by rods carried across the cylinder cover.   Both the engines last mentioned pump into the mains, against an average head of 170 ft. in the stand-pipe.   The five engines are supplied with steam by twenty-four single-flued Cornish boilers, worked at a pressure of 40 lb. per square inch.

During the month of July, 1866, it appears, from the Registrar-General's report, that the Southwark and Vauxhall Company furnished an average daily supply of water amounting to 12,180,000 gallons, this quantity being distributed amongst 73,857 houses.   The total amount

of the impurities in the water was 23.66 parts in 100,000, this including 16.2 parts of carbonate of lime, or its equivalent, and but 0.98
part of organic matter. The total length of the pipes and mains
belonging to the company is at present 675 miles.

THE KENT WATERWORKS COMPANY.

The Kent Waterworks originated in an enterprise to supply the
royal manors of Sayers Court and East Greenwich with water from the
river Ravensbourne, which was started as long ago as the year 1699,
by certain individuals, who obtained a royal charter granting exclusive
powers for 500 years. Water power from the Sheene was employed
for pumping, and eventually the works became the property of the well-
known John Smeaton and of a watchmaker named Holmes, when
Smeaton erected the machinery of which an engraving may be found in
his reports, where it is described under the name of the Ravensbourne
engine.

The Kent Waterworks was one of the many schemes with which Mr.
R. Dodd was connected, and, in the year 1810, a company was formed
to purchase the Ravensbourne works. This—the Kent Waterworks
Company—erected a steam pumping engine, which, together with
Smeaton's water wheel and pump, supplied water to the towns of Deptford and Greenwich, whilst a few years later a duplicate engine was set
up, and the supply extended to Woolwich. Still later the use of filter-
beds was introduced, and in 1851 Smeaton's machinery was taken down,
although it was still perfect; and we may mention here that we have
been informed by Mr. W. R. Morris, the engineer to the company, that
even now the various parts of Smeaton's machinery are preserved at the
works at Deptford. About the date just mentioned also, it became necessary, in order to meet the demands of the increasing district, to provide increased power for distributing the water, and two 70 in. Cornish
engines, of which we shall give some further particulars presently, were
consequently erected for this purpose. In 1860, a very important
change was made in the company's arrangements, as in that year the
use of the Ravensbourne was discontinued, and artesian wells sunk in
the chalk, from which the supply of water has since been obtained.

At the present time the company has six pumping-stations, of greater
or less extent, these being situated at Deptford, Charlton, Plumstead,
Dover-road, Shortlands, and Crayford, respectively. The Deptford
station is the principal one, and at it there are three artesian wells, each
fitted with an engine and pump, besides a pair of Cornish engines for
distributing the water to the low-level district, and a pair of single-

acting fly-wheel engines, which are employed in pumping to the higher levels.

The principal artesian well is furnished with a Cornish beam engine, made by Messrs. Harvey and Co., having a cylinder 60 in. in diameter, with 10 ft. 6 in. stroke, and working a lift-pump 30 in. in diameter, and of the same stroke as the steam cylinder. This engine is fitted with a surface condenser consisting of a number of vertical tubes uniting top and bottom chambers into which the exhaust steam is admitted. The condenser is so placed that the whole of the water raised from the well by the lift-pump flows either over or around it, of course passing between the tubes, and by this means a very good vacuum is obtained. The engine is provided with a " half house " only, that is to say, the cylinder end of the beam only is covered, the pump end being out of doors. By this arrangement, which is common in the mining districts, a considerable expense is saved, and it has consequently been adopted by Mr. Morris in several instances. The lift-pump worked by the engine is situated in the well, at a depth of about 90 ft. below the surface, and, generally speaking, there is about 40 ft. of water over it. The pump valves are of the india-rubber ring kind, invented by Mr. Morris, and used by him very successfully for many years past. We shall, when describing the new engine at the Crayford station, give engravings of these valves, so that at present we need merely state that they consist of a number of flat india-rubber rings made to clip around a central perforated casting, the shape of this casting greatly resembling that of the speed pulleys of a lathe set on end, the smallest pulley being uppermost. The size of the holes in the casting and the thickness of the rings are regulated according to the pressure which the valves have to withstand, and each ring is kept from shifting by an iron clip passed round it near its lower edge.

As the pump in the well is submerged, it is necessary, when the valves or bucket have to be examined, to raise the whole of the pump with its connexions above the water-level, and this lifting operation is readily effected in the following manner: The pump-rod having been disconnected, and the engine made to perform an outdoor stroke, a tackle is attached to the pump end of the beam and the top flange of the second length of the delivery pipe. The engine is then caused to make an indoor stroke, when the delivery pipe, with the whole of the pump, &c., attached to it, is raised to the extent of the length of the stroke, or 10 ft. 6 in. The pipe having been packed up, and the top length removed, the operation is repeated, and so on until the requisite amount of lifting has been performed.

The valve gear of the engine is of the usual Cornish kind, except that it is worked without a cataract, Mr. Morris in this, as in the case of all the other Cornish engines which he has at work, considering that the pump itself is quite capable of regulating the speed of the engine. The engine is supplied with steam by three single-flued Cornish boilers, and we are informed by Mr. Morris that he finds no inconvenience whatever from the use of the distilled feed-water furnished by the surface condenser, the impurities contained in the small quantities of water which have to be admitted from time to time to make up the loss arising from leakage, &c., being quite sufficient to prevent the corrosion which would be apt to take place if the water in the boilers was perfectly pure. The oily matters carried over by the steam into the condenser, and returned with the feed into the boiler, are found to unite with the lime contained in the water supplied to make up leakage, and to form lumps of hard saponaceous matter, which float on the surface of the water, and are easily collected and removed when the boiler is cleaned out. Whilst speaking of the boilers, we may describe the system of firing which is adopted at the Kent Waterworks, and which is found to answer exceedingly well, as the smokeless chimneys testify. Slack coal is used, and each fire is charged with about $2\frac{1}{3}$ cwt. at once, the charges being alternately supplied to each side of the fire-grate. The large quantity of each charge causes a kind of coking process to take place, the gases evolved from the fresh coal being mixed with the heated gases from the clear part of the fire, and with the air passing through it, and thus being effectually consumed. When the charge has become thoroughly coked, it is "broken down" towards the centre of the fire, and a clear fire being thus formed on one side of the grate, a fresh charge can be supplied to the other.

The second artesian well is furnished with a Cornish engine, also built by Messrs. Harvey and Co., this engine being of rather peculiar arrangement. The cylinder, which is 30 in. in diameter, with a stroke of 7 ft., is inverted, the piston-rod working through the lower cover. Instead, however, of the piston-rod being coupled direct to the pump-rod, as in the Bull engine, it is connected with one end of a beam, to the other end of which the pump-rod is attached. The beam has equal arms, so that the lift pump, which is 26 in. in diameter, has the same stroke as the steam cylinder, or 7 ft. The fact of the cylinder being inverted has rendered it necessary to alter the valve-gear somewhat from the ordinary Cornish pattern, but the modifications could scarcely be clearly explained without an engraving. As in the case of the engine previously described, this engine has its steam cylinder and gear housed, but the pump and half the beam are out of doors, the beam being situated close to the ground level.

The pump-rod is guided by a somewhat peculiar kind of parallel motion, which is arranged as follows : The crosshead at the top of the pump-rod (which is connected to the end of the beam by a main link in the ordinary way) has a bracket formed on it, this bracket extending towards the main centre, and its end being bent upwards, so that a centre carried by it is on a level with the centre line of the beam when the engine is at half-stroke. From the centre carried by the bracket a radius link extends outwards to a centre on the beam between the end of the bracket and the outer or pump-rod centre, the length of this radius link being such that the versed sine of the arc which it describes round the last-mentioned centre is equal to the versed sine of the arc described by that centre itself. As the pump is slung in the well, and it is somewhat difficult to maintain it perfectly upright, its top cover has been furnished with a stuffing-box, which allows a certain amount of side motion of the pump-rod to take place without a strain being put upon it. This stuffing-box consists of a short tube containing the usual packing space and gland, and connected with the top cover by a short tube of india-rubber, the stuffing-box being supported in a suitable manner, so that the india-rubber tube is not strained. The engine which we have just been describing is supplied with steam by one single-flued Cornish boiler made of steel.

The third artesian well is fitted with an engine having a cylinder 26 in. in diameter and 4 ft. stroke, working a lift pump of the same stroke and 24 in. in diameter. The quantity of water raised from the three wells by the engines which we have mentioned averages about 5500 gallons per minute ; but a much greater quantity could be obtained, if required, by increasing the speed at which the engines are worked. Although the wells are situated within a short distance of each other, each is found to furnish a perfectly independent supply, the pumping from one not affecting the others. In fact, the Deptford pumping-station is most favourably placed for obtaining a good supply of water from artesian wells, as it is situated just at the point where two very extensive faults in the chalk intersect each other. The water raised from the wells does not require any filtration, and it is, therefore, delivered direct from the lift-pumps into the pump wells of the engines which distribute it over the district. The filter-beds which were employed when the water was drawn from the Ravensbourne are, consequently, now disused ; but one of them is made to act as a reservoir to receive any excess in the quantity of water raised from the wells over that pumped into the mains by the distributing engines. If, on the other hand, these latter engines distribute more than is raised from the wells, the deficit is made up from the store reservoir, the collecting pipes below its bed (which remains in the same state as when it was a filter) being in communication with the pump-wells of the distributing engines.

The water is distributed from the Deptford pumping-station to the lower levels of the district by a pair of Cornish beam engines, made by Messrs. Harvey and Co. These engines have each a cylinder 70 in. in diameter, with 10 ft. stroke, and they each work a double-acting pump of the same stroke, the diameters of the pumps being 18 in. and 20½ in. respectively. The pumps are fitted with Mr. Morris's india-rubber ring-valves already mentioned, and they deliver the water direct into the mains without the intervention of a stand-pipe. A very large air-vessel is, however, provided, this being 30 ft. high and 6 ft. in diameter, and we believe that this air-vessel was the first that was employed as a substitute for a stand-pipe at any of the metropolitan waterworks. The pressure of water against which the pumps work is equal to a head of 170 ft., and the water is supplied to the lower levels of the district, the mains being connected with summit reservoirs at Greenwich Park and on Plumstead Common. A system of fire mains is connected with the former reservoir, for the protection of the Government dockyard and victualling-yard at Deptford, and the Royal Hospital at Greenwich.

The pair of engines for supplying the low-level districts are, like the other engines at the Kent Waterworks, worked without a cataract, but the valve gear of the two engines is connected so that they make alternate strokes. They are supplied with steam at a pressure of 40 lbs. by seven single-flued Cornish boilers, and the cut-off is made to take place at from one-fourth to one-fifth of the stroke.

The upper levels of the district are supplied by a couple of single-acting beam engines with fly-wheels, these engines having been built by Messrs. Boulton and Watt about fifty years ago. They have cylinders 38 in. in diameter and 8 ft. stroke, and each works a pump 16½ in. in diameter, with a stroke of 6 ft. 3 in., the rod of the pumps now used being coupled to the beam at a less distance from the main centre than the piston-rod. Each of the engines is, however, furnished with another pump of the same stroke as the steam-cylinder; but these pumps are not at present worked. The engines are provided with three single-flued Cornish boilers, of which two are generally worked, the pressure of the steam being 16 lbs. per square inch. The effective head of water against which the engines pump is 280 ft., whilst the summit reservoir with which the upper-level mains communicate is situated on Woolwich-common, 228 ft. above Trinity high-water mark, or 240 ft. 6 in. above Ordnance datum. The mains in connexion with this reservoir supply water to the whole of the Government military and naval establishments at Woolwich, with the exception of the Arsenal. The delivery pipes from the pumps of the upper-level engines are, like those from the low-level pumps, provided with an air-vessel; and whilst speaking of this we may mention that Mr. Morris employs no air-charging pumps in connexion with his engines, the loss of air in the air-vessels being made up by the aid of a species of air-lock, of which we shall explain the construction presently, when describing the engine at the Crayford station.

At the Charlton pumping station of the Kent Waterworks Company the supply of water is obtained from two artesian wells, each well being provided with a Cornish beam-engine constructed by Messrs. Harvey and Co., and fitted with a surface condenser. These engines have each a 60 in. cylinder with 10 ft. stroke, and they each work, in addition to a lift pump of the same stroke as the steam-cylinder, a bucket and plunger pump 21 in. in diameter with 8 ft. stroke, the rod of this pump being attached to the beam between that of the lift pump and the main centre. The lift pump of each engine is employed in raising water from the well to which it belongs, whilst the bucket and plunger pumps distribute it over the district. The mains from the Charlton station are in connexion with the services of both the upper and lower levels.

The Dover-road station is situated at the foot of Shooter's-hill, near the Herbert Hospital, and at it there is employed, as an auxiliary lift, a horizontal engine working a doubling-acting pump direct. This engine has a cylinder 20 in. in diameter, with 3 ft. stroke, and is fitted with a surface condenser. The district supplied from this station includes the higher levels of Shooter's-hill, Eltham, Abbey Wood, &c., and there is in connexion with the mains a covered reservoir having a capacity of 325,000 gallons, and situated at an elevation of 311 ft. above Trinity high water.

Near Bromley, on the Mid-Kent line of railway, is the Shortlands pumping-station, where the supply is obtained from an artesian well, which was sunk with considerable difficulty, the boring having to be carried through an outlying bed of sand 70 ft. thick, and charged with water to the surface. The work was, however, successfully accomplished, and a deep boring in the chalk made, and the water now stands in the well at a level 100 ft. above Trinity high water, the supply being full and continuous. The engine with which the well is provided is a direct-acting Cornish engine, with a 40 in. cylinder, and 8 ft. stroke, and was constructed by Messrs. Harvey and Co. It is fitted with a surface condenser, and drives a double-acting pump, 12 in. in diameter. The summit reservoir connected with the

Shortlands station is at Berkeley Park, Chiselhurst; it has a capacity of 450,000 gallons, and is situated at an elevation of 300 ft. above Trinity high water. Mains are now (1866) being laid to connect these works with the other stations.

The works at the Plumstead station were formerly the property of the Plumstead and Woolwich Waterworks Company, to which Mr. Homersham was the engineer, but they were eventually purchased and added to the Kent Waterworks. The water supply is obtained from an artesian well, with headings of the aggregate length of 120 yards driven in the chalk, and this well is provided with a double-acting flywheel condensing engine, having a 29 in. cylinder with 5 ft. stroke. This engine both raises and distributes the water. The mains from the Plumstead station are in communication with the lower level mains from the Deptford and Charlton stations, and also with a covered summit reservoir having a capacity of 800,000 gallons, and situated at the level of 157 ft. above Trinity high water.

When the Plumstead works were in the hands of the Plumstead and Woolwich Company, the water supplied from them was subjected to the "softening" process of Professor Clark, and the same process was also at one time in use at the Deptford station. Its use has, however, now been discontinued at both places; but works have been erected by Government, near the Herbert Hospital, where the water supplied to that establishment is still subjected to the process. Professor Clark's process consists in the addition of a certain quantity of pure lime to the chalk water, the principal salt contained by which is the bicarbonate of lime. The bicarbonate being a soluble salt, the extra quantity of carbonic acid contained in it has a less affinity for the carbonate than for the pure lime, and upon the addition of the latter it unites with it, converting both the bicarbonate and the lime into carbonate of lime, which is insoluble, and is deposited if the water is allowed to rest. Although the process is a simple one, it requires to be carefully carried out in order to obtain good results, as, if more than the correct proportion of quick-lime is added, the water is rendered hard by the excess. It is also necessary that the quick-lime should be thoroughly mixed with the water, and at the Plumstead works this used to be accomplished in the following manner : A cylinder containing prepared lime, or milk of lime, was placed in connexion with the pipe conducting the water from the pumps to the settling reservoir, and this cylinder contained a piston moved by machinery. By the action of this piston, a certain quantity of the milk of lime was delivered at each stroke into the pipe through which the water to be purified passed, and the quantity admitted was of course under control.

At the Crayford station, the works are now (1866) in progress, the artesian well, from which the supply of water will be obtained, being completed, and a horizontal double-acting engine, with surface condenser, being in course of construction by Messrs. Harvey and Co. Of this engine, which works both the lift and distributing pump, we are enabled, through the courtesy of Mr. W. R. Morris, to give engravings, Figs. 1 and 2, on Plate VII., being respectively a general elevation and plan, and the remaining figures on Plate VIII., representing various details. As will be seen by Figs. 1 and 2, the engine-bed is formed of two cast-iron girders, to which the cylinder, distributing pump, &c., are connected, the girders being bolted down to a brick and stone foundation. The cylinder is 24 in. in diameter, with a stroke of 4 ft., and the piston-rod is carried through both covers, and provided with a crosshead at each end. These crossheads work between guide-bars in the usual way, so that the piston is completely supported. To one of the crossheads is coupled the plunger of the distributing pump, and also a pair of connecting-rods extending to cranks on the flywheel shaft, whilst to the other crosshead is attached a short link, which is also coupled to the extremity of the vertical arm of a bell crank, to the horizontal arm of which the lift-pump rod is connected.

The valve chest is placed on the top of the cylinder, and the slide valve, which is of the ordinary kind, is driven, through the intervention of a rocking shaft, by an eccentric on the flywheel shaft. On the top of the valve chest is placed a double beat expansion valve, worked horizontally by a rod extending from a cam on the vertical shaft of the governor. This valve is arranged so that it also forms the starting valve. The governor, which regulates the speed of the engine by varying the amount of the expansion, is geared so as to make two revolutions to one of the engine, and is set so as to give the latter a speed of twenty-five revolutions per minute.

The air pump, which is placed below the crank shaft, is 15 in. in diameter, with 15 in. stroke; it is single acting, and is driven by an eccentric fixed on the crank shaft, as shown in Figs. 1 and 2. The feed pump is 4 in. in diameter, with a 6 in. stroke, and is also driven by an eccentric on the crank shaft. The flywheel is 10 ft. in diameter, and weighs five tons, and the flywheel shaft, which is 6 in. in diameter for the greater part of its length, is carried by four bearings, disposed as shown in the plan. The surface condenser, which is made of wrought iron, is 4 ft. in diameter and 6 ft. 6 in. long, and is placed in the cistern through which all the water passes on its way from the lift to the distributing pump. It contains 160 galvanised wrought-iron tubes, 2 in. in diameter inside, through which the water passes. The tubes, which are $\frac{3}{16}$ in. thick, are secured in the manner shown in the enlarged section, Fig. 7, the holes in the tube-plates being slightly

countersunk, and an india-rubber ring of circular section being forced
into each of these countersinks by a brass nut screwed on the end of
the tube. The tube-plates are 1½ in. thick, and the diameter of the
eduction pipe leading from the cylinder to the air pump is 8 in., whilst
that leading from the condenser to the air pump is 6 in. in diameter.

The lift pump is shown to an enlarged scale by Fig. 3. It is a
plunger pump, the diameter of the plunger being 16 in., and the stroke
4 ft. It is intended to rest upon the bottom of the well, and its case
is made entirely of wrought iron; this mode of construction being
adopted, because, as it is immersed, no repairs could be executed without
lifting to the surface, and lightness, therefore, is very essential. It is
intended, also, that this pump should be used to assist in sinking the
well deeper, should it become necessary to do so. The barrel of the
pump is 21 in. in diameter inside, and is composed of ½ in. plates, the
same thickness of plates being also employed in the construction of the
pipe extending from the top of the barrel nearly to the surface, and
which is also 21 in. in diameter for the greater part of its length. Near
the bottom, however, the diameter of this pipe is increased to 28 in.
inside, so that it forms a chamber for the delivery valves. Both the
top and bottom valves are of the india-rubber ring class generally
employed by Mr. Morris, and to which we have before alluded; and
the top valve is placed, so that its seating forms the top of the pump
barrel, a very neat arrangement. In Fig. 8 there is given an enlarged
view of a portion of one of these valves, with its seating. The
india-rubber rings are ½ in. thick, and cover holes $\frac{4}{10}$ in. in diameter,
with $\frac{2}{10}$ in. spaces between them. The connexion of the upper end of
the delivery pipe from the pump, with the top casting to which the
guide for the pump-rod is fixed, is effected by a stuffing-box, as shown
in Fig. 2. The pump-rod is 2½ in. in diameter, and is cottered into the
top of the plunger, whilst at its upper end it is coupled by a link 12 ft.
long to the horizontal arm of the bell crank already mentioned. The
arms of the bell crank are each 6 ft. long, and the latter is composed of
a pair of plates, each ¾ in. thick, placed 9 in. apart, and having bosses
formed on them. Each arm is 12 in. broad at the root, and 9 in.
broad at the outer end.

The water raised by the lift-pump is delivered through a 12 in. pipe
into the cistern in which the surface condenser is placed; this cistern,
which is 12 ft. long, 5 ft. wide, and 6 ft. deep, being situated as shown
in Figs. 1 and 2. From the cistern the water is led to the distributing
pump, through a pipe 15 in. in diameter, this pipe communicating with
the lower valve-box of the pump. The distributing pump is of the
piston and plunger class, and enlarged sections of it are given in Figs.

4 and 5. The diameter of the piston is 15 in., and that of the plunger 11 in., whilst the stroke is of course the same as that of the steam cylinder, or 4 ft. It has two valves only, and these and the passages connected with them are arranged as shown in the figures. The water rising through the bottom valve is first drawn into the barrel of the pump behind the piston, and on the return stroke it is discharged through the delivery valve, one portion of it being forced into the main, and the other filling the space between the plunger and the barrel of the pump which becomes vacant during the outward stroke. The water thus taken into the inner end of the barrel of the pump during the outward stroke is of course discharged into the main during the suction stroke, as in a bucket and plunger pump, and the pump is thus double acting. The valves are both of the india-rubber ring class, previously described.

On the delivery main from the distributing pump is placed an air-vessel, 4 ft. in diameter inside and about 13 ft. high from the crown to the top of the air-chamber at the bottom. Of this air-vessel we give a vertical section in Fig. 6, which will serve to explain the arrangement which Mr. Morris employs in place of air-charging pumps, and to which we have already alluded. It consists of an air-chamber formed by making the air-vessel with a double bottom, this chamber being connected with the air-vessel by two pipes arranged as shown in the figure. One of these pipes leads from the top of the air-chamber to the open air, and has a branch communicating with the air-vessel, whilst the second pipe is connected to the bottom of the air-chamber, and, like the other, communicates both with the open air and the air-vessel. Each pipe and branch is furnished with a cock, and the way in which the arrangement is worked is as follows: The cocks on the branches leading to the air-vessel being closed, those on the pipes communicating with the open air are opened, and the air-chamber thus filled with air, any water it may contain flowing out through the lower pipe whilst the air enters by the upper one. When the air-chamber has been thus charged, the cocks which have hitherto been open are closed, and those on the branches communicating with the air-vessel opened, when the water in the lower part of the latter flows through the pipe leading to the bottom of the air-chamber, and forces the air contained in it through the upper pipe into the air-vessel. The process can, of course, be repeated as frequently as required. The engine we have just described will be supplied with steam at a pressure of 40 lbs. per square inch by two boilers, each 30 ft. long and 6 ft. in diameter. The distributing pump is intended to force the water to the height of 220 ft., the lift giving, with friction, an effective head of about 290 ft., and the mains from the Crayford station will be in communication with those from all the other stations and reservoirs.

The Kent Waterworks Company supply water to all the towns on the Thames from the Surrey Docks at Rotherhithe to Erith, and their district extends inland to Peckham, Lewisham, Bromley, Chiselhurst, and Crayford, including all the parishes within that boundary. The total length of the mains is 180 miles, and the number of houses supplied is 33,693. According to the Registrar-General's report for August, 1866, the average daily supply was, during that month, 6,835,483 gallons. As the whole of the water is obtained from wells sunk in the chalk, it holds in solution a larger proportion of the salts of lime than that supplied by the other London water companies. In the month of July, 1866—which is the month to which we have previously referred in our accounts of the various waterworks—the quantity of carbonate of lime, or its equivalent, contained in the water supplied by the Kent Company amounted to 24.8 parts in 100,000 of the water, and the organic and other volatile impurities to 1.8 parts of the same quantity.

METROPOLITAN WATER LEVELS.

The Ordnance Survey maps do not give the levels of surfaces of water, but those only of fixed bench-marks on land. In 1856, Mr. R. W. Mylne, C.E., published a topographical contour and geological map of the metropolis, upon which were marked, from his own surveys, the elevations above Trinity datum (12 ft. 6 in. above the Ordnance datum of approximate mean tide at Liverpool) of the great number of elevated sheets of water and reservoirs in and near London. From this map, which is but little known, we have prepared the following table, and for the convenience of engineers, who now work almost exclusively from the Ordnance datum, we have added 12 ft. 6 in. to each of the elevations, as given by Mr. Mylne, above Trinity high-water mark.

	Elevation in feet above Ordnance datum
Ornamental water, St. James's Park (11½ acres) . . .	17.8
The Serpentine (43¼ acres)	50.3
Kensington Gardens Basin (7¼ acres)	81.8
Ornamental Water, Regent's Park	97.1
New River Head, New River Works	94.3
Claremont-square Reservoir, do.	138.5
Camden-square do. do.	172.6
Maiden-lane Reservoirs do.	231.5
Stoke Newington do. do.	100.0

Elevation in feet
above Ordnance datum.

Highgate Archway Reservoir, New River Works . . 326.1

Hampstead Heath do.   do. 446.1

" " Donkey Pond, about 432.5

" " Lower Pond (near Southend) . . 208.8

" " next Higher Pond 231.9

" " do. 245.9

" " do. 247.3

Highgate Lower Pond 210.4

" next Higher Pond 223.3

" do. 236.0

" do. 236.8

" do. 253.0

Kentish-town Reservoir, Artesian well 188.5

Brent Reservoir, full (222 acres) 125.8

East London Filter-beds, Lea Bridge 19.7

Cumberland Basin 98.0

Grand Junction Filter-beds, Kew 33.5

" Reservoir, Campden-hill 133.8

West Middlesex Reservoirs (16 acres) opposite Hammersmith 16.0

West Middlesex Reservoir, Barrow-hill 193.4

Lambeth Waterworks Reservoir, Brixton-hill . . . 196.8

" " " Stockwell 115.1

Chelsea Waterworks Reservoir, Putney Heath . . . 172.6

Kent Waterworks, Filter-beds 16.9

" Service Reservoir, Greenwich Park . 157.0

" do.   Woolwich . . . 238.5

" do.   Plumstead-common 170.3

" do.   Shooter's-hill . . 320.9

Lake, Wimbledon Park (22¾ acres) 58.2

Slade Pond, Richmond Park (16¾ acres) 70.7

Pond, near Slade Pond (6½ acres) 62.0

Pond, Wandsworth Common 70.4

Pond at Snaresbrook 88.8

PART II.

PROPOSED SCHEMES FOR SUPPLYING WATER TO THE METROPOLIS.

MR. BATEMAN'S SCHEME.

THE population of London now amounts to 3,000,000 people. At the commencement of the present century it consisted of one-third; forty years ago of one-half; and twenty years since of two-thirds this number; and, supposing it to increase at the same rate, it is probable that in the course of twenty years from the present time it will number at least 4,500,000 souls. The task of furnishing such a large community with an abundant supply of pure water is no slight one, on the contrary, it is one which demands that the most anxious consideration should be paid to its general arrangement, and careful attention to the construction of the details by which it may be carried out. At the present time its performance is divided between eight water companies, who derive their water partly from the Rivers Thames, Lea, and Ravensbourne; partly from the original sources of the New River Company, and partly from deep wells on the northerly and easterly sides of London. Altogether these companies supply on the average about 108,000,000 galls. daily, equal to about 30 galls. per head on the present population. Of this large quantity rather more than half is abstracted from the Thames, five companies drawing their water from that source. In 1852 several Acts were passed, authorising the withdrawal of water from the Thames, and limiting the quantity so abstracted to a maximum of 100,000,000 galls. per day, the minimum quantity of water then passing Hampton being estimated at 362,000,000 galls. daily. According, however, to observations made in September last year (1865), the quantity which passed down the river, above the waterworks at Hampton, scarcely exceeded 300,000,000 galls. daily, and many complaints have been made, by people residing on the banks of the river, below the points at which the water is abstracted by the different companies, with reference to the diminished volume of the stream and its pollution.

In consequence of complaints made in 1852 about the quality of the water supplied, the London companies have been compelled, since that time to take their water from higher points in the rivers, and they have expended nearly 4,000,000*l.* in the construction of works enabling them to do this, and effecting other improvements. The water now supplied by them contains, according to an analysis made by Professor Frankland, F.R.S., last month (December, 1865), an average quantity of 31.8 lb. of solid matter in each 10,000 galls., or 100,000 lb. of water. Of this quantity the organic matter averages 1.28 lb.; the amount contained in the Thames water being about twice as great as that found in the water from other sources, although the total quantity of solid matter is less. The degrees of hardness, estimated by the quantity of carbonate of lime or its equivalent, contained in the water, were, according to Dr. Clark's scale, 12.39° for the Thames, and 23.6° for the other water; the total average being 20.3°. In Dr. Clark's scale, one degree of hardness corresponds to the presence of one grain of carbonate of lime, or its equivalent, in one gallon of the water, or 1 part in 70,000.

We have been led to the above remarks by a consideration of a scheme which has been lately brought forward by Mr. J. F. Bateman, the engineer of the Glasgow and Manchester Waterworks, for furnishing the metropolis with an abundant supply of pure water, drawn from sources situated amongst the Welsh mountains, and conveyed to London by an aqueduct. Mr. Bateman has published, for private circulation, an excellently written pamphlet* containing an account of his plan, and from this we obtain the following particulars. It is intended that the supply shall be derived from the eastern flanks of the mountain ranges of Plynlimmon and Cader Idris in North Wales, from which spring the upper tributaries of the Severn. Generally it is found that the greatest rainfall in any country takes place in that portion of it which is towards that quarter from which the prevailing winds blow; in the case of a mountain chain, on the contrary, the greatest amount of water is deposited on that side of it which is generally to leeward; this latter fact being apparently due to the warm moist air being deflected upwards by the hills into a colder portion of the atmosphere. The formation of rain-clouds is a necessary consequence, and these discharge their contents on arriving over the sheltered valleys on the lee side of the mountains. As in England, the prevailing winds

* *On the Supply of Water to London, from the Sources of the River Severn.* By JOHN FREDERICK BATEMAN, C.E., F.R.S., F.G.S., &c. Westminster: Vacher and Sons, November, 1865.

are westerly, both the above-mentioned facts would tend to show that a very heavy rainfall might be expected on the eastern side of the Welsh hills, and the observations that have been made fully confirm this. The rainfall in the Cumberland Lake district, which greatly resembles that above mentioned, has been found to average nearly 150 in. annually, while on the Penine range, which separates Yorkshire and Derbyshire from Lancashire and Cheshire, it amounts to about 50 in. Of this latter quantity the net produce which flows off the ground in dry years is found at the Manchester Waterworks, which are situated in the heart of the district, to be 33 in.

Mr. Bateman considers that, in the Upper Severn basin, 45 in. per annum will be available for collection; but in order to be on the safe side, he bases his calculations on 36 in. only. The requisite drainage area he proposes to obtain by two districts, amounting together to 130,572 acres. These are free from metalliferous veins, and are situated on the Upper and Lower Silurian; formations, which yield water of excellent quality, and they afford moreover every facility for the construction of magnificent store reservoirs. The northern district is situated on the eastern side of the mountain range which includes amongst its highest summits Cader Idris and Aran Mowddy. It contains the sources of the Rivers Banw and Vyrnwy, and has an area of 66,380 acres. On the River Vyrnwy it is proposed to form, by an embankment 76 ft. in height, a lake, or reservoir, five miles in length, and capable of containing 1,089,000,000 cubic feet. On the River Banw two reservoirs are proposed, one with an embankment 80 ft. in height, being four miles long, and able to contain 940,000,000 cubic feet; and the other enclosed by an embankment of the same height, having a capacity of 732,000,000 cubic feet.

The southern district forms the drainage ground of the Severn proper; it has an area of 64,192 acres, and is situated to the east of Plynlimmon. It will be furnished with several reservoirs, the principal of which, with an embankment 75 ft. in height, will contain 2,230,000,000 cubic feet. The discharge pipes from the lowest reservoirs in each district will be situated about 450 ft. above Trinity high-water mark.

From the collecting districts the water will be conducted by separate aqueducts to a point near Marten Mere, at which place they will be united into one large aqueduct, extending thence, past the towns of Bridgenorth, Bromsgrove, Henly in Arden, Warwick, Banbury, Buckingham, Berkhampstead, and Watford, to large service reservoirs, which it is proposed to construct on the high land near Stanmore. These reservoirs, which will be of sufficient capacity to hold ten days' supply, will be 250 ft. above high-water mark, and from them the water is to be supplied to London through about ten miles of piping, the service being conducted on the " constant supply " and " high pressure " system. The branch aqueduct from the northern district to Marten Mere will be 19 miles, and that from the southern district to the same point, 21½ miles in length. The length of the principal aqueduct from Marten Mere to the service reservoir at Stanmore, will be about 152 miles, and it will be made capable of carrying 220,000,000 of gallons per day, the two branch aqueducts being each made to convey 130,000,000 gallons daily. The aqueducts will be carried through the mountain ranges between the collecting districts and Bridgenorth, principally by tunnelling. At Bridgenorth the main aqueduct will be conveyed across the Severn by inverted syphon pipes; and the same means will be employed to carry it across the valleys of the Rivers Stour, Avon, and other streams. Between Bridgenorth and London it will consist partly of covered aqueduct or tunnel, and partly of open aqueduct, and its course will be such that it will avoid all the coal-fields near its route, and will pass to the north of Droitwich and its saliferous deposits. The illustrations on this and the next page give the average section of the main aqueducts, the branch aqueducts being similar in

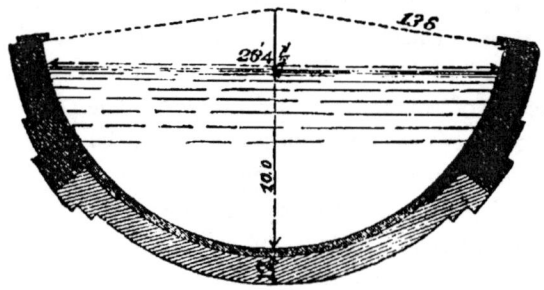

Fig. 1.

general construction, but smaller. The open branch aqueduct is intended to convey 130,000,000 gallons of water per day, with a fall of 6 in. per mile; and the covered branch aqueduct to convey 128,000,000 gallons per day, with a fall of 14 in. per mile. In the case of the main aqueduct, the open portion having the section shown by Fig. 1 will convey, with a 6 in. fall per mile, 224,000,000 gallons daily; and the covered portion represented by Fig. 2 will be capable of conveying 221,000,000 gallons per day, the fall being in this instance 14 in. per mile. The total distance to be traversed by the water from the lowest reservoir on the River Vyrnwy to London (including the length of the piping between the service reservoirs and the metropolis) will be 181 miles, whilst from the Severn reservoirs it will be rather farther, or 183½ miles.

The cost of the undertaking is estimated by Mr. Bateman at 8,600,000*l*., of which, 1,100,000*l*. will be required for carrying out each of the branch aqueducts, with its reservoirs, and the remainder for the construction of the main aqueduct, and the service reservoirs in which it terminates. In this estimate the cost of connecting the service reservoirs with the pipes of the existing companies is included, and 14 per cent. upon the whole cost of works, land, and piping is also allowed for contingencies; but provision has only been made for constructing the syphon pipes, by which the main aqueduct is carried across valleys, of a sufficient capacity to convey 120,000,000 gallons daily, it being proposed to increase the size of these syphons when the increased demand for water renders such a course necessary. Mr. Bateman also considers that it would be unnecessary at first to construct the reservoirs, &c., in more than one of the collecting districts, and the expenditure of 1,100,000*l*. might thus be postponed for some time.

Analyses of the water taken from streams in the collecting districts during dry weather, were made by the late Dr. R. D. Thompson, F.R.S.,

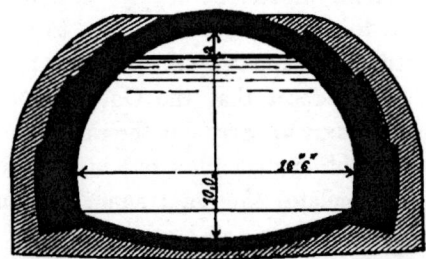

Fig. 2.

and the average amount of hardness was found to equal only 1.6° of Clark's scale, the average quantity of organic impurity being 1.35 grains per gallon, or 1.93 parts in 10,000. Water obtained during floods would probably be even softer than that above mentioned, the water in Bala lake, which is derived from a similar geological formation, having only 0.8° of hardness, whilst the organic impurity amounts to 1.28 grains, and the total impurity of all kinds to but 2.08 grains per gallon, or 2.97 parts in 10,000. The water supplied to Glasgow from Loch Katrine is of 1° of hardness, and the substitution of this soft water for that previously obtained from the Clyde, which varied from 7° to 9° of hardness, has been carefully estimated to effect an economy in domestic establishments alone, "equal to the whole rate there paid for the water supply, or to 36,000*l.* a year, upon a population of 400,000 persons." From this, Mr. Bateman assumes that the saving which would be effected by supplying Lond*ɔ*n with water such as would be obtained from the Welsh hills, in place of that now delivered by the water companies, would amount to at least 400,000*l.* per annum.

The cost of the whole undertaking, great as it is, is not much greater in proportion to the population to be supplied, than the sums which have been already expended in the construction of waterworks by the inhabitants of Liverpool, Glasgow, Manchester, and many other large towns. At Liverpool the cost of new works has been at the rate of about 75,000*l.* for each million gallons per day, while at Manchester it has been 34,000*l.*, and at Glasgow 45,000*l.*, for a like quantity; this last rate will, however, be reduced to 22,000*l.* when the full supply is obtained from Loch Katrine. If to the cost of new works we add the sums which have to be paid to previously existing companies, we find the above rate materially increased. Thus at Liverpool the cost will become 115,115*l.*; at Manchester, 60,000*l.*, and at Glasgow 59,260*l.*, or when the full supply is obtained, 33,645*l.* per million gallons daily. The cost of Mr. Bateman's scheme for supplying the metropolis would be 71,000*l.* per million, whilst the supply consisted of 120,000,000 gallons per day; but this rate would be reduced to 49,300*l.* per million when the full quantity was supplied. Mr. Bateman thinks that it would not be unreasonable to expect that the Government should assist in raising the capital necessary to carry out the undertaking, and that the money might thus be obtained at a low rate of interest, say 4 per cent. Assuming this, he calculates the total annual expenditure to be as follows:—

Interest on capital of 8,600,000*l.* at 4 per cent. . . .	£344,000
Management and working expenses	150,000
Payment of dividends to existing companies, and interest of their borrowed money	450,000
Total . .	£944,000

To meet this expenditure it is proposed to levy two compulsory rates, one a public rate on house property, and the other a domestic rate, and in addition to these rates, it is expected that a considerable sum would be raised by the sale of water for trade purposes, to suburban districts, and to places on the line of aqueduct; and also by the rental of the ground occupied at present by the works of the existing companies. The assessable value of the property in the Metropolitan district was last year 14,524,797*l*., and it is assumed by Mr. Bateman that this value would be increased to at least 18,000,000*l*. by the time that the works, required to convey the water from Wales, could be completed. It is also assumed by him that the assessable value of the dwelling-houses would amount to two-thirds of the whole, or 12,000,000*l*., and from these data he calculates upon the following revenue :—

Probable annual value of surplus property of existing
   companies . . . . £ 50,000
Sale of water for trading purposes, &c. . . . 250,000
Compulsory rate for domestic supplies at 10d. in the
   pound on 12,000,000*l*. 500,000
Compulsory public rate at 2d. in the pound on
   18,000,000*l*. 150,000

                    Total . . £950,000

At both Glasgow and Manchester the waterworks are the property of the corporations, and the system of compulsory rates has been found to work well. At Glasgow the corporation have the power to levy a public rate of 1d. in the pound together with an unlimited domestic rate, on that part of the city which is to the north of the Clyde, and a rate of 1s. in the pound on the part which is to the south of that river. The rates actually levied are 1s. for the domestic and 1d. for the public rate. At Manchester the corporation can also levy two compulsory rates, one being a public and the other a domestic rate, and both being unlimited in amount. The rates now levied are 9d. in the pound for the domestic, and 3d. for the public rate. At both Glasgow and Manchester large sums are obtained by the sale of water for trading purposes, the increase of revenue arising from this source being 35,277*l*. and 56,324*l*. respectively for the two places; and we may judge, therefore, that the sum of 250,000*l*., which Mr. Bateman expects would be annually obtained in the same manner in the metropolitan district is not excessive. Altogether, Mr. Bateman's scheme appears to be a good and thoroughly considered one, and to be well worthy of the careful attention at the present time of both the engineering and general public.

MESSRS. HEMANS AND HASSARD'S SCHEME.

While the metropolis is increasing, not only steadily but rapidly, in population, so, too, are the neighbouring districts from which the metropolis draws its supplies of water. And however we may intercept the sewage, deodorise it, utilise it by irrigation, or otherwise seek to lessen the pollution of our rivers, it is simply impossible to obtain pure and wholesome water from a thickly inhabited collecting area. With the exception of the water from the deep wells in the chalk, the well-waters of London are now regarded merely as the solvents of organic or inorganic impurities, and as the ready distributors of typhus and cholera. But while the surface wells of London, even if they are not the reservoirs of actual poison, are at least unfit for the supply of wholesome water, the surface drainage of the Thames valley is not very much better, and its degree of impurity is constantly and necessarily increasing.

The attention of engineers has for some time been turned to distant sources of water supply for the metropolis, and we have already described in this volume Mr. Bateman's scheme for bringing water to London from the Welsh hills by an aqueduct 183 miles in length. This week* another and a still bolder scheme has been published by Mr. G. Willoughby Hemans, C.E., and Mr. Richard Hassard, C.E., for the supply of the metropolis with water direct from Ullswater, 240 miles away, a lake lying between Westmoreland and Cumberland. Ullswater is nine miles long, from one-fourth of a mile to two miles wide, 210 ft. deep, and its surface is elevated 477 ft. above the sea, not so very much greater, we may remark, than the level of Loch Katrine, the source of supply of the Glasgow Waterworks. It is not, of course, the mere contents of this lake that Mr. Hemans proposes to bring to London, for its whole capacity would not suffice for a lengthened supply to the metropolis, but it is the surplus rainfall of a portion of the lake district which now runs to waste. The area of the metropolis itself is about 125 square miles, while near Ullswater, Haweswater, and Thirlmere are 177 miles of available collecting area, upon which there is an average annual rainfall of 100 inches. We give on Plate IX. a map of this Lake district.

We need hardly say that rain water is practically pure as it falls, it having been originally evaporated from the surface of the earth and thereby separated from earthy impurities. It falls as soft water, and can only become again impure by flowing over or sinking into soils

* August 3rd, 1866.

charged with lime, minerals, organic matter, &c. In the lake district under consideration, however, the soil is thin and but little cultivated, and it overlies the primitive rocks; there is little, if any, peat; and there are but very few dwellings from which any contaminating matter could flow.

Professor Way has analysed samples of the waters taken in January last, after heavy rains, and in their worst state, with the following results:

GRAINS PER IMPERIAL GALLON.

	River Lowther.	Haweswater Lake.	Ullswater Lake.	Thirlmere Lake.
Lime..........................	1·54	0·50	0·81	0·42
Magnesia......................	0·50	0·18	0·20	0·14
Soda..........................	0·80	0·71	0·51	0·45
Chlorides of Sodium and Potassium..................	0·48	0·69	0·69	0·77
Oxide of Iron, Silica, &c.	0·50	0·25	0·20	0·05
Sulphuric acid...............	0·51	0·51	0·37	0·44
Carbonic acid................	2·05	0·82	1·03	0.56
Organic matter..............	0·62	0·62	0·35	0·77
Total impurity...............	7·00	3·99	4·16	3·61
Hardness before boiling...	5·2°	2·0°	2·1°	1·5
Hardness after boiling	4·4°	1·8°	2·1°	1·5

These substances are probably combined as follows:

GRAINS PER IMPERIAL GALLON.

	River Lowther.	Haweswater Lake.	Ullswater Lake.	Thirlmere Lake.
Carbonate of Lime.........	2·75	0·90	1·45	0·75
Carbonate of Magnesia....	1·05	0·36	0·42	0·29
Carbonate of Soda.........	0·70	0·56	0·40	0·20
Sulphate of Soda...........	0·90	0·90	0·65	0·78
Chlorides of Sodium and Potassium	0·48	0·40	0·69	0·77
Oxide of Iron, Silica, &c...	0·50	0·25	0·20	0·05
Organic Matter..............	0·62	0·62	0·35	0·77
Total solid Matter...........	7·00	3·99	4·16	3·61

These analyses show a slight mineral contamination from mineral workings which are to be excluded from the intended metropolitan supply.

From the comparatively small district under notice—a district less than one-half as large again as the actual area of the metropolis itself —an amount of water flows annually to waste sufficient, were it retained, to supply 150 gallons daily to every man, woman, and child in and near London. This amount is, of course, much beyond our requirements, but the people of New York contrive to use and waste 100 gallons daily, per head of the population, of the Croton water, and London ought really to be provided for upon the same liberal scale, with water under constant service, and with a supply for a public fountain in every square. Messrs. Hemans and Hassard have estimated a daily supply, from the district already named, of 250,000,000 gallons. The figures may appear large, and those who do not take the trouble to go into the matter might imagine that no area of water supply could withstand such a drain. But we can bring this vast quantity quite within the grasp of the mind. Let us suppose a stream flowing thirty-eight miles a day, or a little over one and a half mile an hour, a rate which is much below the velocity of streams in hilly countries. At this rate a stream 80 ft. across, and averaging 30 in. deep, would discharge the whole daily quantity above named, viz., 250,000,000 gallons, corresponding to an abundant supply for 5,000,000 people. Such a stream in the northern counties would rank as a trout beck, perhaps, but would be hardly reckoned as a river.

The drainage area embraced in Messrs. Hemans and Hassard's scheme forms the north-western portion of Westmoreland, and a part of Cumberland, and lies just to the west of the Lancaster and Carlisle Railway, between Shap and Clifton. It is elevated from 500 to 3200 ft. above the sea, the mean altitudes being from 1200 ft. to 1300 ft. Windermere and Derwentwater are unavailable, the former being but 134 ft. and the latter 238 ft. above the sea, while the great distributing reservoir near Harrow, and 12 miles from London, is to be elevated 220 ft. But Haweswater is elevated 694 ft., Thirlmere 533 ft., and Ullswater 477 ft. above the sea, thus affording a good head for the supply of the metropolis. It is proposed, moreover, to raise Haweswater 42 ft. in level, and Thirlmere 64 ft., their respective levels thus becoming 736 ft. and 597 ft., and as both these lakes lie in deep, narrow, and lonely valleys, the works requisite for this increase of height would not involve a very great expense. The outlets, however, of these lakes are not only at their northern extremities, away from London, but they discharge into different rivers—Haweswater into the Lowther, Ullswater into the Eamont, and Thirlmere into

the River Greta. The area draining directly into the three lakes is not
large, and would not be nearly sufficient for the required supply.
Messrs. Hemans and Hassard have, therefore, schemed a somewhat
complicated system of intercepting works, whereby all the water of the
Lowther, as far north as Clifton, may be diverted into Ullswater, this
lake being at a lower level than Clifton. At whatever points, too, the
tributaries of Lake Windermere to the south, and Derwentwater to the
west, happen to be higher than Thirlmere, tunnels and conduits are to
be made to divert their waters into that lake. Grasmere is but 208 ft.
above the sea, and it is 325 ft. below Thirlmere, but Edesdale Tarn,
although it at present discharges into Grasmere, and thus through that
and Rydal Water into Windermere, is, nevertheless, at a higher level
than Thirlmere, even when the latter shall have been raised 64 ft., or
to a level of 597 ft. And so a tunnel is schemed to tap Edesdale Tarn,
and tunnels and conduits are to cross the higher portions of the tributaries of Grasmere, and thus carry away their water to the head or
southern extremity of Thirlmere. By like means a portion of the
natural drainage into Derwentwater is also to be brought round the
northern extremity of the Bleaberry Fell into Thirlmere, and a conduit,
several miles in length, will bring to that lake also the upper waters of
the River Greta, which now flow away to the Derwent.

With the drainage of 177 square miles thus intercepted and conducted into Haweswater, Ullswater, and Thirlmere, it would become
necessary either to make a separate aqueduct from each of these lakes
to some common point of junction towards London, or else to bring the
discharge of Haweswater and Thirlmere into Ullswater—which will be
259 ft. below Haweswater and 120 ft. below Thirlmere, when the two
last-named lakes shall have been raised respectively 42 ft. and 64 ft.—
and then to commence a single aqueduct from that lake towards
London. Messrs. Hemans and Hassard adopt the latter course. To
connect Thirlmere with Ullswater a conduit and tunnel are to be made,
the former 6 and the latter 8 miles in length. The direction of the flow
of the water through this communication would be exactly opposite to,
while it would for some distance be parallel with, that of the conduit
bringing down the upper waters of the Greta into Thirlmere. The
tunnel, although 8 miles in length, would admit of shafts being sunk
along its entire course, so that the time occupied in its construction
would be no greater than that required for working the distance
between two of the shafts.

The heaviest single work would be the tunnel from the head or
southern extremity of Ullswater, under the Kirkstone Pass, to Amble-

side. This tunnel, which would form the commencement of the great aqueduct to London, would be $7\frac{1}{4}$ miles long, and for $1\frac{3}{4}$ mile its level would be from 500 ft. to 1500 ft. under the Kirkstone Pass. For this portion no shafts would be sunk, and thus the work would require about three years for its completion from shaft to shaft on either side. The remaining $5\frac{1}{2}$ miles of this tunnel would admit of sinking shafts at any distance apart considered most convenient. Hence to London the water would be conveyed by conduit, tunnel, and iron pipes, past Kendal, down the eastern side of Lancashire, avoiding the Wigan coal-fields, and to the east of Manchester, the Potteries, and the Staffordshire coal district, and to the east of Birmingham, following a route from Coventry nearly parallel with the London and North-Western Railway, to the great regulating reservoir near Harrow, and which would be elevated 220 ft. above the sea. The fall, therefore, for the whole distance would average rather more than a foot per mile, or we will say, the same as that of the Croton Aqueduct, which is uniformly $13\frac{1}{4}$ in. per mile. The Croton Aqueduct has a uniform slope, however, whereas the great metropolitan aqueduct from Westmoreland would follow the natural variations of the surface of the country traversed.

Of the great aqueduct itself, Messrs. Hemans and Hassard's prospectus gives no further particulars, but its construction is no doubt entirely practicable. Its cost is estimated roughly at 8,125,000*l*., while the conduits, reservoirs, and works of collection are set down at 674,000*l*., the tunnel from Ullswater to Ambleside at 350,000*l*., and the regulating reservoirs, &c., near London at 500,000*l*.; making 9,650,000*l*. in all, to which is to be added interest on unproductive capital for an average period of three years, and for other expenses 1,550,000*l*., making 11,200,000*l*. in all. This estimate, too, is framed for 200,000,000 instead of 250,000,000 gallons daily, the total estimate for the works on the larger scale being 12,200,000*l*.

Messrs. Hemans and Hassard have considered very carefully the question of rainfall, and the quantity of rain-water run off, but we need not enter as fully upon this point, inasmuch as it is now quite beyond dispute that 100 in. of average rainfall may be depended upon for the whole district in question, while of this at least 80 in. may, if required, be run off by an aqueduct.

We should just note that auxiliary and compensation reservoirs are contemplated in connexion with each of the three lakes, and we may here reprint the total estimated area and capacity of the whole system of supply.

| Name. | Area of collecting ground in square miles. | Area of Reservoir in acres. | Contents in Cubic feet. | | Total Storage. |
			For supply to Towns.	For Compensation.	
Swindale	38	166		187,000,000	187,000,000
Haweswater		683	235,200,000	961,100,000	1,196,300,000
Martindale	95	255	336,000,000		336,000,000
Ullswater		2300	1,742,400,000		1,742,400,000
Thirlmere St. John's Beck	44	875	1,721,977,600		1,721,977,600
Reservoir		360		380,000,000	380,000,000
	177	4639	4,035,577,600	1,528,100,000	5,563,677,600

equal to 120 days' supply at 250,000,000 gallons per day, and to 157 days' supply at 200,000,000 gallons per day—after giving credit for the average minimum summer yield, which will not be less than 40,000,000 gallons per day — and to 120 days' compensation at 450,000 gallons per square mile of drainage area; this will more than suffice in a district of such constant rain.

There would not be any necessity, in the first instance, for constructing the auxiliary reservoirs in Swindale and Martindale, as, until the towns' supply exceeded 200,000,000 gallons per day, Thirlmere and Ullswater would contain sufficient storage, and would be able, after giving credit for the summer yield, to work up to 135 days' supply, whilst compensation water would be given out from Haweswater, and from St. John's Beck Reservoirs; when the demand exceeds 200,000,000 gallons per day, these auxiliary reservoirs may be constructed, and, if necessary, others in addition, as many sites are available; should the demand eventually exceed 250,000,000 gallons per day, a further area of 53 square miles of collecting ground may be obtained on the southern slopes of the range of hills above Ambleside and Kendal, by constructing reservoirs in the valleys traversed by the Troutbeck, the Kent, the Sprint, and the Bannisdale Beck streams, and an additional quantity of about 75,000,000 or 80,000,000 gallons daily may easily be obtained from these sources of supply.

The surface of Ullswater Lake would be ordinarily maintained at or about its winter level, and water drawn off from it for towns' supply at a depth of 20 ft.; that is at about 460 ft. above the Ordnance datum.

As long as the demand from the district did not exceed 200,000,000 gallons per day, it would not be necessary to lower Ullswater at all, until after a period of 67 days of absolute drought, Thirlmere being able to keep up the supply for that period of time; it would then take about 30 days more to lower Ullswater 8 ft., which would not be very much below its summer level; so that, under these circumstances, 97 days of continuous and absolute drought must occur before Ullswater would be sensibly affected.

When the demand has increased to 250,000,000 gallons daily, and the auxiliary reservoirs have been constructed, with their aid the towns' could be kept up from Thirlmere for a period of 70 days, and it would then take 23 days more to reduce Ullswater 8ft., so that in this case 93 days of continuous and absolute drought would be necessary before the lake was reduced much below its summer level; and there is no record of drought of any such duration ever having occurred in this notoriously wet locality.

Next comes the financial part of the scheme. Here it is proposed to continue to the water companies their present rate of dividends, and the mode of raising the revenue and the sums raised are the same in the first case, and nearly the same in the second, as by Mr. Bateman's scheme for water supply from Wales. We will tabulate the comparative figures as follows:

	Hemans and Hassard.	Mr. Bateman.
First cost	£11,200,000	£8,600,000
Interest at 4 per cent. . . .	448,000	344,000
Collection, management, &c. . .	100,000	150,000
Payments to existing companies .	425,000	450,000
Total annual expense . .	£973,000	£944,000
Sale of water on route . . .	£228,125	
Ditto for trading purposes . .	136,875	£250,000
Rent of surplus property of existing companies		50,000
Compulsory rate upon house property	450,000	500,000
Ditto public	200,000	150,000
Total revenue . . .	£1,015,000	£950,000

Both Mr. Bateman and Mr. Hemans propose compulsory domestic and public rates, such as are now enforced in Manchester and Glasgow. Both adopt the same estimate of the annual value of house property in the metropolis, say 12,000,000*l.*, while the annual value of the entire property is taken as 16,000,000*l.* by Mr. Hemans and as 18,000,000*l.* by Mr. Bateman. The first-named gentleman proposes a domestic rate of 9d. and a public rate of 3d., while Mr. Bateman's estimate is for 10d. and 2d. respectively.

As to the practicability of either Mr. Bateman's or Messrs. Hemans and Hassard's scheme there can be no doubt. We shall not attempt at present to decide upon their relative merits, but we may record our conviction that we must, within a very few years, look, for our London water supply, to sources which are unquestionably capable of furnishing unlimited quantities of soft, pure, wholesome water. None of these sources can be found near London, and nature points clearly to those districts where a great annual rainfall descends upon bare hill pastures and primitive rock, beyond the reach of natural or artificial pollution.

MR. REMINGTON'S SCHEME.

The question of the metropolitan water supply having now become of so much interest as to induce Government to appoint a commission of inquiry, and it being now generally admitted that the present sources of supply are wholly inadequate both as regards the quantity and quality of the water, we think that every proposition by means of which the desired results may be attained should be properly considered; and as we have already given full descriptions of Mr. Bateman's plan for obtaining a supply from Wales, and conveying the water the distance of 180 miles, and also of Messrs. Hemans and Hassard's plan for collecting and conveying the lake waters of Westmoreland and Cumberland the distance of 230 miles to London, we now give a description of Mr. George Remington's plan for collecting the waters of the Dove, the Wye, and the Derwent from the hills of Derbyshire and Staffordshire, at such an elevation as to allow a gravitating supply to all the metropolitan districts excepting the highest parts of Hampstead and Highgate.

The River Dove rises at the foot of Axe Edge, near Buxton, in the formation geologically known as the Yoredale rock, through which it continues to the east of Longnor, where it enters upon the mountain limestone. Its principal tributary is the Manifold, which, rising north of Longnor from the millstone-grit formation, passes through portions of the Yoredale rock and mountain limestone formations, and unites with the Dove at Islam.

The Wye rises at the foot of Black Edge, between Buxton and Chapel-en-le-Frith, and, entering the mountain limestone near Buxton, continues through that formation to Bakewell, where it enters the Yoredale rock, and joins the Derwent at Rowsley. The Wye has many tributary streams running from the high ground near Chapel-en-le-Frith.

The Derwent rises near Dean Head from the millstone-grit formation, through which and the Yoredale rock it continues to Matlock. The whole area of country drained by the three rivers above the respective points of Mill Dale, Monsal Dale, and Calver, near Stoney Middleton, is about 262 square miles, three parts of which consist of millstone-grit and Yoredale rock, the remainder of mountain limestone. In many places the hills attain an elevation of from 1700 to 2000 ft. above the level of the sea, and these districts are subjected to heavy rains, at times swelling the Dove so rapidly as to flood the low grounds in the neighbourhood of Ashborne, Uttoxeter, and Tutbury, extending to the Trent, and the waters of the Derwent, also falling into the Trent below Derby, cause that river frequently to overflow from Burton-on-Trent to Nottingham, thereby causing much damage.

Taking the rainfall at 48 in. per annum on the 262 square miles of high land gives 182,077,621,862 gallons, or 498,842,799 gallons daily, *one-sixth* part of which, or 83,140,466 gallons, would be more than equal to the quantity now supplied by all the existing metropolitan water companies, and, taking the number of houses at 500,000, would give each an additional daily supply of 166 gallons.

Some years ago Mr. Remington explored the country with the view of ascertaining the most favourable route for a line of railway from London to Manchester, and, with that object, took sections of the valley of the Dove to its summit near Axe Edge, and it appears that the head of the Dove is 976 ft. above Ordnance datum, the Dove at Ludwell 726 ft., and at Mill Dale 586 ft.; and, assuming that the waters falling upon the high districts above Mill Dale could be collected at various levels by the construction of weirs, dams, and embankments, and aqueducts and tunnels constructed from Ludwell, on the Dove, to Lees Bottom, on the Wye, length about 5 miles, and from Monsal Dale to Calver, near Stoney Middleton, on the Derwent, the waters running into those valleys would be concentrated to Mill Dale, and a short tunnel would also unite the Manifold with the intended main aqueduct.

It is intended to commence the main aqueduct at Mill Dale, from an extensive reservoir, and to proceed in the direction of London partly in open cutting along Dove Dale; but nearly the whole length would be in tubes, pipes, and tunnels, excepting at the intermediate reservoirs, which would be constructed on the high grounds separating the valleys of the Trent, the Soar, the Welland, the Nen, the Ouze, the Ivel, and the Colne. These intermediate reservoirs, if the present line of section be adopted, would be at Battle Flat, near Bagworth, Kibworth Harcourt, Rothwell, Souldrop, Ampthill, Barton Hill, and Barnet, the latter 350 ft. above Ordnance datum, the relative levels allowing an average fall of 18 in. per mile from Battle Flat in the direction of London, but the part from Mill Dale to the Trent would fall more rapidly. A map showing the course of the aqueduct is given on Plate X. The aqueduct, where in tubes or pipes, would in many parts be in undulations, the tubes being supported on piers of brickwork or masonry.

The total length of the main aqueduct would be about 138 miles, but it is said that this distance may be reduced by making certain alterations in the line surveyed, and Mr. Remington estimates the cost of the works required for collecting the quantity of water assumed—viz., 83,000,000 gallons per day—and conveying it to London, at 5,000,000l.

It may be mentioned that Manchester, Huddersfield, Sheffield, and other large towns obtain water from the northern and eastern sides of the contiguous hills, but not from the slopes of the Dove, the Wye, and the Derwent.

METROPOLIS WATER SUPPLY.

The coming session (1866) of Parliament, as well as the current session of the Institution of Civil Engineers, can hardly close without exhaustive discussions upon the best modes of increasing the quantity and improving the quality of the water supply to the metropolis. And however we may complain of the delay and often unsatisfactory conclusions of royal commissions, we believe that her Majesty's Ministers cannot do less than support a petition for the royal reference customary in cases of such vast importance to the public health and convenience. At present we have upwards of three million people drinking water from the Thames and the Lea—water collected from wide cultivated districts, and unquestionably contaminated with the impurities of town drainage, or, in more familiar and unmistakable phrase, sewage. Nature filters rain-water by percolation and organic decomposition at considerable depths, and the London water companies imitate the process by a rapid straining of the contents of small pools of water through three or four or five feet of sand and gravel, a straining which is even more effective than could be expected, but which is not sufficient to purify the water, although it is only a question as to what extent of comparative purification is necessary to render water fit to drink. The lesson of this year (1866) is that cholera may accompany an impure water supply; and, if we may judge from the comparative exemption of Glasgow, Manchester, and Sheffield, that it is kept off by pure water, makes the question of purity one of the most pressing importance. Construing the purity of water with some allowance of degree, nearly all are agreed as to its importance, but the difference between the liquid treasures of Loch Katrine and the (now well known to have been) unfiltered water which carried death last summer to the East London Company's district is only one of degree.

It is only upon the question of the degree of impurity which may be tolerated in drinking-water that engineers differ and doctors disagree. To the outside public it would seem that, however little these differences may be, we ought to select the purest water we can obtain. We know we cannot obtain it from the Thames nor the Lea, and it is questionable whether we can obtain it from the chalk; but we can obtain water of great comparative purity from Wales and from Westmoreland. It is a fearful responsibility to incur, if by bringing sewaged water into London—and all the water now drunk here is sewage, highly diluted—we invite pestilence; and although human life ought to be reckoned priceless, it costs the country a considerable sum for the growth of each adult human being. Taking this simple basis of calculation, a heavy money loss was incurred this year (1866), when cholera carried off at least 10,000 of the population of London.

Since it has been declared law that the towns upon the Thames above London shall no longer discharge their sewage into that river, it has been maintained by a considerable body of engineers that Thames water will, after filtration, always be sufficiently pure for drinking. Mr. Bailey Denton recommends that the London water supply be taken from the district within which the Thames has its sources; but here, although we should avoid the impurities of the lower portions of the river, it is more than doubtful whether the drainage of a comparatively low-lying district having only a very moderate rainfall would be sufficient for the full supply of London. We require at least fifty gallons per head of population daily, or upwards of 150,000,000 gallons daily, and our prospective sources of supply must be sufficient to give a stream equal to 100 ft. wide, 4 ft. deep, and moving at the rate of one mile an hour. Any one who knows the upper Thames knows that, even were that stream to be directed into an aqueduct, the entire head waters of the Thames drainage area would afford no such supply.

Others tell us that the chalk contains all the water we require, although no experiments upon percolation have been made to give the least probability to the notion that the chalk will supply even one-fourth of the water required for London. We have visited nearly every one of the large breweries in the metropolis, and we know that most of them have deep wells, into the chalk, which have lowered from 2 ft. to 3 ft. per year for a long series of years. Messrs. Combe, Delafield and Co.'s wells have lowered 60 ft. in twenty-five years, and at other breweries the wells have failed altogether. So far as percolation goes, we can count upon but little in the London clay district, almost as impervious as the block-paving and macadam of London itself, and we are to bear in mind that the metropolis includes nearly 125 square miles. Most of the water in the chalk must have percolated into out-crops far away, and the rate of transmission through the chalk is so slow that, in any case, an extensive and costly series of wells and pumps would be necessary to collect this water of percolation, and render it available for a steady supply.

The philosophy of the water-bearing and water-carrying powers of the London chalk was well set forth by Mr. Hawkshaw, on the occasion of the discussion, at the Institution of the Civil Engineers in 1859, of Mr. C. E. Amos's paper on the Trafalgar Square Waterworks. He said :

"I was called upon some years ago to report upon a scheme for supplying London with water from Watford by sinking a large well adjacent to the river Colne, and I then found, as appeared to be still the case, that there existed some misconception upon what I consider to be a very simple question. Water cannot be pumped from wells sunk into the chalk, or into any other water-bearing stratum, beyond a certain quantity, without affecting the level of those wells. This will be evident upon a little consideration. Subterranean reservoirs, as I may perhaps be permitted to call them, are similar to all other reservoirs, and follow precisely the same law. If a well be sunk into a subterranean reservoir, in which the water happens to come in faster than it is pumped out, that reservoir will remain full; that is to say, it will continue at the precise level which happens to be determined by the natural point of overflow or escape. But if the water is pumped out faster than it comes in, then the level must of necessity be reduced. This rule will apply to all wells, whether under London or elsewhere. A certain given quantity of water only can be obtained from the chalk. Whenever that quantity is exceeded, the level of the reservoirs from which the water is pumped will be lowered. I think a part of the confusion that seems to prevail on this subject arises from the disposal of the rainfall which it is usual to make, and which has been repeated during the discussion, that one-third is disposed of by evaporation, one-third by the rivers, and one-third by absorption or infiltration, and that this last portion alone is available for pumping. Now, there is no such thing as infiltration in this sense; vegetation absorbs a certain portion of water, and another portion sinks into the ground. But it is evident that so much of the rainfall as sinks into the earth, and is not taken up by vegetation or by evaporation, merely passes below the surface to again run out elsewhere—if not immediately into the sea, then into streams or rivers. Consequently the water which flows along the streams and rivers, or finds its way into the sea, must be the measure of that portion of the rainfall which penetrates the ground by infiltration. I am surprised, therefore, to find that it is still considered possible to sink a well into the chalk and pump from it an unlimited quantity of water, without affecting either the level of the well or the quantity carried off by the rivers. I do not dispute the statement that there are places where large quantities may be pumped without lowering the level, because there may be at those places a much greater influx than the quantity abstracted; but there is no water-bearing stratum anywhere from which it is not possible to pump such a quantity of water as will gradually exhaust it. In some cases this may be a slow process, because, in addition to the annual quantity obtained from infiltration, a supply may be drawn from water lying below the level of what may be termed the natural outlet, and accumulated there during long periods of years."

It will be reasonably apparent from Mr. Hawkshaw's remarks that we have no unfailing supply of water from the chalk, and we are left, then, to choose between neighbouring and distant drainage areas. To us it appears that we should consider only which water is best, and that the cost of carrying out the requisite works should form a secondary consideration. Even if the cost be ten or twenty millions, London cannot afford to tolerate a supply of impure water from private and practically irresponsible sources, as is now the case; and however the coming inquiry may terminate, we think we see approaching the end of the existing water companies.

PART III.

MISCELLANEOUS ARTICLES ON WATERWORKS AND WATER SUPPLY.

WATER SUPPLY.

Nothing is more essential to the health and well-being of a community than an abundant supply of pure water, and yet there are at the present time numbers of cities and large towns both in this country and on the Continent where such a supply is wanting. The inadequacy of the present water service of the metropolis is well known, and so is the scarcity of water at Liverpool and many other large manufacturing towns; and besides these, there are many smaller places at which the supply is either insufficient in quantity or is of bad quality. On the Continent, Paris is short of water, and so are Vienna, and Florence, whilst at Leipsic and several other places extensive works are now being carried out.

The improvements which have been made in this country within the last few years in the drainage of towns, and in our sanitary arrangements, have had an important influence upon the question of water supply. In the first place, they have rendered a larger supply of water necessary; and in the second place, they have made, or are making, unavailable many sources from which water was formerly drawn. Hitherto a great number of our towns have depended for their supply of water upon the rivers in their immediate neighbourhood; but these are now, in very many cases, so polluted by the influx of sewage and of the refuse from manufactories along their banks, that their water cannot be used for household purposes with any degree of safety. Such, for instance, is the case with the Thames, the condition of which we have described in another part of the present volume. The Thames receives more or less directly the drainage of fifty-six towns situated within its basin, above the pumping stations of the Chelsea and other Metropolitan water companies at Hampton; and the more perfect the sewage arrangements of these towns are made, the more will the water of the Thames be polluted. An analysis, made in February, 1866, of the water supplied from the Thames by the London water companies, showed that the solid matters contained in it amounted to 31.14 parts in 100,000; the organic and volatile impurities forming, in one case, as much as 2.0, and in another, 2.59 parts. Of the inorganic matters, 21 parts were carbonate of lime or its equivalent. The quality of the water is improved by a drought, heavy rains increasing the amount of the impurities. The quantity of water in the Thames certainly has not increased during the last few years; on the contrary, there seems to be good evidence that it has decreased. In 1852, when several water-works' acts were passed, the minimum quantity of water flowing past Hampton in the course of one day was estimated at 362,000,000 gallons; it has been stated by the engineer to the conservators of the Thames that in 1864 the least daily quantity which passed over Teddington Weir was 380,000,000 gallons; but careful observations made at Hampton in September, 1865, showed that the daily quantity flowing down the river rarely exceeded 300,000,000 gallons. By the terms of their respective acts, the total maximum daily quantity which those of the London water companies which draw their supply from the Thames are permitted to abstract from that river is 100,000,000 gallons, and of this quantity they are now probably taking from 50,000,000 to 60,000,000 gallons. Some of the companies draw a further supply from other sources, such as the rivers Lea and Ravensbourne, the New River, and deep wells in the neighbourhood of the metropolis; and altogether the London water companies are estimated to have supplied during 1865 a gross daily quantity of about 108,500,000 gallons. This supply was distributed to about 470,000 houses through mains and branches extending to a total length of 3290 miles.

At the present time * the population of London and its suburbs within the area of a circle struck from Charing Cross, with a radius of 15 miles is nearly 3,500,000 souls, and to this number the water supply, which we have just mentioned, would give an average quantity of about 30 gallons per individual. This average amount, however, will not enable us to form an opinion as to the adequacy or inadequacy of the supply, as the water is very unequally distributed, and in some of the poorer parts of the metropolis the quantity furnished is fearfully insufficient. In the course of a letter from Dr. Horace Jeaffreson (the late medical resident officer of the Fever Hospital), published in the *Times* on the 3rd of January, 1866, that gentleman states that some

* April, 1866.

courts, containing eight two-roomed houses and sixty-four inhabitants, are supplied merely by a ⅛-in. pipe projecting a few inches within the walls of the court, the water being turned on for about twenty minutes only in the course of the day. In other instances twenty persons were found to be supplied from a single butt holding 80 gallons, and having the water flowing into it for from ten minutes to half an hour per day; and other similar or even worse cases could be quoted. On Sunday, when no water is obtained from the mains, the small stock in the districts to which we have alluded is soon exhausted, and a further supply has to be begged by the inhabitants as best they can.

It is but fair, however, to state that the insufficient supply of water to the poorer parts of the metropolis can scarcely be charged to the water companies. It is in a great measure due to the parsimony of the proprietors of house property, who do not furnish sufficient storage accommodation. The fact of there being an insufficient supply, however, teaches one thing, and that is that in any estimate which we may form of the quantity of water which will be required in future years, we must, in addition to allowing for the increase of population, allow for a greater quantity of water per head than is at present furnished. Glasgow furnishes a good example of the manner in which improvements in sanitary arrangements cause an increased demand for water. In that town the quantity of water used in 1838 amounted to 26 gallons per head of the whole population per diem; in 1845 it had risen to 30 gallons per day, and in 1852 to 35 gallons per head on the north side and 38 gallons per head on the south side of the Clyde. The present supply amounts to 45 gallons per head, of which 3½ gallons per head are sold by meter for trade purposes, leaving 41½ gallons per head for household use. We have stated that the present population of the metropolitan district amounts to nearly 3,500,000, a number twice as great as it was forty years ago. The census returns show that the annual increase is at the rate of about 2 per cent., and we may, therefore, assume that by the end of the present century between 5,000,000 and 6,000,000 people will have to be supplied with water by the London companies. At 40 gallons per head per diem, from 200,000,000 to 240,000,000 gallons of water daily would thus be required, and it seems quite certain that the excess of this quantity over that now supplied could not be permitted to be drawn from the Thames, even if the purity of that stream rendered it advisable to do so, and other sources of supply must therefore be sought out.

We have hitherto confined our remarks to the London water supply and to the state of the Thames; it must not be considered, however, that the latter is the only river the condition of which requires attention. The Severn furnishes another prominent instance, as the evidence given last year in committee on the Cheltenham Waterworks Bill proves. The Severn has eight tributaries above Tewkesbury, and each of these has six or seven smaller streams falling into it. The Severn is thus made to receive the drainage from a number of towns containing altogether nearly 1,000,000 inhabitants, and in the opinion of some of the witnesses before the committee we have mentioned, its water is in the neighbourhood of Worcester quite unfit for drinking purposes. Many other rivers might be mentioned which are in a similar state, but our space will not permit us to do more than allude to them. The observations made by Dr. Stevenson Macadam on the contamination of the Leith water by the sewage of that town and of Edinburgh, furnish us with some instructive information. This investigation proved that the amount of oxygen contained in the water was materially diminished by the admixture of sewage. About 29 per cent. of the total quantity of gases held in solution by good water is oxygen, and water taken from the springs which supply Edinburgh, and that drawn from the sources of the Leith water, formed no exception to this rule. After the Leith water had mixed with the sewage, however, it was found that in some parts of the stream the quantity of oxygen had diminished to 10.20, and in others to as little as 4.1 per cent. of the total amount of the gases.

The influence which the purity or impurity of water exerts upon the health of the people using it was strikingly shown during the visits of the cholera to the metropolis in 1848-9 and 1853-4. In the latter years the Lambeth Company pumped from the higher parts of the Thames, and supplied water equal in quality to any furnished at that time by the other companies. The Southwark and Vauxhall Company, on the other hand, drew their supply from lower down the river, and the water then furnished by them has been stated to be " perhaps the filthiest stuff ever drunk by a civilised community." The Lambeth Company supplied 24,854 houses, containing about 166,906 people, and amongst these the deaths from cholera amounted to 611, or were at the rate of 0.37 per cent. of the population. The Southwark and Vauxhall Company supplied 39,726 houses, containing about 268,171 inhabitants, of whom 3476 died from cholera, the death rate being in this case 1.3 per cent., or about three and a half times as high as in the district supplied with purer water. That the difference in the mortality in the two districts we have mentioned was mainly due to the difference in the quality of the water supplied to them is curiously corroborated by observations made in 1848-49. At that date the water furnished by the Lambeth Company was worse than that sup-

plied by the Southwark and Vauxhall Company, and the proportionate
death rate in the former was then greater than in the latter district.
Owing to the increase of the population and extension of the drainage,
the water supplied by the Southwark and Vauxhall Company in
1853-4 was worse than that pumped up by the same company in
1848-9, and this deterioration in the quality was accompanied by a
higher mortality, the death rate in 1853-4 being about 10 per cent.
higher than in 1848-9. The presence of organic matter in water is
far more injurious than that of inorganic impurities ; indeed a certain
quantity of the latter appears to be essential.

Although, from what we have stated, it will be seen that the water
of those rivers which pass through populous districts is generally
unfit for drinking purposes, yet it must not be supposed that, taking
this country as a whole, there is likely to be any serious deficiency in
our water supply. In many parts of the country, artesian and other
wells will furnish an abundant supply of pure water. Thus, at Croy-
don, two wells sunk in the upper chalk have each supplied 1,000,000
gallons per day, and Brighton draws a daily supply of 1,080,000
gallons from wells sunk in it. The South Essex Company also pump
161,000 gallons daily from the large chalk pits at Grays, and we
believe that 2,000,000 gallons may be drawn from the same source.
In other parts of the country, as in Wales and in the lake district, the
rainfall is out of all proportion to the population to be supplied, and
this has led engineers to consider the possibility of supplying some of
our principal towns from these tracts. We have already described in
this volume the schemes proposed by Mr. John F. Bateman for supplying London with water led from the mountain ranges of Cader
Idris and Plynlimmon in Wales, and there is also that of Mr. Thomas
Dale, the engineer of the Hull Corporation Waterworks, furnishing some of the principal manufacturing towns of Lancashire and
Yorkshire with a supply of water drawn from the lake districts of
Cumberland and Westmoreland. Both are grand schemes, and both
deserve the most careful consideration. It is estimated by Mr. Bateman that the works necessary for a supply to the metropolis of
130,000,000 gallons daily from the Welsh hills could be constructed
for an outlay of 8,600,000*l.*, and the supply might be increased to
220,000,000 gallons daily by an extra expenditure of 1,100,000*l.*
Mr. Dale, on the other hand, estimates the cost of carrying out his
scheme at 11,960,000*l.*, this outlay covering the cost of works for a
supply of 131,000,000 gallons of water daily, divided between nineteen
different towns. The sums which we have just mentioned are no doubt
large ones, but it is evident that without the expenditure of such large

sums, and the execution of grand works, it will be impossible to carry out the present and more particularly the future water supply of our metropolitan and manufacturing districts in anything like a satisfactory manner.

THE WATER SUPPLY OF PARIS.

In Paris, as in so many other capitals, a question of great present interest is that of increased water supply.

With a population of 1,700,000 souls, Paris now (1866) receives a total supply of 240,000 cubic metres, or about 53 millions of gallons per day, giving an average of 31 gallons per head, part of which is due to some works very recently constructed. A further item of 16,000 cubic metres is expected to be added within a very short time by the completion of the works which collect the water of the river Dhuys, and to this a total additional supply of 196,000 cubic metres is proposed to be procured by the collection of the sources of the river Vanne, by pumping water from the Marne river, and by boring two new artesian wells.

The present waterworks are divided into two distinct branches, which are entirely independent of each other, both with regard to the sources of supply and with regard to the reservoirs and service pipes. They are distinguished as " spring water " and " river water " service, the former supplying the water for domestic use, while the latter serves for the so-called public use, *i.e.* for cleaning the streets and sewers, for filling the public reservoirs, artificial lakes in the parks, ornamental fountains, &c. Each street of Paris is supplied with two different systems of pipes, viz., a spring-water service pipe and another for the supply of river water.

The principal source of the spring water is the river Dhuys. The water from this river is collected and brought into Paris by an aqueduct of 134,000 metres in length, of which a length of 118,000 metres is constructed in brickwork and 16,000 metres length consists of cast-iron pipes. The section of the brick culvert is ovoïdal, of 1.40 metres in greatest width and 1.76 metres height, internal measures; the iron pipes have an internal diameter of 1 metre and a thickness of 0.021 metre for the lower pressures, and 0.025 metre for the higher pressure.

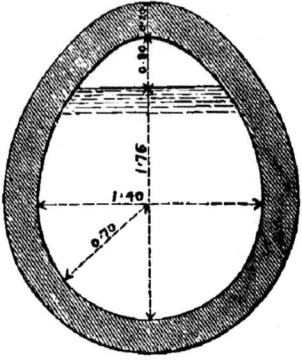

These differences of pressure are due to the different altitudes of the districts supplied with water.

The fall of the brick aqueduct is 1 in 10,000; the fall or loss of head in the iron pipes is about 1 in 2000. The Dhuys water is delivered into the upper part of the recently constructed great reservoir of the Menilmontant, containing 100,000 cubic metres, and a small part is pumped some 30 metres higher up, into the upper reservoir of the Telegraph, which supplies the highest parts of Paris, viz., Montmartre, Belleville, &c.

The other sources of spring water are those of Arceuil, collected in the reservoir of the Pantheon and the artesian well of Grenoble, all of which communicate with the first and with each other through the service mains.

The spring water is supplied at three different heights; the low level reaching to a height of 48 metres above the level of the Seine, the high level from 48 to 81 metres, and the small district of Montmartre, &c., to which the water is pumped from the high-level reservoir.

There exists another source of spring water, which has, however, not yet been made use of for domestic purposes, and is at present employed in feeding the artificial lake of the Bois de Boulogne. This is the great artesian well of Passy, with a yield of 8000 cubic metres per day.

The total present supply of spring water, including the well of Passy, is 35,600 cubic metres, and, with the completion of the Dhuys waterworks, will be shortly 51,600 cubic metres per day.

The river water is obtained by pumping from the canal of the Ourcq, and from the Seine and Marne rivers.

The canal of the Ourcq is entirely open, and serves also for navigation. It supplies the reservoir De la Villette, containing 200,000 cubic metres. From this reservoir an aqueduct of nearly 4 kilometres length leads to the reservoir of Monceaux, containing 100,000 cubic metres. It branches off at different places, supplying the main service pipes and some smaller reservoirs distributed over the town.

The Seine water is pumped into the reservoir of Passy, containing 40,000 cubic metres of water, and into the reservoirs of Gentilly, Charonne, Charenton, Montmartre, Batignolles, Passy, Vaugiraud, and Pantheon. The Marne water is raised to the lower reservoir of the Menilmontant and of the Telegraph.

All the reservoirs supplying river water are equally in communication with each other through their respective service pipes, so that the irregularities of supply and the consequences of accidental stoppages of machinery are equalised all over the town. By this arrangement great regularity and constancy is obtained in the supply of water to all parts of Paris.

The river water is delivered at two levels—the low and high level—corresponding to those of the spring water supply.

The water level of the Seine river, at Pont Royal, is 25.04 metres above the sea, and the highest parts of Paris are at 130 metres, giving a greatest height of about 105 metres for the delivery of river water by the pumping-engines of Paris.

Of the proposed new works, the two artesian wells are in progress of excavation; the aqueduct of the Vanne, although sanctioned by the authorities, is still under consideration of the engineers with regard to its details, which have not yet been entirely decided upon.

For the data of the above description we are indebted to an eminent American engineer connected with the water supply of New York, who is at present in England collecting valuable information about the waterworks of the principal European cities. At his request, and in reply to his inquiries, M. Belgrand, the chief engineer of the Paris Waterworks, in the most courteous and obliging manner compiled a complete and valuable series of answers, of which we have been permitted to avail ourselves.

To the information supplied by M. Belgrand we add the following account of the reservoir at Menilmontant.

The Menilmontant reservoir has been recently constructed to receive the waters of the Dhuys and the Marne.

The Dhuys, which falls into the Surmelin, a tributary of the Marne, is all brought to Paris by a covered aqueduct 2 metres in height by 1.40 metres span at springing.

The hill of Menilmontant, where the reservoir is situated, lies at 107.85 metres above the level of the sea, and at 82.61 metres above the low-water mark of the Seine or the zero at the Pont de la Tournelle. The upper reservoir, which receives the waters of the Dhuys, has an area of 2 hectares, or 5 acres; and as the depth of the water is fixed at 5 metres, it would contain 100,000 cubic metres, or 22,009,675 gallons for distribution.

In plan it is a semicircle of 94 metres radius, flanked by a rectangular part. The semicircle lies towards the slope of the hill, and as the reservoir is excavated in the green marl which lies on the top of the gypsum, this form gives more resistance to the pressure of the earth. Besides, it contains the greatest area within the smallest amount of wall. The nature of the ground rendered it necessary to excavate to the solid ground. This extra height has been availed of to build a lower reservoir, of the capacity of 32,000 cubic metres, to receive the waters of the Marne, pumped up from St. Maur. By the amount just mentioned, it will be seen that the whole of the lower reservoir is not required, but was necessary to be constructed in order that the piers might be carried down to a good foundation. The reservoir is divided into two equal and symmetrical parts by means of a thick wall. These two compartments are quite independent of each other, so that whilst one is being repaired the other can contain half the total supply of water.

The external distributing reservoir of the waters of the Dhuys serves as a junction between the supply-pipe and the large reservoir. In this reservoir there are three gun-metal valves, to regulate the three conducting-pipes, two of which communicate with the two compartments of the reservoir; the third crosses but does not communicate with it, and conducts the water directly to a distributing-pipe of 1 metre diameter.

At the bottom of each compartment of the reservoir is a sluice that enables the water to be discharged into the lower reservoir. The bottom is arranged sloping 1 in 1000 towards the centre, to enable it to be perfectly emptied.

The waters of the Marne reservoir can be diverted into the culvert which contains the distributing-pipes.

The depth of water in the two reservoirs is limited to 5 metres above the bottom, by means of a vertical tube, which communicates with the discharge culvert.

The waters of the Marne are brought by two conduits. There are, likewise, two sluices that communicate with both the lower reservoirs.

The piers of foundation are placed at a distance of 6 metres from centre to centre on the gypsum which lies under about 7 or 8 metres of green marl. The side walls, at the level of the foundation, support a pressure of 5 to $5\frac{1}{2}$ kilogrammes when the upper reservoir is filled to a depth of 5 metres with water.

The external wall of the Dhuys reservoir is 1.70 metres in thickness. The masonry is bound together by iron chains, and firmly fixed by holdfasts 70 centimetres in depth.

The arches of the lower reservoir are 40 centimetres in thickness at the key.

The coverings of the upper reservoirs are formed by arches of two courses of bricks. They have a rise of 60 centimetres, and have only to support a thickness of 50 to 60 centimetres of earth covered with turf. This covering slopes slightly towards the centre of the reservoir, to enable the rain-waters to fall into the lower reservoir by means of a vertical pipe. The front wall of the reservoir is protected by a slope of earth.

No dressed stone, with the exception of a small quantity required for the setting of the metal work, has been used in this great work.

All the facing is Vassy cement, called Gariel cement. For works intended to contain water, whether reservoirs or cisterns, it is most important that the surfaces should be smooth; otherwise the water charged with any matter, however little, deposits it, and perfect cleaning becomes difficult when the reservoir is emptied. The Vassy cement is well adapted to fulfil these conditions.

The quantity of earth excavated amounted to 200,000 cubic metres, and the masonry to 70,000 cubic metres. The total cost was 3,700,000 fr., or 148,000l.; so that the cost per cubic metre for storing the water was 28 fr.

This grand work was designed and constructed by M. Huet, ingénieur des Ponts et Chaussées, under the direction of M. Belgrand. Its construction was entrusted by the municipality of Paris to Messrs. Garnuchot and Loroque, and executed in the space of two years. This celerity, due in a great measure to the activity of the contractors, has not been prejudicial to the works.

The regularity of the distributing service is ensured by the immense size of the reservoir. There are deposited all matters held in suspension, and the reservoirs are sheltered from the action of the sun, so that no vegetation can be developed.

The Menilmontant reservoir is a work of public utility, being the largest in Paris; and the only ones that approach it in size are those of Passy and Belleville, and they contain but 40 and 36 thousand cubic metres of water.

Even looking back to the thermæ of Diocletian and Caracalla, this work seems worthy of the Romans, our masters still in the management of the water supplies to large cities.

THE BROOKLYN PUMPING ENGINE.

The pumping engine of which we give illustrations on Plate XI. and the following page, is one of a pair made for the Brooklyn Waterworks, near New York, by Messrs. Woodruff and Beach, of Hartford, Connecticut, from the designs of Mr. William Wright. According to the contract, the "duty" of the engine was not to be less than 600,000 lb. raised 1 ft. high by the consumption of 1 lb. of coal, and the engine was also to be capable of raising 10,000,000 of New York gallons of water (equal to 8,000,000 imperial gallons) into the reservoir in sixteen continuous hours, the actual height of the lift being 160 ft. In calculating the duty, the weight of water was to be taken at 62½ lb. per cubic foot, and the friction of the water in the pipes was to be accurately ascertained by gauges, and when this was done the necessary allowance was to be made by considering the resistance caused by friction as an additional height lifted.

THE BROOKLYN PUMPING ENGINE.

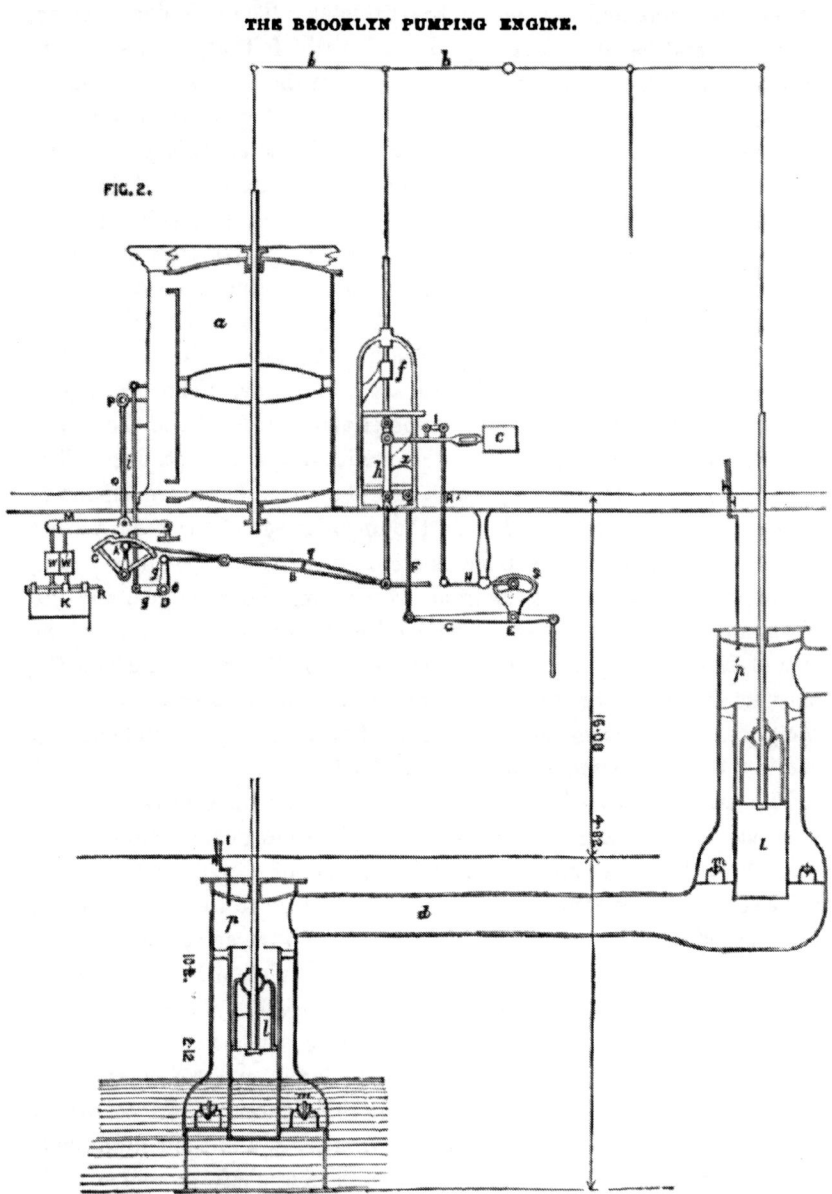

FIG. 2.

THE BROOKLYN PUMPING ENGINE.   107

The engine is double acting, the cylinder being 90 in. in diameter,
and made to accommodate an extreme stroke of 10 ft. 3½ in.; the stroke
at which the piston is intended to work is 10 ft. The double bedplate
to which the cylinder is fastened extends the whole length of the engine,
which is placed directly over the pump-well. The piston is 1 ft. 6 in.
deep in the centre, and 8½ in. deep around the circumference; and the
piston-rod, which is 8¼ in. in diameter, passes through stuffing-boxes
at both the top and bottom of the cylinder. The cylinder is steam
jacketed, and is also carefully cleaded with felt and black walnut
lagging; its base is above the water-level in the boilers. The valves,
which are worked by a peculiar arrangement of gear, as will be described presently, are balanced puppets, the diameters being 14 in. and
14½ in., and 16 in. and 16½ in.; they are swelled out around their stems
in order to reduce the waste of steam. The steam and side pipes are
1 ft. 8 in. in diameter. The piston-rod, which passes through the top
of the cylinder, is connected by the ordinary arrangement of parallel
motion to the end of a cast-iron beam, 36 ft. long between end centres,
7 ft. 2 in. deep in the middle, and weighing 25 tons. The web of the
beam is 5¾ in. thick, and the flanges are 16 in. wide. The bearings of
the main centre are 1 ft. 1 in. in diameter and 2 ft. long, and the height
of their centre above the floor of the engine-room is 26 ft. 3 in. The
arrangement of the frame by which the plummer-blocks are supported
is shown by Fig. 1, Plate XI. To the opposite end of the beam to that
to which the piston-rod is coupled is attached the rod of the upper pump,
and at intermediate points the frame for working the valve gear and the
air-pump-rod are connected. The condenser, which is one-third of the
size of the cylinder, is placed at the centre of the engine beneath the
floor, as shown in Fig. 1; the injection water can be drawn either from
the pump-well or from the force-pipe. The air-pump is double acting,
and is 3 ft. in diameter, with a stroke of 5 ft.

The arrangement of the valve gear is, as we have already stated,
peculiar. It differs from that usually employed in Cornish engines, inasmuch as the valves are moved by the piston of a water cylinder, the
valves of which are moved by the frame connected to the engine beam;
the cataract is, however, retained. In Fig. 2 we give an outline diagram
of the valve gear of the Brooklyn engine, which will enable us to
explain its action. In this diagram, a is the steam cylinder, and b the
main beam of the engine, and to this beam is connected the frame f,
which, in combination with the water cylinder, c, and roller levers, h,
works the valves. The upper ends of the roller levers, h, are connected
by links with the piston of the water cylinder, c, and their lower ends
by links, q, with the arm, g, of the lower rocking shaft, e; and another

arm, *g*, on the same shaft, is coupled by means of the vertical links, *i*, to the upper rocking shaft, which is placed in bearings between the side pipes. The frame *f* is connected by the link F with the lever G, fixed upon another rocking shaft E, this shaft carrying the cam, S, which works the valves of the water cylinder by means of the lever and link, H and H', and the bell crank, I. An arm on the rocking shaft, E, is also connected by the bar B, with the arm A, fixed upon another rocking shaft D, upon which there is also fixed the segment C. This segment is adjustable by hand, so that it can be arranged to shut the steam valves at any desired point in the stroke of the piston. Its face is formed to two different radii, as shown in the diagram, the difference of these radii being equal to the lift of the steam valves. The stems of these valves are connected by means of the levers P and links O to a pair of levers M N, one end of each of which is attached to a fixed fulcrum, N, whilst the other, M, is coupled to the plunger of one of the cylinders of the cataract, K. These plungers are weighted by means of the weights *w w'*, and each is furnished with a catch bolt, R, which bolts, when the plungers are lifted, fall into sockets and keep them raised. Each of the catches is forced into gear by a spring at the back of it, and is withdrawn by an arm fixed upon the rocking shaft, *e*. The action of this valve gear is as follows: Let us suppose that the piston is at the middle of the up-stroke, the lower steam valve being still open, and the cataract plunger connected with it being at the bottom of its cylinder, and the latch, R, withdrawn. When, in the course of its upward motion, the piston arrives at the point at which the steam is to be cut off, the segment C is moved by the action of the frame *f*, and the connecting links, &c., until the projecting part of its face comes under the lever, M N. This lifts the lever and closes the steam valve, at the same time raising the corresponding plunger of the cataract, which is then held by one of the catches, R. Further on in the stroke the incline, *x*, fixed upon the frame, *f*, comes in contact with the roller upon the upper end of the roller lever, *h*, pushing it over and opening, by means of the rods *q* and *i*, and the levers *g g'*, the lower exhaust valve. Near the end of the stroke, the valves of the water cylinder being moved by the cam S through the gear already described, the piston of that cylinder forces the roller lever right over quickly, and thus draws back the catch holding up the cataract plunger connected with the upper steam valve. The weights on this plunger then cause it to fall and open the valve, admitting the steam to the upper side of the piston.

As will be seen by Fig. 1, the engine is placed directly over the pump-well, this latter being 37 ft. 3 in. deep and 60 ft. by 10 ft. inside. The

side walls are of granite, and are from 5 ft. to 6 ft. 6 in. thick, the bottom
being formed by a flat arch, 2 ft. 6 in. thick, resting on a plank floor
placed on a bed of solid gravel. The depth of the waterway is 7 ft. There
are two pumps, both placed beneath the floor of the engine-house, as
shown in Fig. 1, one of them being at a lower level than the other. The
lower pump is worked by the extension of the piston rod through the
bottom of the steam cylinder, and the other by a pump rod attached to
the opposite end of the beam; both the rods are $8\frac{1}{4}$ in. in diameter. The
arrangement of the pumps and valves is shown by the diagram, Fig. 2,
from which it will be seen that each pump has two barrels, l and m, the
inner barrels in which the buckets work being 3 ft. and the outer ones
4 ft. 6 in. in diameter. The delivery or force pipe is led from the top of
the upper pump, and the bottom of this pump is connected with the top
of the lower pump by a pipe 3 ft. in diameter. Each bucket is fitted with
a double-beat valve, and eight similar valves are placed at the bottom
of the annular space between the barrels of each pump. The action of
these pumps is as follows: When the piston in the steam cylinder is
making an up-stroke, the bucket of the lower pump lifts the water
above it, and forces it through the valves in the annular space and
descending bucket of the upper pump; when the reverse stroke is
made, the bucket of the upper pump lifts the water, the space between
the two buckets becoming filled by the flow of water through the valves
of the lower pump. The quantity of water delivered at each single
stroke of the engine is thus equal to the contents of one pump barrel
(less of course any loss arising from the valves not closing quickly, or
from other causes), and as the water is always flowing in one direction,
all loss of momentum is avoided.

The delivery pipe, reaching from the upper pump to the reservoir, is
3 ft. in diameter and 3450 ft. long, and is furnished with a check-valve
at the middle of its length. It is laid with but one curve, and that of
800 ft. radius, and has an overfall discharge into the receiving chamber.
An air chamber, 25 ft. 4 in. high, 6 ft. $6\frac{1}{2}$ in. in diameter, and projecting
13 ft. 10 in. above the floor of the engine-room, is placed upon the
force-pipe close to the upper pump, as shown in Fig. 1. This air-
vessel is furnished with a diaphragm plate, fitted with valves, which
can be arranged so as to throttle the return pressure of the air; the
loss of air arising from leakage, &c., is made up by a supply forced in
by an auxiliary pump worked from the air-pump rod. Each of the
pump rods has a loaded counterweight chest attached to it, as shown in
Fig. 1, that on the rod of the upper pump being placed just below the
beam, and that on the rod of the lower pump being situated beneath
the cylinder; in addition to these a vibrating counterweight, placed on

a countershaft, is also connected to the lower chest in such a manner as to increase the load upon the piston during the first half of each stroke, and diminish it during the latter half. These counterweights amount altogether to 46 tons, and the total weight of the engine, boilers, and appurtenances is 440 tons.

The engine, the whole of the details of which are finished in the best manner, is placed in an engine-house having an engine-room 84 ft. by 77 ft., and two wings or boiler-rooms 66 ft. 6 in. by 45 ft. This engine-house will afford accommodation for four engines and their boilers. The boilers of the engine which we have been describing, are three in number; they are of the return drop-flue class, and are 30 ft. long by 8 ft. in diameter. The upper flues are 1 ft. 6 in., and the lower or return flues 9 in. in diameter. Each boiler is furnished with independent stop, feed, and safety valves, so that either can be shut off at pleasure. They are fed by an independent engine, which draws the water, by means of separate pipes, either from the hot-well, the pump-well, or from the force-pipe, as may be desired; the feed-water is heated by passing it through coils of pipe placed in the lower return flues. A measuring tank is placed in connexion with the donkey-pump, in order that the amount of water evaporated by the boilers may be exactly ascertained when it is desired to do so. The boiler flues are connected with a chimney 100 ft. high, and 4 feet in diameter inside.

After the engine had been set to work, two sets of experiments were made with it, the one to ascertain the "duty," and the other to find out the quantity of water pumped into the reservoir in a certain time. From the report of the experimenters, Messrs. Erastus W. Smith, Fred. Graff, and W. E. Worthen, and the notes of Mr. Samuel McElroy, the assistant engineer to the Brooklyn Waterworks, we find that the following results were obtained: The actual height to which the water was lifted, measured from the average level of the pump-well to the point of discharge, was 160 ft.; the friction of the water through the pumps and force tubes, as measured by indicator cards taken from the pumps, was equal to an additional lift of 10 ft., making the total equivalent lift 170 ft. The trial for "duty" lasted 26 hours 3 min., during which time the engine made 14,965 double strokes, or about 9.57 per minute on an average. The average length of stroke of the pumps, as deduced from numerous observations, was 9 ft. 10½ in.; their capacity at this stroke is 849.6 gallons, whilst the quantity delivered, as measured in the reservoir, amounted to 835.2 gallons per stroke. The loss occasioned by the action of the pumps was thus only 1.69 per cent., an extremely good result. By comparing the pressure shown by the indicator diagrams taken from the cylinder with those taken from the pumps, it was found that in the former case there was an average pressure of 12 lb. per square inch over 6375 square inches, and in the latter an average pressure of 73.91 lb. per square inch on 959.31 square inches, the actual loss of pressure occasioned by the friction of the engine being thus only 7.4 per cent. of the steam pressure. Account was taken of the quantity of fuel consumed in the following manner: The engine, after having been at work some hours, was stopped, the steam blown off from the boilers, and the fires drawn; the firing was then recommenced, and an account taken of all fuel used up to the end of the experiment, when the engine was allowed to run until it exhausted all the steam and stopped of itself. The grates were then cleared out, and the coal remaining separated from the cinders and ashes, and the amount subtracted from the coal fired. The pressure of the steam was 15 lb. According to the report of Messrs. Smith, Graff, and Worthen, the fuel used was as follows:

Wood 1200 lb., or equivalent of coal . .	600 lb.
Total of coal fired	35,700
	36,300
Less residuum of coal	870
Net quantity of fuel used	35,430 lb.

In the report above mentioned, the duty is estimated from the average pressure on the pump buckets, and the result obtained is a duty of 609,982 foot pounds by the consumption of 1 lb. of coal. According to Mr. McElroy's notes, the net quantity of fuel burnt was 34,772 lb., and the total quantity of water delivered into the reservoir was 2,000,000 cubic feet. The duty, thus calculated, was thus

$$\frac{2,000,000 \times 170 \times 62.5}{34,773} = 611,114 \text{ foot pounds}$$

performed by 1 lb. of coal. Neither of the above duties was so high as have been obtained from English engines; but in the case of the Brooklyn engine, the pressure of the steam was lower, and it was also cut off later in the stroke than is usually the case here.

The second set of experiments were made to ascertain the quantity of water delivered by the pumps in a given time, in order to see whether the engine complied with the terms of the contract, which, as we have already mentioned, required that it should deliver 10,000,000 New York gallons or 8,000,000 imperial gallons into the reservoir in the course of sixteen hours. The duration of the trial was sixteen hours, and water delivered was measured, as in the case of the " duty " trial, both by guages applied to the reservoir and by the flow of the water over a weir. The results, as given in the report of Messrs. Smith, Graff, and Worthen, were as follows:

Water delivered.

By reservoir measures	. .	8,234,481 imp. gal.
By weir		8,076,100 „

The quantity delivered was therefore in excess of that required by the contract. From Mr. McElroy's notes of the second trial, we find that engine made 9708 double strokes during the sixteen hours, or an average of 10.11 per minute; the average speed for four hours was 10.36 double strokes per minute. The total quantity of coal burned was 26,528 lb. Mr. McElroy gives the quantity of water raised during the trial as 8,286,449 imperial gallons.

We have no doubt that many of our readers will freely criticise the Brooklyn pumping engine of which we have given a description. Its design is not one to be recommended, embodying as it does an imperfect application of the Cornish principle of working. In order to work to a considerable degree of expansion, the initial cylinder pressure must be correspondingly greater than the constant resistance to be overcome, the terminal pressure in a single cylinder being at the same time less than the constant resistance. If the piston drove the pump pole directly against the constant resistance of the water, only an insignificant amount of expansion could be permitted, as no machinery can be made to withstand the shock of communicating sudden impulses to large volumes of water, especially when they are under great pressure. In the Brooklyn engine, the piston does work directly against the constant resistance of the water in both directions, and 46 tons of dead weight, divided upon the two pump poles, is added, so as to permit of the accumulation of a certain amount of force at the beginning of each stroke, in order to give an opportunity for expansion towards the end. But in order to generate sufficient momentum in these weights, so as to render them of real service for expansion, they must be put into sudden motion, and this motion must be permitted to exhaust itself gradually towards the end of the stroke. But the water can only accommodate itself to these impulses after opposing a sudden and severe resistance, amounting to a shock upon all parts of the engine. So far is this the fact, that the following are the indicator diagrams taken from the engine, and we need not say how these contrast with the highly expansive diagrams of first-class Cornish engines, in which the action of the steam is only in one direction, the work done being the lifting of a weight, no steam pressure being ever applied to the water itself. The diagram shows great throttling of the steam, and an expansion of not more than one-half of the stroke. With an evaporation of $8\frac{1}{4}$ lb. of water per pound of coal, it is no wonder, therefore,

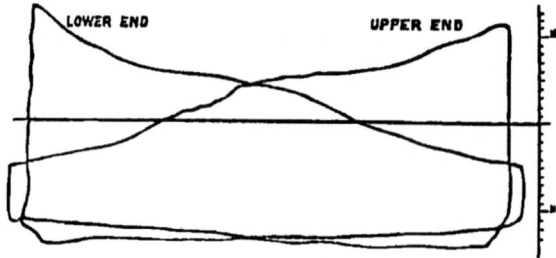

that the actual consumption of coal was $3\frac{1}{4}$ lb. per effective horse-power per hour, being slightly less than 3 lb. per indicated horse power. It was found that the engine would not bear full steam for any considerable part of the stroke, not even with additional weight on the pump poles.

In a later engine of much smaller dimensions, made for the same waterworks, a crank and heavy flywheel were adopted, two pumps being worked, one from near each end of the beam. These gave good diagrams with a high rate of expansion, and compare well with good rotative pumping engines of the ordinary construction.

TURBINES AT THE PHILADELPHIA WATERWORKS.

The three Jonval turbines in use at the extension of Fairmount Waterworks, Philadelphia, are the largest wheels of that class that have as yet been erected, although, as they are worked with a low fall of water, they are by no means the most powerful. At the time when the extension of the works was determined upon, an examination was made of the water power available at the Fairmount dam, and it was found that, for more than ten months of the year, the amount of water wasted by flowing over the dam was greater than could be passed through the nine wheels then in operation. The dam at Fairmount extends completely across the River Schuylkill, which river has, between the dam and Columbia Bridge, a point rather more than $1\frac{3}{4}$ miles above it, a mean sectional area of 8254 square feet. The average velocity of the flow at this part of the river is about two miles per day, the daily discharge being thus equal to over 540,000,000 gallons. The mean depth of water at the dam is 11.3 ft., and the greatest depth 35 ft. After some consideration it was determined to provide the additional pumping power required, by the erection of large turbines, and an extensive series of experiments was carried out in order to ascertain the form of wheel best adapted to the work. Altogether, nineteen series of trials were made of model wheels of various kinds and proportions, furnished by twelve different makers; these wheels being all tested under an uniform head of water of 6 ft., and the power exerted being measured by dead weights of from 500 to 1600 lb. lifted to heights of from 14 to 25 ft. The quantity of water used by each wheel whilst under trial was, of course, accurately measured, and the results obtained showed that the actual power utilised by the models varied from 47.34 to 87.77 per cent. of that due to the quantity and fall of the water. It was found that those wheels, such as the Jonval, through which the water passed vertically, gave the highest useful effects; next in order came those which delivered the water centrifugally, or from the centre, whilst the lowest in efficiency were those in which the water escaped centripetally, or towards the centre. Our space will not allow us to enter into the details of these experimental trials, although they were very interesting; the final results were, however, that three wheels, those constructed by Mr. J. E. Stevenson, Mr. Emile Geyelin, and Messrs. Andrews and Kallbach were found to be nearly equal in efficiency, the per-centages of useful effect obtained being 87.77, 82.1, and 81.87 per cent. respectively. The three makers above mentioned, and also Mr. Levi Smith, were invited to tender for the supply of three wheels with the necessary gearing, and eventually the bid of Mr. Emile Geyelin (who was at one time with Messrs. Koechlin and Co., of Mulhouse, where the Jonval wheel was first brought out) was accepted. The first two wheels were constructed for the contractor, Mr. Geyelin, by Messrs I. P. Morris and Co., of Port Richmond, and of one of these we give illustrations on Plate XII.

As the dam at Fairmount backs up the water of the river for about seven miles, and as any accident to it would cause the destruction of a large amount of valuable property, the operation of putting in the head arches and flumes for conveying the water to the wheels had to be conducted with the greatest care. The works were commenced by constructing a strong coffer-dam on the north or upper side of the dam, and inside this, after an excavation had been made to the proper depth, a bed of broken stones was formed. Upon this bed was laid a platform of 12 in. pine logs, around which sheet piling was driven; the interstices between the logs were then filled up with broken stone, and cement grout was run in so as to bind the whole mass together. The platform or bed thus formed was then covered with 3 in. pine planking, and upon this the front wall, head arches, and gates were erected. The gates and flumes are of cast iron, faced with brass, and the gates, which open a waterway of 65 square feet for each wheel, are raised by screws. After the face wall had been carried to its full height, and the flume led into the embankment for such a distance as to ensure safety from any accident arising from the pressure of the water, the works were commenced upon the south or down-river side of the dam. On account of the great depth required for the wheel pits, and the looseness of the materials of which the dam was composed, the construction of a cofferdam on the south side of the dam was found to be a matter of considerable difficulty. Notwithstanding that excavations were made into the dam as far as safety would permit, and piles freely used, a large quantity of water leaked into the cofferdam at high tide, and gave much trouble. After a depth of about 16 ft. had been excavated, a deep stratum of river mud was reached, and into this were driven three hundred and fifty piles. These piles were driven through the mud and a substratum of gravel from 3 ft. to 5 ft. thick, making in all a depth of from 16 ft. to 23 ft.; the mud was then excavated around the heads of the piles to a depth of 1 ft. 6 in., and the space filled in with broken stone, as shown in the figures. A platform, 113 ft. by 23 ft., made of 12 in. timbers, was then placed upon the heads of the piles, and surrounded by a double row of jointed sheet piling. The interstices between the timbers were then filled with broken stone, into which cement grouting was run, and the whole was covered by a double thickness of 3 in. planking. This platform forms part of the foundations of the buildings and machinery, the wheels being supported directly upon this floor. The foundations for the pumps are formed partly upon the dam itself, the loose stones, of which the embankment is composed, being levelled to a proper depth, and the interstices filled up with cement grout, so as to form one solid mass: 33,500 cubic feet of grout were used. The mill-house is roofed with brick arches covered with flagging, and supported by wrought-iron girders. The arrangement both of the roof and foundations is shown in the illustrations.

In order to avoid the danger which would have been incurred by excavating far into the dam, the turbines are placed at the south or down-river end of the mill-house, and each wheel is supplied with water by an elliptical tube 36 ft. long, the horizontal diameter of the tube being 12 ft. 10 in., and its vertical diameter 7 ft. 2 in., giving a clear water-way of over 70 square feet. The cover of the wheel casing is strongly ribbed on the outside, and is slightly arched so as to join the inlet tube. Each wheel stands in a pit 15 ft. by 20 ft., the floor being 4 ft. 4 in. below mean low tide, and 10 ft. 4 in. below mean high tide; the extreme variation of the tides, however, is 8 ft., and this, of course, greatly affects the power developed by the wheels. The centre of the wheel is 2 ft. 8 in. below the surface of an ordinary tide of 6 ft.,

and the mouth of the casing from which the tail water escapes is
1 ft. 9 in. below low-water mark. The form of the wheel casing, and
the arrangement of the wheel, is shown in the section, Fig. 2, from
which it will be seen that the guide curves of the stationary or guide
wheel are fitted into a conical part of the casing, which unites the wheel
casing proper with the upper chamber, the latter being 12 ft. in diameter.
The guide curves are seventeen in number, and are 1 ft. 7 in. high;
the area of discharge through them is 2050 square inches, or 14.236
square feet, this being about 30 per cent. in excess of the area of discharge through the revolving buckets. The revolving wheel is made
of wrought iron, cast to a cast-iron centre, and bound by a wrought-
iron rim. The buckets, of which there fifty, are 9 ft. in diameter outside, 6 ft. 4 in. inside, and 12 in. deep. They are 1 ft. 4 in. long, and
the total area of discharge afforded by them is 1575 square inches, or
10.9375 square feet. The wheel is turned true, and the buckets and
guide curves are ground smooth. The main shaft is 8 in. in diameter,
and to its lower end is keyed a cast-iron socket, hollowed on its under
side to fit upon the top of a block of lignum vitæ 15 in. in diameter
and 8 or 9 in. thick. This block is fixed in a socket supported by a
short column resting on the foundations, the upper end of the column
being steadied by arms connected with the draft-box, as shown in
Fig 2. The draft-box, or discharge tube, is supported by stands resting
upon the base ring, these stands and ribs cast upon the outside of the
draft-box forming guides for the gate. The gate consists of a short
ring or cylinder 10 ft. 5 in. in diameter and 2 ft. 6 in. high, raised and
lowered by single gearing. When raised, it uncovers the whole of the
mouth of the discharge tube; and when lowered, it fits water-tight on
the base ring and on the mouth of the discharge tube. The total
height of the draft-box, cylinder, chamber, and cap is 17 ft., and the
bottom edge of the wheel is 7 ft. 1 in. above the ground joint on the
bottom plate, on which the bottom edge of the gate fits.

The arrangement of the gearing by which the shaft of the wheel
connected with the crank-shaft for working the pumps is shown in the
Figs. 1 and 2. It consists of a pair of bevel wheels which transmit the
power from the vertical shaft of the turbine to a horizontal countershaft, and a pair of spur wheels connecting this shaft with the crank-
shaft. The total ratio of the gearing is as 35½ to 13, and the average
speed of the crank-shaft is 12 revolutions per minute. In both pairs of
wheels the pinions are of cast iron; the wheels are of cast iron, with
hickory cogs. The crank-shaft carries at each end of it a disc wheel in
which are fixed the crank pins to which the pump connecting rods are
coupled. The pumps themselves are 1 ft. 6 in. in diameter, with a

stroke of 6 ft., and are fixed horizontally upon a bed plate, as shown in Fig. 1. The pump pistons are packed by wood placed with the grain abutting endways upon the bore of the pump barrel, and forced outwards by means of a cone placed within the wooden ring of each piston. The valves are of the double-beat class, and are contained in chambers connected with the ends of the pumps. An air-vessel is placed over each set of valves, and another on the connecting pipe between the chambers, as shown in the figures; the suction pipes which draw the water from the flumes supplying the wheel are also provided with air-vessels.

From the pumps of the three wheels the water is led to near the foot of the upright pipe leading to the reservoirs by means of three 30 in. mains, these being connected with the upright pipe by a single main 4 ft. in diameter. The upright pipe, which is 64 ft. high and 5 ft. in diameter, is made of wrought iron, and is closed at the top. A branch, 3 ft. in diameter, is led from the upright pipe at a point 7 ft. below the top, the space between this branch and the cover of the pipe forming an air-vessel. This branch pipe, being only 3 ft. in diameter, checks to some extent the flow of the water; it is, however, the size of the connexions on the old stand-pipe to which it leads. The upright pipe is enclosed in an ornamental stone tower, and is connected with the side of the hill by an arch carrying and enclosing the 3 ft. branch pipe. The lift under which the pumps have to work is 115 ft., and the average fall of water for driving the wheels is 11 ft. As we have already said, the average speed of the pumps is 12 double strokes per minute, and at this speed the whole of them would have a pumping capacity of about 13,000,000 gallons per day. It was stated in a report made by the chief engineer of the works, Mr. Henry P. M. Birkinbine, soon after the wheels were erected, that the amount of power developed by these wheels was a little over 70 per cent. of that due to the fall and quantity of water used. This duty was less than that obtained from Mr. Geyelin's model, and not quite so great as that guaranteed by the contract; but this result was attributed by Mr. Birkinbine to the injudicious arrangement and limited size of the ascending mains, and to some imperfections in the gearing, and he stated that when improvements had been made in these details he had no doubt but that the wheels would give the full guaranteed duty.

OBSTRUCTION OF WATER-MAINS.

The town of Torquay is supplied with water through about thirteen miles of 10 in. mains, the source of supply being about 1100 ft. above the sea. The mains were laid down about eight years ago by Messrs.

Easton, Amos, and Sons. The size of mains to which they were limited was hardly sufficient for the full requisite quantity of water, and the wants of the town have also increased considerably since the mains were put down. Within the last year or two, however, the deficiency has become very serious, and it appeared clear that the supply was much less than it formerly was. It was known that the water at the source of supply was much aërated, and also that the mains had not been protected internally by any preservative substance or composition. These facts served to indicate that the cause of the lessened delivery was the formation and accumulation of oxide of iron in the mains, although we are not certain that this was suspected until after Mr. William Froude had, by the application of a series of pressure gauges at regular intervals along the pipe, ascertained that there was no local obstruction at any one or two points, the readings of the gauges giving an uniform hydraulic gradient from the source to the point of discharge.

When the character of the obstruction came to be understood, it became a matter of interest to know how it could best be removed. The late Mr. Appold had visited the mains, and with a ready instinct he suggested that a scraper be sent through the main, under the pressure of the water itself. This proposition was discussed among a number of engineers, including Sir William Armstrong, and it was the general opinion that the scraper, if it got on at all, would, after a certain quantity of matter had been scraped off, stick fast against it. Mr. Froude, however, resolved to try the experiment, and he had constructed a sheet-iron piston with a cupped leather behind it, and projecting in front of it was a stalk mounted with eight scrapers, placed obliquely to the axis. Each scraper covered about 45° of the circumference of the pipe, and the scrapers were set in two series, so as together to meet the whole interior surface of the main. Each scraper was held up to its work by a spring, and could "give" and pass by any obstruction too hard for removal. The full pressure of water in the mains, at a mile or two below the source, would of course be very considerable; but instead of giving the full force of the water, which was not required, openings were made through the piston so as to give a total available difference of pressure, on its two sides, of from 800 lb. to 900 lb. On being started in the mains, it went along at a maximum rate of three miles an hour, cutting away great quantities of oxide of iron, sometimes in nodules of the size of the thumb. The position and progress of the apparatus were made known by its sound, the mains being laid 2 ft. only beneath the surface of the ground, and it could be easily and certainly followed by those walking near the course of the pipes. The mains have not yet (1866), however, been cleared out for their whole length, but for a distance, we believe, of two miles, and from this portion alone some tons of oxide have been removed. It will be understood that the water, passing through the piston of the apparatus, is in itself a powerful carrying agent, and it is indeed the help of the water which enables the apparatus to go forward instead of sticking, as was predicted, against the accumulated mass of obstruction. The apparatus has stuck on one occasion, but as the mains have stop-valves at distances of two miles its removal was not attended with much difficulty. When the whole work of cleaning out the mains is completed, it is expected that the present water supply will be increased by nearly 70 per cent.

THE DUBLIN WATERWORKS.

For several centuries previous to the year 1775, the whole of the water supply of Dublin was obtained from the River Dodder, the water being led by an open conduit, called the "city watercourse," from a point near Templeogue, about five miles from Dublin, where a weir had been constructed across the river above mentioned. In 1775, owing to the badness and insufficiency of the water supply, arrangements were made by the Corporation for obtaining what was at that time thought to be an ample supply from the Grand Canal; and in 1806 this supply was augmented, and an additional quantity obtained from the Royal Canal. At the present time the north side of the city is supplied with water from the Royal Canal, which is received into the city basin; whilst the south side of the city is furnished with water from the Grand Canal and city watercourse, the supply being received into the James-street and Portobello basins. The levels of the water in the north and south basins are respectively 78 ft. and 76 ft. above ordnance datum, or the low-water level of a 12 ft. tide; the surface levels of the city along the quays ranging from 20 ft. to 28 ft. above datum, whilst some parts of the city lie too high to be supplied with water from the basins above mentioned.

The water of the Dodder is soft, but is much polluted by the refuse from the paper and other mills situated on the course of the river; the water from the canals, on the other hand, is very hard, the hardness being from 15° to 16° of Dr. Clark's scale, this agreeing to 15 or 16 grains of carbonate of lime, or its equivalent, in each gallon of the water; the canal water is also greatly polluted. This want of an abundant supply of good water at a high pressure for the city of Dublin and its suburbs has caused various plans to be proposed for obtaining it. A proposition to draw the supply from the canals at a higher level was brought forward in 1857, and afterwards it was proposed to take the water from the Liffey at a point about 20 miles above Dublin. A proposal was also brought forward for obtaining the supply from wells; but this idea was abandoned, partly on account of the number of wells that would have been required, and the hardness of the well-water; partly because it was doubtful whether a sufficient supply could have been obtained, and partly because the scheme, if carried out, would have required the continual employment of pumping power. Ultimately, in 1860, the whole matter was referred to a royal commissioner, Mr. Hawkshaw, who recommended that the Dublin water supply should be obtained from the River Vartry. An Act for carrying out this recommendation was obtained in 1861, and in November of the following year the works were commenced, the contract for the whole being taken at 274,000*l.* In addition to the sum just mentioned, about 60,000*l.* will be spent in the extension and improvement of the system of pipes within the city.

The source of the River Vartry is at the southern base of the Great Sugarloaf Mountain, and for about ten miles it flows through a very thinly populated country to the Devil's Glen, where it passes over the fall. After this its course continues down the glen to the Broad Lough, and it finally flows into the sea at Wicklow. The point chosen for the formation of the storage reservoir is Roundwood, about 7½ miles below the source of the river, and about 20 miles from Dublin in a straight line, the length of the course followed by the pipes, &c., being about 24½ miles. Above the storage reservoir, the drainage area of the river amounts to 13,992 acres, or about 22 square miles, and the area of the reservoir itself will be 409 acres. Rain gauges set up in different positions within the collecting area just mentioned have shown that the average annual rainfall within the district was, in 1861, 60.87 in.; in 1862, 60.48 in.; in 1863, 44.85 in.; and in 1864, 48.39 in. This rainfall is far more than sufficient to secure an ample supply of water for the purposes required, all mill rights, &c., along the course of the river having been bought up. The water of the Vartry is almost identical in analysis with that by which Glasgow is now supplied from Loch Katrine; it is collected from a clay-slate district, and is particularly soft and pure, and during the greater part of the year colourless.

The storage reservoir at Roundwood will hold about 2400 millions of gallons of water, this being equal to 200 days' supply, at 12 millions of gallons per day. The present population to be supplied is 340,000, but the quantity just mentioned would give a daily supply of 25 gallons per head to 400,000 persons, and leave 2,000,000 per day for manufacturing purposes. The supply of 25 gallons per head per diem above calculated upon is considerably less than that provided at Glasgow; but the quantity used at the last-mentioned town for manufacturing purposes is far greater than it would be at Dublin—a circumstance which would raise the general average. At Manchester the supply is less than 21 gallons per head daily. The defective state of the taps and house-fittings in many cases causes a very great waste of water, and it has been stated that in Glasgow probably nearly 15 gallons out of every 39 gallons per head have been uselessly expended through leakage. In other large towns similar results have been noticed, and as in Dublin especial care is being taken to ensure that all the house-fittings shall be maintained in the best possible condition, there is little doubt but that the supply of 25 gallons per head per diem will be found ample. The embankment forming the reservoir at Roundwood will be 2000 ft. long at the top, and will have a greatest height of 66 ft., the maximum depth of water within it being 60 ft. When the reservoir is full, the level of the water will be 692 ft. above ordnance datum. The entire width of the embankment at the top is 28 ft., and a carriage road, 24 ft. wide, is carried over it; its thickness at the base is 380 ft. at the deepest part, the outer slope being $2\frac{1}{2}$ to 1, and the inner slope 3 to 1. The puddle wall, which is in all parts carried down to the solid rock, is 6 ft. thick at the top and 18 ft. thick at the level of the surface of the old river bank. The by-wash, or waste weir, which discharges into the old course of the river, is 300 ft. wide, and the total quantity of earthwork in the embankment amounts to 320,000 cubic yards.

An outlet tunnel, leading from the reservoir, is formed by excavating an open cutting through the rock under the eastern end of the embankment, and then turning a semicircular arch of ashlar masonry, 4 ft. thick, over it. The tunnel is 14 ft. high by 14 ft. wide at its broadest part, and at the centre of it a brick plugging, 20 ft. thick, is built, the brickwork being carefully notched into wedge-shaped recesses formed in the solid rock. Two pipes, respectively 33 in. and 48 in. in diameter, are laid through this plugging, the 33 in. pipe being led into a water-tower erected at the inner end of the tunnel, and provided with openings in its sides at different levels. These inlet openings are furnished with valves on the inside, so that the water can be drawn from various depths, as may be desired. The 33 in. pipe is for conveying the water to the distributing basin, whilst the 48 in. main, which is to be continued into the tail of the by-wash, is intended to be used as a sluice for rapidly lowering the water-level in the reservoir when required; a complete arrangement of stop valves, however, placed in a valve chamber at the outer end of the tunnel, enables either main to be used for either purpose at pleasure. From the distributing basin the water passes by open conduits to the filter-beds and pure-water tanks, which, together, cover about six acres. Each of the seven filter-beds is 205 ft. long by 110 ft. wide, and is composed of sand, gravel, and broken stone. Six of these only will be required to be at work at one time, and one can thus be always spared for cleansing and repairs. The filter-beds are placed three on the one side and four on the other side of the two pure-water tanks, which hold 2,730,000 gallons each; a sand-cleansing machine and store for the sand are situated close by.

The water will be led from the tanks by means of a cast-iron main 42 in. in diameter, laid with a fall of 6 ft. per mile. This pipe will be about 700 yards long, and will be led 120 yards into a tunnel, which forms one of the principal works to be executed. This tunnel, which is now approaching completion, is being cut through very hard Cambrian rock, full of veins of quartz. It is 4367 yards, or nearly 2½ miles, in length, and is 8 ft. high by 5 ft. wide, the fall being 4 ft. per mile. It is being excavated by working right and left from twenty-one shafts sunk in the line of its course, and up to August last 3160 yards, or about 1¾ miles, had been tunnelled, the hardness of the rock and the quantity of water met with rendering the work tedious and difficult. It is on this tunnel that Mr. Low's boring-machines are being * employed. Six shot-holes, 20 in. deep and 1¾ in. in diameter, are usually fired at each blast, these six holes being completed by one machine in about 3¼ hours. The machines are worked at about 600 blows per minute, and the actual rate of boring is about 1 in. per minute, the remainder of the time being occupied by changing the tools, shifting the machine, &c. Two chisels are used for boring each hole, the first 9 or 10 in. being bored by a rose tool having two chisel edges at right angles to each other, and the remainder with a chisel tool having the cutting edges formed to three bevels slightly inclined to each other in both directions. The tools require regrinding after the completion of one hole. The chisels are not withdrawn for the purpose of clearing the hole, the latter being kept free from loose material by a water-jet directed into it. Before firing the charges, the machines are run back upon their tramways to a place of safety, the distance that they are thus removed varying with the progress of the work. The rate of advance of the tunnel where the machines are employed is from 6 in. to 8 in. per day, the rate at which the holes can be bored by the machines being from five to eight times as fast as they can be by hand-labour, whilst the saving in tools is very great.

* May, 1866.

A relieving tank and measuring weir will be constructed at the lower end of the tunnel, the surface of the water in the tank being 606 ft. above ordnance datum. From this tank the water will be led by a 33 in. main to the distributing reservoirs at Stillorgan, a self-acting stop-valve being placed where the main joins the tank so as to prevent flooding in the event of a pipe bursting. The main, which is laid with an average falling gradient of 20 ft. per mile, passes the village of Newtown Mount Kennedy, where another self-acting stop valve is introduced, and thence along the coach road through the glen of the Downs, to the relief tank at Kilmurray. This tank, which is about 7 miles from the lower end of the tunnel, is circular, and is excavated out of a gravel bed; it is lined with puddle covered with pitching, and the surface level of the water in it is 473 ft. above ordnance datum. A 33 in. double-acting stop-valve is placed at the end of the main delivering into the tank, and a self-acting stop-valve at the mouth of the outlet main. From this tank the main is again led along the road to the Kilcrony relief tank, a distance of 3 miles. The Kilcrony tank is situated on the top of the southern bank of the Dargle; it is excavated out of loose quartz rock and lined with puddle, and the surface level of the water in it is 414 ft. above datum, the inlet and outlet mains being furnished with valves as in the case of the Kilmurray tank. The main is next carried for a distance of 3½ miles to the Rathmichael relief tank, passing on its way under the Dargle and Cookstown rivers. The Rathmichael tank is square, and is excavated out of the rock and puddled. It is situated just on the junction of the granite with the clay slate, the tank being cut partly out of the one and partly out of the other; the level of the contained water is 341 ft. above datum, and the entering and issuing mains are furnished with similar valves to those applied in the other tanks. From Rathmichael the main is continued to the distributing reservoirs at Stillorgan, a distance of nearly 4 miles, its course being partly along the Wicklow Railway. A self-acting valve and a stop-valve are inserted about the middle of the length.

At Stillorgan, which is about 16¾ miles from the lower end of the tunnel, are situated the two reservoirs from which the water will be supplied direct to the town. Their area is 18 acres, and their average depth about 20 ft., so that they will together contain about 90,000,000 gallons; this will form an available reserve in case of an accident occurring to the line of mains from Roundwood. The reservoirs are 4¾ miles from the city boundary, and the level of the water in them will be, in the case of the upper reservoir, 274 ft., and in that of the lower 271 ft. above Ordnance datum. Both reservoirs are connected

with the 33 in. main leading from Roundwood, stop-valves being provided, so that either can be used at pleasure; a connecting pipe is
also laid through the embankment dividing the two reservoirs. The
valve-house and screening-chamber are situated near the lower reservoir. The screening-chamber is furnished with screens of copper wire,
which the arrangement of valves will allow to be cleaned by means of
a hose and jet, without interfering with the supply; and into this
chamber are laid mains from each reservoir, and also one leading
direct from the Vartry main; the use of this latter in hot weather will
enable the water to be supplied direct to the town without being
exposed in the reservoirs. From the screening-chamber a double line
of 27 in. mains extends to the city boundaries, a distance of 4¼ miles;
these mains are furnished with air-valves at all summits, and scouring-
valves at all depressions, and they are connected with each other at
three intermediate points, groups of stop-valves being supplied for
turning the water from one to the other at pleasure.

The water supplied to houses will be charged for by a compulsory
rate of 1s. in the pound on the rental, whilst that used for manufacturing purposes will be sold by meter at rates to be determined
upon. In Dublin, a public valuation is made of all property, and the
assessment is, on the average, 25 per cent. below the rent actually
paid; the charge of 1s. above mentioned is therefore really only equivalent to 9d. in the pound—an exceedingly reasonable charge. The
whole management of the water supply is in the hands of the corporation. The information respecting the Dublin Waterworks, contained
in the present notice, has been obtained principally from a paper "On
the Dublin Corporation Waterworks," read by Mr. Parke Neville, the
Engineer to the Corporation, before the Institution of Mechanical
Engineers on the occasion of their meeting at Dublin, in August last;
partly from a paper, "On a Rock-boring Machine," read by Mr.
George Low at the same meeting, and partly from the discussions
which followed these two papers.

THE CHICAGO LAKE TUNNEL.

One of the most remarkable examples of American engineering has
just (December, 1866) been successfully executed. It is a tunnel, two
miles in length, formed under the bed of Lake Michigan, at Chicago, for
the purpose of supplying that city with pure water. The city, now containing a population of 259,000 inhabitants, stands on the western shore,
and near the southern extremity of the lake, which is there about forty
miles wide, widening to sixty miles at Milwaukie, 120 miles farther
north, while the whole length of the lake from north to south is about

250 miles. The annexed sketch gives an outline of the position of the city, with the Chicago river, and its North Branch and South Branch, as its tributaries are named, discharging into the lake. These rivers are of but a very few miles' total length, and form together the port of Chicago— a port from which are now shipped more timber, more grain, more live

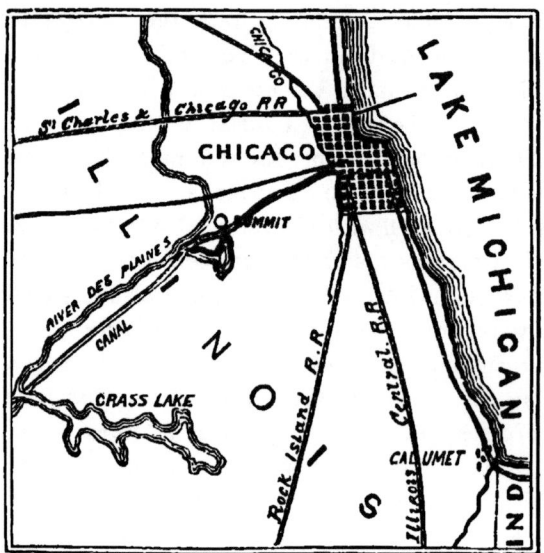

stock, and more salted meats than from any other place in the world. The river has innumerable slaughter-houses, distilleries, and manufactories on and near its banks, and receives the sewage of the whole town. To the west is an almost boundless prairie, rising very gently for a distance of eight miles, whence it slopes as imperceptibly away; and from this point, so near Lake Michigan, which drains through Lakes Erie and Ontario into the River St. Lawrence, and thus into the North Atlantic, the water-shed is part of the vast valley of the Mississippi, whose outlet is the Gulf of Mexico. We may just add that Lake Michigan is hardly 600 ft. above the sea, and that the dividing ridge near Chicago is but about 40 ft. higher.

The water has for several years been pumped from the lake at the northern end of the city, or what was the northern end when we last visited Chicago, ten years ago, the city having, we believe, since extended much further in that direction. And although intake pipes were carried out some distance into the lake, the foul discharge of the Chicago river, washed directly along the shore, was sufficient to greatly lower the standard of purity of the water pumped. The lake water itself is of the greatest purity, equal in this respect to the Loch Katrine

water with which Glasgow is supplied. It was resolved therefore,
in 1863, by the Board of Public Works, to make a tunnel directly out
from, and at right angles to, the shore, for a length of two miles, the
depth of water outside being 35 ft. This resolution was adopted after
careful borings had shown that a compact bed of fine blue clay, at
least 100 ft. in thickness, extended under the bed of the lake the
whole way out, the clay being overlaid with surface earth and sand of
very moderate depth.

The work was commenced at the shore end in March, 1864, and the
outer or lake shaft was begun somewhat later, the tunnel having been
driven from both ends, gangs of men, working eight-hour shifts, being
employed day and night with the exception of Sundays.

The shore shaft is 77 ft. deep, and for 30 ft. down, through the
surface earth and quicksands, is 9 ft. in internal diameter, the remainder being 6 ft. internally. The upper portion of the shaft is
formed of iron cylinders, three high, each 10 ft. long, 9 ft. inside
diameter, and $2\frac{1}{2}$ in. thick, the weight of the three cylinders being rather
more than 40 tons. These cylinders were undersunk in the usual
manner, an additional length being bolted on when the one beneath
it had entered for its full length. From the bottom of the shaft thus
formed, and which was well within the clay, and below the reach of
water, the ironwork was contracted to 8 ft. diameter, and undersunk
47 ft. further into the clay, and then lined with 12 in. of brickwork, in
three rings laid in cement. The bricks were hard burned, well formed,
and free from lime; their size 8 in. by 4 in. by $2\frac{1}{4}$ in., and the cement
was mixed with but an equal measure of clean sharp sand. These particulars apply to all the brickwork in the tunnel, four million bricks
having been used.

The most interesting work was the lake shaft, through 35 ft. of
water and 31 ft. down into the clay beneath. This shaft was commenced
within a cofferdam, 40 ft. high and nearly 90 ft. in diameter, the dam
having five sides measuring 58 ft. along each face. It was built on
shore, and had three walls formed of 12 in. squared timber, braced
apart with great strength, and having fifteen water-tight compartments
within the walls, while the inner wall formed a well 25 ft. in diameter
for the whole height. All the walls were caulked and payed on both
sides in the manner of ship-caulking, and the five outer angles were
protected from ice by iron armour $2\frac{1}{4}$ in. in thickness. Upwards
of 50,000 cubic feet of timber were used in the construction of this
work, besides 60 tons of iron bolts, and 400 bales of oakum were used
in caulking. The cost of this cofferdam was upwards of 100,000
dollars, or, in gold, about 14,000l.

In June, 1865, this coffer-dam was launched, and towed to its intended position two miles out. Its fifteen compartments were then filled with 6026 cubic yards of clean rubble stone, thus sinking it to the bed of the lake, where it was securely moored by strong cables reaching in every direction to large mooring-screws, holding 10 ft. in the clay. The coffer-dam being 40 ft. high, it then stood 5 ft. above the ordinary surface of the lake. Although we have called this structure a coffer-dam, it was what is known in America as a crib, and it was not pumped out, but served merely to secure a well of still water within which to sink the pipes forming the shaft. These pipes formed a column 64 ft. high, in seven lengths, the pipes, like those in the shore shaft, being 9 ft. in diameter and $2\frac{1}{4}$ in. thick, their total weight being $90\frac{1}{2}$ tons. They were connected successively together, and let down 9 ft. at a time, as each pipe was bolted on, until they reached the bottom, and, by their own weight, went through a thin bed of sand into the clay. The column of pipes was then continued to its full height above the water, being in the meanwhile pumped out; and a closed cap having then been placed upon it, it was exhausted, and thus sunk by atmospheric pressure, amounting, with complete exhaustion, to nearly 60 tons.

The lake shaft having been cleared of clay, the tunnel was started from below—the bottom of the tunnel at this point being 66 ft. below the ordinary surface of the lake. It falls 4 ft. towards the shore end, being there 70 ft. below the surface of the lake, and 77 ft. below the surface of the ground, so that the tunnel may at any time be pumped dry from the shore end, the inlet gates in the lake shaft being easily closed.

The tunnel, which is exactly two miles in length, is of nearly circular section, 5 ft. 2 in. high and 5 ft. wide inside, the variation from a true circle being made on account of the keystone of the arch. It is lined with two rings of brickwork, of a total thickness of 8 in., the bricks, laid lengthwise, being of the sizes and quality which we have given in connexion with the shore shaft. The excavation made in the clay was about 7 ft. in diameter, about 16,000 cubic yards having been removed. A railway of narrow gauge was laid in the tunnel, from each end, as the work progressed, and upon this mules were employed to draw wagons, loaded, in the outward direction, each with one and a half cubic yards of clay to be hoisted up the shaft, and inward with brick and cement. The railway had passing stations and turn-tables. In each end of the tunnel the men were divided into two gangs of five each, one gang of miners and one of bricklayers, the latter following within a few feet of the former. One miner drove a driftway, $2\frac{1}{4}$ ft. wide, another followed him breaking down the earth, a third trimmed the work to shape, and two loaded the wagons. A complete system of ventilation was maintained, and the men got on very comfortably. Occasionally a seam of inflammable gas was cut, and now and then a narrow fissure filled with water; but although these caused temporary alarm, and a sudden rush to the bottom of the shaft, no accident to life or limb happened during the two and a half years of the progress of the work. We may add, however, that one man was killed in a quarrel with a fellow-miner within the tunnel. About a hundred and twenty men were employed upon the entire work.

The great iron column forming the lake shaft is closed at the top, and has inlet gates below, and on different sides of the shaft, one 5 ft., the next 10 ft., and the highest 15 ft. above the bed of the lake. Either or all these can be used according to winds or other circumstances, each gate being under perfect control by suitable gearing. In any case the water cannot be drawn from a point less than 20 ft. below the surface of the lake. The openings of these gates have flumes or penstocks passing through the surrounding crib, the openings being heavily grated with iron on the outside. The inlet openings are each 5 ft. high and 4 ft. wide.

The rubble stone in the great timber crib is to be taken out of the fifteen water-tight compartments in successive portions, and is to be then replaced, carefully laid in hydraulic cement, so as to form a continuous tower of masonry. This is to be carried up several feet above the surface of the lake, in heavy courses of granite, cramped and bonded together, and a lighthouse is to be erected upon the whole, the lake at this point being greatly thronged with steamers and sailing craft, many of the former of great size. The whole work is to be completed with every regard for permanence, and is expected to endure for ages.

The whole work was originally let by contract for 315,139 dollars (gold), or say 63,000*l.*, exclusive of charges for extra work consequent upon any changes made in the plans. The actual cost is believed to be at least 700,000 dollars currency, or say 100,000*l.* gold; but it is understood that the City Government will not only make up the deficiency, but, by the expressed decision of the citizens, add a net profit of 100,000 dollars. The engineer to the work was Mr. E. S. Chesborough, and the contractors, Messrs. Gowan and Dall.

THE WATERWORKS OF ALTONA.

The town of Altona, in the Duchy of Holstein—virtually a suburb of Homburg, from which town it is separated only by a ditch, and by political boundaries now rapidly disappearing—contains about 50,000 inhabitants. The waterworks of this town, which form the subject of our illustrations on Plates XIII. and XIV., were completed in 1859 from designs made by Mr. T. Hawksley, C.E., and carried out by Messrs. York and Co., contractors, for a company formed by capitalists of Altona and Homburg. Mr. William Lindley, engineer of the Homburg Waterworks, acted as consulting engineer to the company.

The town is situated near the mouth of the river Elbe, and, after some consideration, a site was chosen for the works by the side of that river, but removed a considerable distance from the town. The pumping-engines have been placed close to the river, and at the foot of a hill about 300 ft. in height. On the top of this hill are placed the filter-beds and reservoirs, from which the water descends by gravitation to all parts of the town.

Fig. 1 represents a section through the engine-house, boiler-house, and a small building containing the air-vessel; Fig. 2 shows the same in cross section, and Fig. 3 in plan. These buildings contain two 60 horse-power engines, made by Messrs. Hawthorn and Co., of Newcastle, four Cornish boilers, and the necessary store-rooms for coal and other material. The engines are double-cylinder Woolf engines, with crank and fly-wheel on the pump-side of the beam, and the high and low pressure cylinder, with air-pump and feed-pump, on the opposite side. The low-pressure cylinder, 35 in. in diameter, 7 ft. stroke, works with a radius of 12 ft. 6 in.; and the high-pressure cylinder, 20 in. diameter, is placed at three-fourths of that distance from the centre of the beam, its stroke being 5 ft. 3 in.

Steam is admitted to the small cylinder at 28 lb. boiler pressure, and cut off at $\frac{1}{8}$ths, $\frac{3}{4}$ths, or $\frac{8}{8}$ths of the stroke, and expanded thence into the large cylinder. The capacities of the cylinders being, respectively, 46.75 cubic feet and 11.5 cubic feet; this gives an expansion to $5\frac{3}{4}$, 7, and 8 times the original volume of steam, corresponding to an ultimate pressure of $3\frac{1}{2}$ lb. on the square inch of the low-pressure piston in the extreme case, independent of the loss of pressure due to condensation and other causes, which, however, are partly counteracted by a steam jacket on the large cylinder receiving steam from the boilers direct. The fly-wheel is 20 ft. 8 in. in diameter, and of 16 tons weight, 10 tons 15 cwt. being carried in the rim, which is 16 in. broad by 18 in. deep. The eight spokes are of H section, bolted to the nave and keyed to the rim. The fly-wheel shaft is 11 in. diameter, and makes fifteen revolutions per minute, giving to the rim of the wheel the velocity of 1035 feet per minute at the periphery.

The bearings of the fly-wheel shaft are each $16\frac{1}{2}$ in. long, by 9 in.

K

diameter, and the plummer blocks are held down by $2\frac{1}{2}$ in. bolts, which pass through the foundation walls. Each of the two engines is independent of the other, having its own fly-wheel, and working a separate pump. The pumps, being placed at one-half the radius of the beam, have 3 ft. 6 in. stroke. Their cubical contents give $8\frac{3}{8}$ cubic feet per stroke; the quantities stipulated by the contract, viz. $7\frac{1}{3}$ cubic feet delivery per stroke, equal to 700 gallons per minute when making fifteen double strokes, being thereby exceeded in actual practice. The air-vessel is 5 ft. diameter, 18 ft. high; and the pipes from both pumps, each 15 in. diameter, lead into it, whilst the supply of air is kept up by two small air-valves fixed to the pumps, which admit a small quantity of air at each stroke. This has the additional advantage of cushioning the shock of the water in motion at each change of the position of valves. The suction pipe, 21 in. in diameter, is composed of cast-iron pipes, in lengths of 9 ft., turned and bored out at the joints, and caulked with lead. It is 735 ft. long, and leads into a strainer, which is enclosed in a square casing 10 ft. long by 8 ft. square. This lies imbedded in the river upon a foundation of piles, so as not to interfere with the navigation in any manner, nor to be interfered with by the latter.

The consumption of fuel was stipulated by the contract not to exceed 224 lb. of Newcastle coal per hour for raising 700 gallons of water per minute to the height of the top reservoir, placed at 275 ft. above the mean water-level of the Elbe. This, being equal to the work of 58.52 horse-power, gives a consumption of 3.33 lb. per effective horse-power per hour. At the trials made with these engines, each trial lasting twenty-four hours, the actual work performed was 62.45 horse-power, with a consumption of 3.63 lb. of coal when using two boilers; and 62.80 horse-power, with all three boilers working, were obtained with 3.34 lb. per horse-power per hour. The results of practical working through several years, which have since been observed and published by Mr. W. Kümmel, the resident engineer of these works, are, of course, higher in the relative figures, which is due partly to the intermittent working of the engines and partly to other accidental causes. The engines use 4.84 lb. of coal per horse-power per hour, without the fuel wanted for raising steam and other accidental additions, which raise the gross quantity of coal used to the considerable quantity of 6.08 lb. per effective horse-power per hour as an average throughout one year.

The water is pumped into the highest reservoir, from which it passes through strainers into the other compartments destined for settling and filtering. The first reservoir is 129 ft. long, 66 ft. wide, capable of holding water to a depth of 7 ft. The surplus passes through overflow openings of 5 ft. width, three situated on each side in the adjoining strainers, which are filled with gravel to the height of 5 ft., and allow the water to pass through that layer into the two settling reservoirs. These are 138 ft. long, 66 ft. wide each, and 11 ft. deep at the sides, the bottom inclining towards the centre, at which the depth of water is 12 ft. They deliver the water to the filters, each reservoir supplying two of the latter, which are on the principle introduced by Mr. Simpson at the Chelsea Waterworks, and have the dimensions of 138 ft. length, 66 ft. width, and 11 ft. depth. These four filtering-beds are capable of filtering over three million gallons per day, giving an average supply of 62 gallons per head in a town of 50,000 inhabitants.

The reservoir for holding the purified water is covered with brick arches carrying a stratum of earth 3 ft. thick on the top. The bottom is formed of a layer of Portland cement 1 ft. in thickness. This reservoir is divided by partition walls into twenty-four compartments, which are in communication with each other, the walls serving only as supports for the arches. The water stands 12 ft. deep in this reservoir, and the bottom of each compartment is formed of clay covered with a tile flooring. The total quantity of water stored in all the reservoirs is 457,000 cubic feet. The delivery pipes are 16 in. diameter for a length of 20,700 ft., and 15 in. diameter for a length of 13,300 ft.; the total system of pipes measures about 150,000 ft., or nearly thirty miles in length. All pipes are of cast iron made by Messrs. Losh, Wilson and Co., and Messrs. Bell Brothers, of Newcastle; they are tested to a pressure equal to a column of 600 ft. of water, and are laid 5 ft. below the pavement to protect them from frost. The arrangement for supplying water to fire-engines, and for similar purposes, is illustrated in Figs. 7 and 8.

The great distance of the reservoirs and engines from the town made it desirable to have an extra reservoir within the town itself, to supply a considerable quantity on an emergency, in case of an accident happening to the pipes or machinery of the waterworks. For this purpose an elevated reservoir has been constructed by Mr. Lindley in the vicinity of the railway station at Altona. This reservoir contains 16,000 cubic feet of water at a height of 135 ft. over the river level. It is filled from the waterworks with filtered water, but in case of need could be supplied with water from the river direct by setting the stationary engine at the railway station to work at a pump. This reservoir consists of a cast-iron tank, 42 ft. in diameter and 12 ft. deep. It rests upon a massive building, consisting of walls, arranged as shown in the figures 9 to 12 on Plate XIV. These foundations are arched over so as to form a basement story, and the reservoir rests upon the top of all the arches. The pillars supporting the arches are continued above, and carry a wrought-iron roof, which rests upon them independent of the reservoir, so as to give the latter no other strain but the weight. The total cost of these works, including all expenses, was about 80,000*l.*, of which the engines, with boilers and fittings, cost 7000*l.*, and the reservoir at the railway station 3000*l.*

The water is not only used for household and public purposes, but it also supplies power for working machinery, to which it is particularly suited, on account of the high pressure at which it is supplied, varying from 95 lb. to 100 lb. on the square inch in the lower parts of the town. This great pressure necessitates considerable caution in the manner of opening and closing valves, so as to prevent too rapid action and destructive shocks. The valves found most suitable are Lambert's patent and Aird's screw-piston valves.

THE ABERDEEN WATERWORKS.

Her Majesty consented to inaugurate, on October 16th, 1866, the Aberdeen Waterworks. The ceremonial took place at Invercannie, the point at which the water is taken from the River Dee. Invercannie is 20 miles above Aberdeen, and 30 miles below Balmoral. The water is diverted from the River Dee at a point on the lands of Cairnton about three miles west of the village of Banchory. At the intake, the channel of the river has been deepened for a short distance along the north side, and a cutting has been made in the bank sloping to the depth of three feet below the bed of the river, almost at right angles to the stream, which, while admitting the water freely, will not allow it to run in with too great velocity. At the end of the aqueduct there is thus about six feet of water. A strong wall of granite masonry is constructed on the foreshore of the river, with an opening seven feet wide and ten feet high, protected on the outside by a strong iron haking to keep out salmon, and on the inside by a finer grating of galvanized-iron wire to sift the water of smaller substances—leaves, &c. A yard or two further in is a large measuring tank, built of solid granite masonry, about fifteen feet square, which contains a floating gauge or measure-pipe. This gauge is placed at the end of the aqueduct, and acts as a mouth-piece. It is kept constantly on a level with the surface of the river—rising and falling with it, by two large copper balls, two feet six inches in diameter, filled with air. The mouth of the pipe is

7 ft. wide by 18 in. deep, and admits exactly the required quantity—6,000,000 gallons daily—stipulated for in the Police and Waterworks Act, when the water flows over the gauge 7½ in. deep. The tunnel and the works at Invercannie are thus protected from any sudden influx of water such as might otherwise be caused by a sudden rise in the river during the night, or when the sluice-keeper may not be at hand to shut off the water.

To the end of the tunnel—a distance of about 100 yards down the river—the water is conveyed by a brickwork aqueduct 4 ft. 6 in. by 3 ft. 6 in. in internal diameter. The length of the tunnel is 760 yards, and the depth of the one shaft is 95 ft., and of the other 103 ft. Its dimensions are 5 ft. high, by 4 ft. wide ; the rock being so compact and solid that it was unnecessary to make room for any lining of either brickwork, cement, or puddle. Indeed, instead of being diminished, the quantity of water will be very considerably augmented from the number of springs that have been struck in the tunnel—of excellent water, cool and limpid. The work of excavating this tunnel has been one of extreme difficulty. In the first place, the rock—principally a species of whinstone—was found to be exceedingly hard. Then the bore was too small to permit of more than one man striking on the umper at one time. And, lastly, the quantity of water that was encountered greatly impeded the workmen, the average proportion being twenty buckets of water to one of stone taken up the shaft. The work, however, was pressed on with great energy. The men were kept working at it twenty out of the twenty-four hours, in two relays, one for the day and one for the night; yet the average rate at which each heading was driven was only from 6 in. to 8 in. a day, or 3 ft. over all, during the two years and a half occupied in the excavation. It was principally ordinary blasting powder that was used in the work, but there was also a good deal of gun-cotton tried. The latter was found to cut the rock better than the former, and to be much cleaner; but it seemed to emit some sort of gas injurious to the health, and which there was not enough of ventilation to carry off, for the men always complained of headaches after having used it once or twice. Where there is plenty of ventilation, however, there is no doubt that gun-cotton is much superior to the ordinary blasting powder. The sides of the tunnel have been roughly dressed, but quite as well as it required, and as the hardness of the rock and other adverse circumstances would permit.

The brickwork aqueduct recommences and continues for about half a mile, conveying the water to the Invercannie reservoir, calculated to hold 15,000,000 gallons. It is constructed in a hollow between the Burn of Cannie and the rising ground to the south. The aqueduct brings the water along this rising ground, so as to discharge it into the reservoir within a few feet of the top of the embankment. First of all, to make it water-tight, it is furnished with a flooring of clay puddle, 18 in. deep and well beaten. A vertical wall of the same material and the same thickness forms the centre of the embankment. This is supported on either side by a mixed bank of sand, earth, gravel, and stone, with slopes of 2 to 1. On the outer surface grass has been sown, and is already growing luxuriantly. The inner surface is covered with a bed of lime concrete, six inches thick, above which is laid a protection of stone pitching. The dimensions of the embankment are 60 ft. broad at the base, about 17 ft. high, and 8 ft. broad at the top, along which is a gravelled walk. The water will come up to the height of 15 ft., and the diameter of the reservoir is, at the top, 450 ft., and at the bottom 390 ft. On the inner slope, at the west side, the representation of a salmon has been very neatly made in the stone pitching, being formed with red stones with a background of blue granite. He measures 50 ft. " from the point of the nose to the tip of the tail," as showmen say; and according to the Act all the fish caught in the reservoir belong to Sir James Burnett, except this one !

Before the water enters the reservoir, it passes through a second measuring tank, at the south side, where the ceremony of opening the works will be performed by the Queen. The sluice drawn by her Majesty is constructed at the end of the aqueduct. It is 2 ft. in diameter, and, when opened, it allows the water to flow through a gauge weir 12 ft. in circumference, and fall over the edge about 4 in. deep—giving the necessary quantity—into the tank. Two smaller sluices communicate with the reservoir, and will convey the water through the embankment into its pond within a few feet of the top of the slope.

At the east side of the reservoir the outlet machinery is situated. This consists of two pipes, about 20 ft. long, with pepper-box apertures at the top, placed in a horizontal position, and made to work upwards and downwards upon joints, like a pair of arms. They are supported by a balance-weight apparatus, constructed upon two brick piers, with planking running out 40 ft. from the top of the embankment, and will be floated by two copper air-balls, 2 ft. 6 in. in diameter, which will maintain them at a constant level of about 2 ft. below the surface of the water. A large pipe passes through below the embankment, and goes between the filters, two branch pipes, of 15 in. diameter each, discharging the water into the surface of the filter-beds. Should the reservoir become too full, a spill-water has been provided at the north side, by which any surplus will be discharged through a pipe into the

Burn of Cannie. There is also another overflow about 100 yards above the measuring tank in the aqueduct, which will let off the water should the quantity coming from the tunnel exceed that required at the reservoir.

The filters are 136 ft. each in diameter, and are furnished with slopes and puddle walls, very similar to the reservoir. The beds are composed of sand and gravel, 5 ft. in depth, through which the water percolates into a brick drain in the bottom, which communicates with a small tank, the filtered-water well, on the east side, and where the aqueduct commences. There is space reserved for two additional filters, if required. The ground enclosed for the reservoir and filter-beds, including the approach roads, &c., is about ten acres in extent.

The aqueduct commences at the east end of the filters. It is a brickwork construction of an oval form, with an internal diameter of 3 ft. 9 in. high by 3 ft. 3 in. wide. The bricks used are perforated with two holes, and are much larger than ordinary, being 9 in. long by 6 in. broad and $3\frac{1}{2}$ in. thick. They are moulded to the radius of the curve, and are cemented with a fine lime, known as Lord Elgin's lime, brought from Fifeshire, and which has more the appearance and character of cement than ordinary building lime. The brickwork is rendered water-tight by a casing of clay puddle, 9 in. thick, placed all round the outside. This mode of structure is continued with but little variation along the turnpike road and through various private grounds—for a distance of 18 miles—to the Lower Service Reservoir at Pitfodels. The Burn of Cannie is crossed by a cast-iron pipe 40 in. in diameter, which passes through below the bridge constructed for the new road. The Burn of Crathes is crossed by another 40 in. pipe. At the moss of Belscavie, where the level of the ground is too low, an embankment, about half a mile in length and 15 ft. high, has been constructed to carry the aqueduct across. The Burn of Culter is crossed by a 40 in. syphon pipe supported by two piers built of granite, 25 ft. high. The pipe extends to a length of 400 yards, and at its east end the aqueduct recommences as before. Throughout almost its entire length the line of the aqueduct is scarcely discernible, being quite covered up, and having grass and other crops growing above it the same as on the adjoining land. Air-escapes and man-holes are placed all along at equal distances for the ventilation and cleaning of the interior. Although only required to discharge 6,000,000 gallons a day, the aqueduct is capable of discharging much more—probably about 8,000,000 gallons. It has a uniform fall throughout of 2 ft. per mile, which gives a velocity of 21 in. per second.

The lower service reservoir is calculated to hold a day's supply of

water for the town—6,000,000 gallons.   It is 270 ft. in diameter and
17 ft. deep.   The bottom is laid with clay puddle, similar to the main
reservoir; but instead of the inside of the embankment being sloped,
it is a vertical wall of masonry, backed by clay puddling of the
usual thickness, and with a very strong dyke of earth and gravel
outside.   For a short distance west of the reservoir, 36 in. pipes are
laid to carry the water to the top of the reservoir wall, and so discharge it into the basin.   The floor immediately below the waterfall
is laid with flags, to prevent it being worn away.   A line of 27 in.
iron pipes is laid from the end of the aqueduct past the north side of
the reservoir, which communicates with the latter by two sluices; and
the water may be shut out of the reservoir altogether if necessary, and
sent into town by these pipes, without passing through it at all.   This
main continues along the Cuparstone-road and Holburn-street, and
joins the existing main pipes at the Waterhouse at Union-place.

The level of the lower service reservoir is 160 ft. above high water,
and it will be capable of supplying about nine-tenths of the city with
water.   The remainder will be provided for by a smaller tank, called
the high-service reservoir.   Its elevation is 396 ft. above high-water
level; it is 80 ft. in diameter, the same depth as the lower one, and
similarly constructed, and will hold 600,000 gallons of water.   The
water will be pumped into it through a 10 in. pipe, by a hydraulic
engine, erected near the river side, below the village of Cults.   This
will be worked by spare water from the aqueduct, conveyed to it by an
18 in. main pipe, 400 yards long, with a fall of 150 ft.   The quantity
of water taken off daily will be 1,350,000 gallons, and of this quantity
350,000 gallons daily will be pumped up to the high-service reservoir.
The remainder serves to give the necessary hydraulic force, equal to
about 50 horse-power, for pumping, and is then allowed to run off into
the Dee.

The quantities of material which have been used in the construction
of this work have been bricks, upwards of seven million—about 42,000
tons weight—equal to about twelve million of common bricks, those
used being considerably above the ordinary size; of clay puddle, about
70,000 tons for the reservoirs and aqueduct; pipes and other ironwork,
2500 tons.   The extent of earthwork excavation required for the
aqueduct was about 300,000 cubic yards, and of filling in about
170,000 cubic yards.   Of rock excavation in the tunnel there was
nearly 60,000 cubic yards. The number of men employed on the works
varied from 1000 to 1500.

The works have been constructed from plans by James Simpson,

Esq., C.E., F.G.S., London. The original survey in 1855, as well as the subsequent survey in 1861, were carried out by his assistant, Mr. Robert Anderson, C.E., resident engineer, who prepared all the plans under Mr. Simpson's superintendence. Mr. Easton Gibb is the contractor, with Messrs. J. Abernethy and Sons as sub-contractors for ironwork, with the exception of the large pipes, which were cast in Glasgow. The hydraulic engine has been constructed to the order of Messrs. Abernethy, by Sir William Armstrong and Company. The total outlay for the works will not exceed 115,000*l*.

BOMBAY WATERWORKS.

In 1852, before the great importance of sanitary improvements had been recognised generally throughout India, the municipal committee of the town of Bombay called for a report of its sanitary state and requirements, and the duty of drawing up the report was entrusted to H. Conybeare, Esq., superintendent of repairs to the Bombay Board of Conservancy.

At the above date the town of Bombay contained about half a million inhabitants. Any data upon which to draw up a scheme for sanitary reform were altogether wanting; there was not even any trustworthy census or annual mortality return, and no complete or systematic surveys or levels had ever been taken of the town. In the absence of any such data, however, it was not unreasonable to conclude that (arguing from English sanitary statistics), if it be shown that the existence of open drains and cesspools, &c., in a crowded town invariably occasions a certain, specific, and very considerable increase in the mortality of their neighbourhood, similar nuisances should prove even more deleterious when exposed to a tropical sun, in an atmosphere so surcharged with moisture as that of Bombay, and that, too, in a town so overcrowded as regards the number of square yards to each inhabitant, far beyond all European precedent. In all large towns every part is not found to be equally healthy, the annual death-rate being far less amongst the inhabitants of first-class houses than amongst those who live in confined alleys and courts; but in Bombay the difference between the death-rate in the healthiest and most unhealthy districts was found to be considerably greater than in any towns of England: thus, as far as the returns obtainable could be relied on, the death-rate of the Fort (the only district which was altogether provided with covered drains) was only 9.9 per 1000, while that of some of the subdivisions of the native town, where open drains, or rather receptacles for every kind of filth, abounded to an extent unparalleled elsewhere, was as high as 60 per 1000. Out of the entire population of Bombay, 337,169 occupied the six urban subdivisions of the native town, containing 6659 acres, or an average of only 9.5 square yards to each inhabitant, which is only about one-thirteenth of the English average. The whole of Bombay, including the Fort, was found to contain only 14 miles of sewers and 130 miles of road; what sewers there were, too, were not water-tight, and were laid close to the surface of the roads, so that, owing to the dryness of the climate, the thirsty soil abstracted all the moisture within its reach, and the consequence was that the sewers were found to contain a very large proportion of solid matter, which had to be removed by hand. The average annual expenditure by the Board of Conservancy amounted only to 21,320*l.*, and the actual progress of drainage works averaged less than 2 miles per annum.

Under such circumstances it was not to be wondered at that the death-rate of Bombay should have been high when compared with that of English towns; but, in addition to the defective sewerage, other circumstances tended to increase the ratio of mortality, and amongst the most important and prominent of these might be ranked a defective water supply.

Although measures for the general sanitary improvement of Bombay were not seriously entertained until the year 1852, the very great scarcity of water there in 1846, owing to the paucity of rain during the preceding year, necessarily led to the consideration of measures to be adopted with a view of securing at all seasons a plentiful supply of wholesome water. No permanent works were at that time put into operation; but in order, as far as possible, to ensure an adequate supply of water for the current season, the public tanks and wells were placed in charge of the police, with the view of preventing waste or pollution; temporary wells were opened in different parts of the Esplanade, to provide additional places from which to draw water when its scarcity began to be felt, and an opening, 20 ft. square, was constructed into which the water from a number of washerwomen's wells on the Esplanade, near the Native Town, was filtered; a stop was put to the appropriation of water in public tanks and wells to purposes of irrigation, and the water standing in certain quarries in the island was secured to the public. The shipping also was prohibited from laying in their water at the Presidency, and was therefore obliged to obtain supplies from the opposite coast, and from the neighbouring islands of Elephanta and Kenera. Special constables were appointed to guard certain private wells, and a dam was constructed to keep out the sea from a freshwater spring in the sand, towards the north end of the Colaba causeway, so that it might be kept pure for drinking purposes.

The above measures, being merely of a temporary character, served but to mitigate the evils of a drought for the season. Officers were deputed to examine sites for reservoirs, and submit schemes whereby some permanent provision might be made against the recurrence of a similar visitation ; but by 1850 no such provision had been made, or even commenced, and the fall of rain during the monsoon of that year was so scanty that serious apprehensions were entertained of great distress amongst the population of Bombay from a scarcity of drinking-water during the ensuing hot season. In 1845, the year preceding the previous drought, the fall of rain amounted to only 54.73 in.; in 1846, it was 87.48; in 1847, 67.31 ; in 1848, 73.42 ; in 1849, 118.88 ; and in 1850 it was as low as 47.78 in. Measures, similar to those adopted in 1846, were at once put in force, and the experimental construction of a small reservoir on the Esplanade, with diverging channels into a red sandstone, was commenced, for the purpose of ascertaining whether by such means a sufficient quantity of water could be obtained for the future supply of the town.

Again in May, 1854, the people of Bombay were suffering from the effects of a scarcity of water. A large portion of the wells in the island were wholly exhausted, and in all the remainder there was a great deficiency : thus, for example, out of one hundred and thirty-six tanks and wells, but thirty-seven contained any water, and of that number eight only contained good water, that in the others being green, bad, dirty, and brackish. The scene at the wells at that time can hardly be described : they were literally besieged night and day by crowds, each person carrying a canvas bucket, and clamorously struggling for a place, in which women and infirm persons naturally contended at a great disadvantage. With a view to obviate extreme calamities, and mitigate as much as possible existing distress, water was introduced into the island in casks, and both the railway and shipping were employed in that service.

Many of the tanks and wells in Bombay owe their existence to private native liberality. That the natives of India consider the construction of such works not only an act of benevolence, but also one of religious merits, is proved by some of their writings, of which we subjoin a few translated extracts. From the " Vishnoodhurmotárá Pooran :" " No satisfaction is felt without water in the three worlds, heaven, earth, and hell ; therefore, a wise and learned man should cause reservoirs, tanks, wells, &c., to be made." From the " Yámá Pooran :" " A person that makes wells, gardens, establishments for distribution of water, also he that causes trees to be planted, gives his daughters in marriage to others, causes bridges, dams, &c., to be made over rivers, and all these for charity's sake, obtains a perpetual bliss in paradise." " Also a person in whose pond or lake there is a constant supply of water, obtains perpetual felicity without question." From the " Bhuvishyotárá Pooran :" " O thou son of Kunti, get large supplies of water made at the sacrifice of your whole property ; for the man at whose reservoir the cow becomes satiated of her thirst becomes the preserver of his family."

Before the construction of waterworks, the tanks and wells in Bombay derived their supply of water principally from the water-bearing strata of the island, which consist of moorum or laterite and a littoral concrete, the former resting on a retentive stratum of rock, the latter, usually one of clay. In some cases the arrangement of the various strata is such as to convey to one locality, in the shape of springs, water which has fallen as rain over a wide extent of country many miles distant. Some springs continue to flow all the year round, others become exhausted after a continuance of dry weather. Perennial springs are of course much rarer in countries, as in India, where a short rainy season is succeeded by many months of continuous dry weather, than in countries situated within the zone of constant precipitation, in which the rainfall is distributed over the whole year. None of the water in the public tanks, with the exception of that of Framjee Cowasjee, on the Esplanade, could be considered wholesome, as they were all more or less filled by drainage, at the best times impure and subject to the taint of a large town.

From Fort George, northward to Mazagon, the water-shed of the eastern side of the island of Bombay is composed of a mass of trap rock, varying from 16 to 60 ft. in height above high-water mark. The wells in this portion of the town, which comprises the suburbs of Mazagon, Oomercary, Mandoee, and the eastern portion of the Fort, were generally mere reservoirs of rain-water. Springs are occasionally to be met with, but the majority of them are very brackish immediately after the rains, and become quite salt before the end of the hot season. The trap formation has its line of water-shed very close to the harbour margin, and after gradually declining towards the west for about 350 yards, it again dips beneath the surface, and is overlaid by a porous stratum of moorum or laterite, and this is again covered by a thin stratum of stiff clay, known as the Langoon formation. The moorum formation is very porous, and the rock on which it rests is generally impervious and retentive. The moorum is consequently a water-bearing stratum wherever it attains any depth, but from being generally below high-water mark, and having been until the present century overflowed at high water, it is in many places so impregnated with salt as to render the water stored in it of little use; the salt is, however, being gradually washed out of the lower portion of it, and the upper has always contained sweet water. Along the bottom of the eastern escarpment of the Malabar hill ridge, this moorum formation contains the best wells in the island. In the market, Dhobee Talao, Girgaum, and Chowpatty subdivisions, the retentive clay stratum, known as the Langoon formation, sinks below the surface, and is overlaid by a highly porous formation of littoral concrete, which contains, in proportion to its thickness, an enormous quantity of water, and is riddled with wells. These wells are not sunk quite down to the Langoon formation, for fear of reaching salt water.

In sinking wells in many parts of the island, particularly at Mazagon, Byculla, and the new and old town districts, though springs are to be expected, it is quite a lottery whether those reached will be salt or fresh, as there are instances of two wells in the same garden, and within forty yards of each other, containing the one good water and the other water too salt for use. Sometimes the salt is merely an impregnation of the soil, which becomes washed out after the well or tank has been drawn for a few years, and the water then becomes sweet. The wells in Colaba are, with one or two exceptions, in trap rock, like those of the town, and are generally little more than reservoirs of rainwater, drying up, if drawn upon, as the season advances. Besides these wells, some of the native houses of the best class have extensive reservoirs beneath them, into which the rain-water from the roof is collected.

In point of numbers and capacity the wells and tanks of Bombay would have proved amply sufficient had they been available for public use all the year round. For some time after the monsoons the supply of water continued abundant, and, in the wells, of good quality; but as the season advanced the majority of the wells and many of the tanks dried up, and the water remaining in the few of the latter that contained any became too contaminated with organic impurities to be used with impunity for drinking purposes without filtration. Water was, however, always abundant in the wells of the littoral concrete of Chowpatty, Girgaum, and the Oart districts, in those on the east side of the Esplanade, and in many of the wells in the Fort; but towards the end of the dry season the old and new town districts mainly had to depend for their supply of water on underground aqueducts, which conveyed the spring-water of the Oart districts to the reservoirs at Duncan-road, Poydownee, and Musjid Bunder.

Rain-water, when stored in open tanks in the town, always became rapidly contaminated, and an establishment had to be kept up for removing the so-called "vegetation" from its surface. During the monsoon of 1852 these tanks were covered with a floating green slime, which, on examination, proved not to be vegetation, but an aggregation of myriads of little green animalculæ, called the *Monas grandis*. By the close of the following hot season the amount of decomposing animal matter in the tanks became enormously increased, and the evolution of gaseous products proved too great for the existence of animal life, and that to such an extent that labourers had to be employed in removing dead fish from the waters.

The three most promising schemes submitted for securing a permanent supply of water to Bombay were, 1st, the construction of a cut-stone well or reservoir in the sandstone formation of the Esplanade, with long feeding channels cut into the sandstone, and filled with loose rubble stone, through which the water would filter continually, and keep up a supply within the reservoir; 2nd, the collection of the surface drainage of the Malabar-hill in a reservoir situated at the foot of the hill, and, 3rd, by forming a reservoir near Vehar, in the island of Salsette, by throwing a dam across the Goper valley, and conveying water thence to a reservoir in Bombay by about sixteen miles of iron pipes. The last of these schemes seemed to promise the most favourable results, and has since been undertaken and completed under the direction of Mr. Conybeare. The object of the present article is to give a detailed description of the works undertaken in connexion with this project.

Surface-collection was the only source by which Bombay could be efficiently supplied with water, and the only valley debouching in the neighbourhood from which such a supply was obtainable is that of the Goper. The island of Bombay forms, in fact, a continuation of this valley; so much so that, before the construction of the embankment between Sion and Worlee, the Goper used, when in flood, to traverse the island of Bombay on its way to the sea. The capabilities of this valley in respect to the water supply of Bombay were first pointed out by Major Crawford in 1846.

The Goper debouches on the mangrove marsh which separates Bombay from the islands of Salsette and Trombay, at a point about nine miles distant from Bombay Cathedral. Ascending it from thence, the hills, at first detached and distant, gradually approach and unite into ranges, till near Puspolee, about sixteen miles from Bombay, the valley suddenly contracts into a narrow gorge. Below this point the ground in the neighbourhood of the Goper offers no facilities for the construction of dams or reservoirs; but the gorge above Puspolee, which is about a mile in length, contains two exceedingly good sites for a dam. Above this gorge the valley expands into a wide plain or basin, surrounded with very high-wooded hills, in the centre of which was formerly situated the village of Vehar. The basin of Vehar offered peculiar facilities for the storage of water, its bottom being extremely flat, and covered with a tenacious clay, of which brick and common pottery were made, while the hills which form its sides rise abruptly, and are composed of compact unstratified rock. The gorge through which the Goper escaped was the lowest, but not the only breach in the circle of hills surrounding the basin of Vehar, other weak points presenting themselves along the southern margin of the proposed reservoir, across which dams had to be constructed.

The average rainfall over the Vehar gathering-grounds exceeds somewhat 100 in. in the year, of which it was estimated that at least six-tenths would become available to the supply of storage reservoirs. The surface of the country drained by the Goper, above the point where its channel is intercepted by a dam, is 4682 acres, or 7.316 square miles, which, with an available fall of 60 in. of rain, would give a total supply of 6,355,211,091 gallons.

In the early part of 1855, after having completed a survey of the Vehar valley, Mr. Conybeare came to England in order to obtain such information as would enable him to test the accuracy of his estimates, and to make himself acquainted with the practical working of any of the latest improvements in hydraulic engineering, which might be of service in facilitating the perfect completion of the works projected in Bombay. In consequence, however, of his non-return to India at the expected time, Government set about the commencement of the works, and entrusted their superintendence to Mr. West, who had assisted Mr. Conybeare in preparing the surveys and plans.

Works were commenced on 31st January, 1856, with the main dam at Syce, a point a little above the Puspolee datum. The formal inauguration of the work at its commencement was presided over by Lord Canning, on which occasion the Government offices in Bombay were closed at noon, in order to enable all who were desirous of witnessing the ceremony, which took place at 5 o'clock in the afternoon, and extra trains were run by the Great India Peninsular Railway for the conveyance of passengers towards the spot.

Having completed his detailed estimates and specifications for those portions of the works, which it was proposed should be undertaken by contract, and having obtained tenders for the same, Mr. Conybeare did not return to India, there to superintend the execution of the works, as had been originally intended, but he remained in England, and undertook the responsible duties of consulting engineer to the East India Company for the Bombay Waterworks, and proved and inspected the pipes and other materials previously to their shipment for Bombay, and Mr. J. D. Walker was sent out as engineer in chief at Bombay.

The main dam was, as we have before stated, placed at Syce, where the valley of the Goper is contracted by a chain of hills into a narrow gorge. The construction of this dam, together with the two other embankments necessary for completing the reservoir, and of a waste weir, inlet tower, and masonry connected therewith, and laying of pipes through the embankments, was undertaken, under a contract, by Messrs. James Bray, Son, and Champney for the sum of sixty-seven thousand and twenty-one pounds.

The site of the reservoir was cleared of all trees, hedges, stone dykes, and other fences; houses and other buildings pulled down and removed by, and at the expense of, the Bombay Government.

The whole of the surface of the ground to be covered by the three embankments was in the instance stripped of all loose earth, soil, and rotten rock, so that the embankments might come into close contact with, and rest upon, solid rock or clay. The excavation for the trench to receive the puddle walls of the embankments was carried down to a permanently secure bottom, and was stepped into the hill sides, so that the puddle might have a proper vertical bearing on its seat. The top width of the Syce, or principal embankment, is 24 ft., and that of the other two embankments 20 ft.; the inner slope of all three embankments being 3 to 1, and the outer slope $2\frac{1}{2}$ to 1. The puddle walls are all 10 ft. in width at the top, with a regular batter on each side at the rate of 1 in 8. The clay for the puddle walls and material for embankments were taken from within the water-line of the reservoir; that for the puddle walls was formed in regular layers of about 4 in., and that for the embankments in layers of about 6 in. thick; the materials of each layer being broken up and evenly distributed, and then watered and beaten with wooden pounders. The puddle walls were kept on a level of 6 in. above the adjoining portion of the embankment during construction; and, in order to allow for settlement, the contractor was bound to complete the embankments and puddle walls to a height greater than their required permanent height, by half an inch for every foot in height. The slopes, external and internal, of all three embankments, as well as their top surfaces, are covered with 12 in. in depth of rough stone pitching, set by hand, and resting on an additional inch of broken stone. The earthwork in the principal embankment consists of about 255,700 cubic yards, and in the other two embankments of about 43,620 and 106,745 cubic yards respectively.

One line of cast-iron pipes, of 41 in. interior diameter, is laid through the main embankment at an uniform level, in a trench sunk below the natural surface of the ground, and where the pipes cross the puddle wall, they are supported on a solid bed of masonry. At their joints the sockets of the pipes have laps of yarn tightly driven in, and a layer of lead of an uniform depth of $2\frac{3}{4}$ in. run in by means of a clay fillet, and afterwards well caulked down flush with the face of the faucet, the weight of lead in each joint averaging about 60 lb.

The waste weir, which is situated at a short distance from the Syce dam, is constructed on the same principle as the embankments, and is faced throughout with chisel-dressed ashlar set in the best Portland cement.

Inside the main dam is situated the inlet tower. In the construction of this, the earth was first excavated in order to obtain a solid foundation. The foundation of the tower consists of two courses of stones 8 in. thick. The tower itself is built of rubble masonry, faced inside and outside with chisel-dressed ashlar masonry set in the best cement. The tower is octagonal in form, and is surmounted by an ornamental iron roof; four inlet pipes and the supply-pipe are let through the masonry of the tower, and round each pipe a recess, cut in the masonry to the depth of $3\frac{1}{2}$ in. and $\frac{1}{4}$ in. on the face, was run in with lead to make the joint water-tight, and caulked down flush with the outside of the tower. A gangway forms the means of communication between the top of the embankment and the inlet tower.

Outside the embankment is the sluice-house, into which the 41 in. supply-pipe from the inlet tower is led, and where it is connected with the sluice valve for regulating the supply of water from the reservoir to the conduit pipes.

The conduit for conveying the water from the sluice-house into Bombay consists of cast-iron pipes, of 32 in. internal diameter, $\frac{15}{16}$ in. thick, and 12 ft. long, exclusive of the faucet, laid in trenches 5 ft. below the surface of the ground, and then well covered over with the soil again. The distribution of water throughout the town is effected by means of pipes varying in internal diameter from 28 in. to 3 in. The greater part of the pipes, both for the conduit and distribution services, were obtained from Messrs. Stewart and Bowser of Glasgow.

L

The rate at which the supply of water from the Vehar reservoir was calculated, was 20 gallons per head of population per day. This may doubtless be thought a small allowance for an Eastern city, but it must be remembered that the sources whence such supplies were formerly obtained still exist, and that 20 gallons per head per day was therefore in addition to the supply formerly enjoyed by the inhabitants of Bombay.

The Vehar Waterworks were completed and taken over by Government from the contractors on the 13th of May, 1859, and the reservoir began to fill immediately on the setting in of the ensuing rains. On the 1st of June following the gauge showed 32 ft. 7 in.; on the 2nd of July, the water had risen to 35 ft. 7 in.; on the 1st of August, to 43 ft. 8 in.; on the 2nd of September, to 48 ft. 4 in.; and by the 6th of October it had attained a height of 50 ft. 1 in. above the lip of the lowest inlet pipe. The real depth of the lake was, however, nearer 80 ft., about 30 ft. lying in the bottom of the valley.

The water of the reservoir was, on analysis, found to contain only 2.20 grains of saline matter in 10,000 grains of water, and this saline matter consisted of chloride of sodium, with a minute quantity of chloride of calcium.

During a greater part of the hot season of 1865 the Vehar water was in a more or less impure state, and animalcules and particles of aquatic plants were discovered in the water drawn from the distribution-pipes; aquatic vegetation was also so abundant in the neighbourhood of the inlet tower as to choke its strainers, and there was a layer of foul mud several inches thick in the lower part of the bed of the reservoir. The water drawn from near the bottom of the reservoir, through the lowest valve of the inlet tower, had an offensive odour, while that taken from the surface was nearly free from it; a sample of the water drawn from below for examination had lost its offensive smell when it arrived in Bombay. This general offensive condition of the water was no doubt caused by the decomposition of both vegetable and animal matter, the greater intensity of the foul odour at the greater depth being due to the water in contact with the mud at the bottom being more fully impregnated with the gas evolved during the putrefaction of organic matter, while this gas became dissipated or destroyed by oxidation when the water came into contact with the atmosphere. The water, though temporarily deteriorated, was found, on chemical analysis, after being freed from suspended impurities, to hold dissolved in each gallon only six-tenths of a grain of organic matter.

Although at the time of commencing these waterworks the population of Bombay was only between five and six hundred thousand, and it is now above eight hundred thousand, there is no reason to fear that the town will again suffer from the painful calamity of a scarcity of water, since, by raising the embankments which enclose the Vehar valley, the reservoir may be made capable of containing as much again as at present, and thus the supply of water from it be doubled.

The purchase of the Vehar estate by Government cost 15,000*l.*, and the amount of the several contracts for making the reservoir, laying the pipes, and supply of pipes and other materials, including the cost of freight to Bombay, were estimated, in the first instance, at 257,448*l.* 7s. 10d. The value of stores sent from England, including freight and shipping charges, up to the end of 1862, was 120,175*l.*, and the total cost of the works up to that date had amounted to 454,239*l.* Of this sum it has been determined, by Act II. of 1865, of the Bombay Council, that 373,005*l.* shall be repaid to Government by the municipality of the town of Bombay, by annual payments of 17,500*l.*, which sum shall include interest at 4 per cent. per annum on the unpaid portion of that sum, the balance being devoted to the formation of a sinking fund towards paying off the principal.

PUMPING ENGINE AT CINCINNATI.

We give, on Plate XV., an engraving of a direct-acting pumping engine recently completed at the Waterworks at Cincinnati, U.S., from the designs of Mr. George Shields, the engineer in charge. This engine has a cylinder 100 in. in diameter, with 12 ft. stroke, and it drives a double-acting pump 45 in. in diameter, the stroke being, of course, the same as that of the steam-cylinder. The steam-cylinder is placed directly over the pump, at a considerable height above the latter, and there is no balance-beam, as is usual in the case of direct-acting or " bull " engines. The air-pump is double acting, and is placed below the steam-cylinder; the air-pump, being worked direct from the steam-piston, as shown in the engraving. The condenser is situated on one side of the engine, at a short distance below the floor of the engine-room, and it is supported on beams built into the masonry. The valve-gear is of the Cornish kind. The engine-house is situated by the side of the river Ohio, and the suction-pipe is arranged as shown in the illustration, the gearing of the sluice near its mouth being worked by means of a pitch-chain leading to a hand-wheel in the engine-house, as shown. Both the suction and delivery pipes are provided with air-vessels, that belonging to the latter being of large size. The extreme rise and fall of the Ohio river at the part where the pump is situated is 60 ft., and the maximum lift against which the pump has to work is

170 ft. The engine is worked with very little expansion, and its pumping capacity is 800,000 gallons per hour. At present the engine is supplied with steam by a set of old boilers, which are not fully capable of doing the work; but this state of affairs will, no doubt, be altered. This pumping-engine at Cincinnati is, we believe, the largest yet erected in America.

MADRAS WATER SUPPLY.

Sir Arthur Cotton has persistently stated that the one great and paramount requirement throughout India is water; and although we may, perhaps, somewhat demur to accepting this assertion to the extent to which that officer intended it to apply, there can be no doubt entertained as to its correctness generally.

The supplying of Madras with an abundance of pure water is a question which has occupied the attention of the Government there for many years, having been often forcibly brought to its notice by the repeated complaints of the gradually increasing impurity of the water drawn from the wells, which at present form the only source of supply. The gradual deterioration of the Madras wells is notorious. The town is built upon a portion of the belt of silicious sand which runs along the Coromandel coast, and which, in its uncontaminated state, yields, nearly everywhere, a very pure fresh water; owing, however, to the filthy state of the surface of the ground and the constant flushing of drains, the porous subsoil has absorbed much sewage and other impurities, the result being that many of the wells are not only unfit for use, but offensive. From an analysis of the waters of the "Seven Wells" enclosure at the north side of Black Town, from which the troops in Fort Saint George are supplied with water, it appears that the amount of solid ingredients in one imperial gallon varies from 23.10 up to as high as 70.10 grains; the largest amount of organic matter contained in these waters is 7.85 grains, and of inorganic matter 64.40 grains per gallon, and of almost all the wells it was remarked that their waters gave clear evidence of the presence of animal life as well as vegetable growth, and in one instance animalculæ were discovered.

In 1855, Lieutenant (now Lieutenant-Colonel) O'Connell, of the Royal Engineers, having been deputed to investigate the subject of improved water supply to Madras, submitted a report, with plans and estimates, showing that a scheme for that purpose was perfectly feasible. No action was, however, taken on his proposals, nor on those subsequently put forward by others, until Mr. Fraser, C.E., suggested the probability of being able to improve upon Colonel

O'Connell's design, and he was forthwith directed to undertake a rein-vestigation of the whole project, the result of which was a report which has since been recommended for adoption.

The plan now proposed for introducing a supply of pure water into Madras is by throwing a dam, 600 ft. in length, across the Cortilliar river at a point about 12 miles from the Red Hills, and cutting thence a supply channel, $8\frac{1}{2}$ miles long, and with an inclination of 2 ft. to the mile, to the Cholavaram lake, which, it is proposed, should be enlarged by raising its level 6 yards above the present surplus weir. From the Cholavaram lake a channel, $2\frac{3}{4}$ miles in length, and with an inclination of 3 ft. per mile, would carry the water on to the Red Hill lake, which, it is also proposed, should be enlarged by raising its level to 5 yards above the present escape weir, and thence a delivery-channel would be cut to the Spur Tank in Madras, a portion of which it is proposed should be converted into the last settling reservoir.

The present population of Madras is estimated at about 470,000, and provision has been made for the storage of 40,000,000 cubic yards per annum, or an average of $37\frac{1}{4}$ gallons per head per day, from which, however, deductions would have to be made on account of eva-poration, waste, &c., from the several tanks, in estimating the amount available for actual use.

The discharge of the Cortilliar at the site of the proposed dam, during a portion of the north-east monsoon, has been ascertained to amount to about 450,000,000 cubic yards. The floods generally keep up their maximum height for four or five days, and then run about 3 ft. deep for thirty or forty days more, whence there would appear to be an ample supply obtainable for filling all the lakes. By placing the dam at the lowest possible point, the discharge due to 30 miles of the Cortilliar proper is secured, as well as that from the Trittani and Nagiri rivers, which latter streams include within their drainage area the greater portion of the Nagiri mountains, and their basins are about 770 square miles in extent.

The supply channel will cross two drainage streams which at present carry to the Cortilliar the surplus waters—amounting to about twenty millions of cubic yards per annum—from a large number of tanks which lie on the north of the railway, and which it is proposed to divert into the supply channel, thus furnishing an additional quantity for filling the lakes.

The Cholavaram and Red Hill lakes were both formed centuries ago, by bunding across valleys surrounded by low hills of laterite rock and gravel. They have been hitherto dependent for their supplies on the surface drainage of their respective basins during the monsoons;

with the additions now proposed to be made to the height of their
waste weirs, their cubical contents will be 36,427,473 and 101,981,815
yards respectively, the Cholavaram being raised 18 ft., and Red Hill
lake 15 ft. above the crown of its present calingula. The capacity of
the two lakes collectively will thus be 138,409,288 cubic yards. The
Mirassidars who own existing wet lands near the lakes possess an here-
ditary right to a certain portion of the water, and this would therefore
have to be deducted before calculating on the quantity actually available for the Madras water supply; but, after allowing for their rights
to this water, there would remain a storage capacity for 100,000,000
of cubic yards, which would give 60,000,000 available for irrigation
after supplying Madras.

Most of the waste land under these lakes is of a very fruitful character, consisting generally of an alluvial deposit; it is also well
situated for irrigation, as it descends in a slightly inclined plane towards the sea. Taking Sir Arthur Cotton's estimate of 7000 cubic
yards of water as sufficient to irrigate one acre of rice, the surplus
60,000,000 of cubic yards of water would be sufficient for 8571 acres,
which is, however, but about one-third of the extent of land available
for cultivation; and the entire project, therefore, includes irrigation as
well as water supply to Madras.

Dr. Wyndowe, the Government chemical examiner, after analysing
the water of the Red Hill lake, reported that, as regards sensible pro-
perties, the water was free from odour or taste, but cloudy (even after
filtration) from suspended impurities, but which would no doubt subside,
after a time, if the water were left at rest. Chemically speaking, he
considered it to be by far the best specimen of drinking water he had
examined at Madras. The salts held in solution amounted only to
6.98 grains per gallon, and the amount of organic impurity was not
great. The grosser particles held in suspension would, it is anticipated,
be deposited in Cholavaram lake, the finer particles in the Red Hill
lake, so that water comparatively pure would be delivered to the Spur
Tank, where it would pass through proper filtering-beds into the pure
water basin, which would be covered in. From this basin, which it is
proposed should be capable of holding three or four days' supply, the
water would pass from the pump-well, placed at some central point,
where it would be raised, probably, into an elevated cistern, and thence
distributed through iron pipes to the several parts of the city.

The present scheme, estimated to cost, irrespective of distribution,
63,752l., is principally intended to meet the requirements of the
northern portion of the town only; but there exists in connexion with
it an additional scheme for the separate supply of the southern quarters

of the town from the basins of the Kooum and Adyar rivers, as well as a plan for the junction of those two rivers and of the northern and southern portions of the East Coast Canal.

It has not yet been decided by what agency these works shall be carried out, although they have already been commenced by Government, who will probably desire to retain the irrigation portion in their own hands, as it promises to be very remunerative. The municipality of Madras is poor, and is already burdened with many obligations present and perspective, so that it is doubtful whether they will be in a position to carry out the more important part of the scheme by themselves. The demand for good water is, however, now urgent; and if water be not soon introduced from the country, the garrison and different public establishments in the town must be furnished with subterranean tanks for storing water from the roofs of the buildings. That, however, could at best but afford temporary relief; and as the larger work must ultimately be undertaken, the sooner means are devised for raising the required capital for that purpose, the better it will be both for the Government and the town.

THE CROSSNESS WORKS, METROPOLITAN MAIN DRAINAGE.

Those who have not seen the Crossness pumping-station have probably little idea of its extent, its architectural beauty, not to say splendour, nor of its almost entire freedom from any unpleasant odour from the vast mass of offensive matter upon which it is continually at work. When we visited the works, there was hardly any evidence to the senses of what was going on in the vast subterranean reservoirs, and in the thirty-two great pumps beneath the engine-house. It is not too much to say that, for size, loftiness, and especially in internal decoration, the Crossness engine-palace surpasses anything of the kind yet erected. Nor is there reason for believing that solidity or excellence of workmanship has been in any way sacrificed to display.

The sewage is brought to the Crossness pumping-station from Deptford by a circular sewer 11 ft. 6 in. in diameter inside, this sewer being laid under the ground at depths varying from about 1 ft. 6 in. to 78 ft. beneath the surface, the latter depth occurring in the course of its passage under Woolwich. For the greater part of its length this 11 ft. 6 in. sewer is formed of four rings of brickwork; but under Woolwich, where, as we have already mentioned, it is laid at a great depth, the thickness is increased to five rings. The sewer has a fall of 2 ft. per mile, and the sewage passes through it with a velocity of about four miles per hour.

The 11 ft. 6 in. sewer joins the various culverts with an easy curve, and from the point of junction an outlet leads direct to the river. This outlet passage is termed the deep outlet, and discharges the sewage 8 ft. below low-water mark, or about 26 ft. below high-water level. There are also two other high-level outlets, the use of which will be described presently; these latter discharge the sewage about 2 ft. below low-water level. At the junction of the sewer with the works at Crossness, penstocks or sliding-valves are introduced, by means of which the sewage can either be turned at once into the deep outlet, or can be caused to pass into the lowest story of a triple culvert, which is laid across the end of the reservoirs between them and the river, and parallel to the latter. The triple culvert consists of three culverts, one above the other; the lowest one, into which the sewage can be turned direct from the sewer, being 12 ft. 6 in. wide, by 9 ft. 3 in. high in the centre. The bottom of this culvert is formed by an invert 1 ft. $10\frac{1}{2}$ in. thick, and the sides by walls 3 ft. 9 in. thick. The top, which also forms the bottom of the middle culvert, consists of brick arches turned between cast-iron girders. The middle culvert is 13 ft. 9 in. wide by 7 ft. 6 in. high, and it is roofed over by York landing-stone carried by cast-iron girders, another layer of York landings, supported by the same girders, forming the floor of the top culvert. The last culvert is 13 ft. wide by 12 ft. 6 in. high in the centre, and has a semicircular top formed of four rings of brick-work, this top being strengthened by suitable counterforts. The manner in which these culverts are used we shall now proceed to describe.

As we have already said, the sewage arriving by the 11 ft. 6 in. sewer can be turned direct into the deep outlet, and thus discharged at low water; this, however, is but rarely done, the practice being to discharge the sewage at or near the time of high water. To enable this plan to be carried out, it is necessary to raise the sewage considerably above the level at which it is supplied by the sewer, and it is therefore, by means of a penstock, turned from the latter into the lowest culvert of the triple culvert which we have been describing. Each main penstock consists of a cast iron sliding-door or valve bearing against a seat, also of cast-iron. The door is $1\frac{1}{4}$ in. thick, and is strengthened by ribs at the back; it is raised by chains worked by gearing above the ground level. From the lowest culvert the sewage is led by two branches into the pump chambers, which are each 32 ft. 6 in. long by 21 ft. $7\frac{1}{2}$ in. wide, and are 42 ft. deep below the floor of the engine-house. This floor is, however, considerably raised above the surrounding ground level. By the pumps, which, together with the engines, we shall describe presently, the sewage is raised and discharged into the top story of the triple culvert, and by this it is led to the reservoirs.

The reservoirs are four in number, and hold altogether 4,840,000 cubic feet. This capacity, large as it is, is, however, less than that of the Barking Creek reservoirs, connected with the nothern outfall works, which hold 6,485,000 cubic feet. The reservoirs are arched over with brick vaultings, supported by brick piers, and each reservoir is furnished with sixteen openings or passages, 3 ft. 9 in. high, eight leading to the top and eight to the middle story of the triple culvert. Each of these passages is fitted, at the end next the reservoir, with a sliding cast-iron door or valve, bearing against a cast-iron seat, and capable of being raised or lowered by gearing above the ground level. By raising the valves belonging to the passages leading from the upper culvert, the sewage is allowed to flow from the latter into the reservoirs, where it remains until near the time of high water. The valves of the passages communicating with the middle culvert are then opened, and the sewage discharged, by the action of gravity, through this middle culvert into the deep outlet, whence it flows into the river. The bottom of the top culvert is slightly above the level of the floor of the reservoirs, whilst the bottom of the middle culvert is below that level. The middle culvert is also connected with the two high-level outlets mentioned above; these are generally only used to relieve the reservoirs in cases of emergency; they only lead as far as the river wall of the works, whereas the deep outlet is taken some distance out into the river. One of the high-level outlets was opened for a short time during our visit, the tide being nearly low at the time, and the powerful stream of black sewage which rushed from the mouth of the culvert certainly did not appear to be nice stuff to deal with.

On its way from the lowest culvert to the pump-chambers, the sewage is passed through screens which separate the coarser matters from it. The first of these screens consists of 4 in. meshes, and the last of parallel bars 2 in. apart. Originally, the chambers in which the screens are placed were furnished with filth-hoists, worked by the pumping engines, these hoists each consisting of a number of buckets fixed to endless chains passing over drums at the top and bottom of the lift. The buckets of these hoists were intended to raise the solid matters from the bottom of their chambers, and at the same time clear the screens in front of which they were placed. It was, however, found that the power required to work them was very great, and that, owing to the complicated manner in which rags and other refuse matters entwined themselves about the bars of the screens, they did not perform their work efficiently. Their use has consequently now been abandoned, and the solid matters are raised from the screen-chambers by buckets filled by hand labour, and hand labour is also employed to clear the screens themselves.

Of the pumping engines and boilers at Crossness we give engravings on Plates XVI. and XVII. respectively. The pumping engines, which are four in number, and are named the "Victoria," the "Prince Consort," the "Alexandra," and the "Albert Edward," were made by Messrs. James Watt and Co., from designs furnished by Mr. Bazalgette, and are fine specimens of workmanship. They are beam engines, each having the cylinder placed under one end of the beam and the fly-wheel shaft under the other, whilst the pump plungers, of which there are eight to each engine, are worked from points on the beam between the centre and ends. As the engines are all alike, a description of one of them will serve for all. The beam is made double, the two parts, which are 6 ft. deep in the middle, being about 5 ft. apart. The length between end centres is 40 ft. 6 in., whilst the horizontal distance between the centres of the cylinder and crank shaft is 40 ft. The cylinder is 4 ft. in diameter, with a stroke of 9 ft., and the piston-rod is coupled to the one end of the beam by the ordinary arrangement of parallel motion. The connecting-rod, which is of wrought iron, and is 28 ft. 9 in. long between end centres, is coupled to the other end of the beam and to an overhung crank on a shaft carrying a fly-wheel 27 ft. in diameter. The rim of the fly-wheel is furnished with teeth for a portion of its width, these teeth being employed for turning the engine round by hand by the aid of suitable gearing.

The steam and exhaust valves are of the double-beat class, and their spindles are connected to arms fixed to rods sliding vertically in guides fixed to the cylinder. The lower ends of these rods bear upon cams placed on a cam shaft running under the floor of the engine-room, close to the back of the cylinder, and parallel to the fly-wheel shaft; this cam shaft receiving its motion, through a pair of bevel wheels, from a longitudinal shaft, which is in its turn driven from the fly-wheel shaft by means of bevel gearing. The cams for moving the steam valves are made with three steps for cutting off the steam at different points in the stroke, and, by means of an arrangement of levers, either of these steps can be brought under the ends of the steam-valve rods at pleasure. This valve gear appears to work exceedingly well, as the annexed diagram, which has been reduced from one supplied to us by Messrs. James Watt and Co., will show. This diagram was taken from the bottom of the cylinder of the "Albert Edward" engine on the 30th of May, 1866, the engine at the time that it was taken making $12\frac{1}{2}$ double strokes per minute, and the steam being

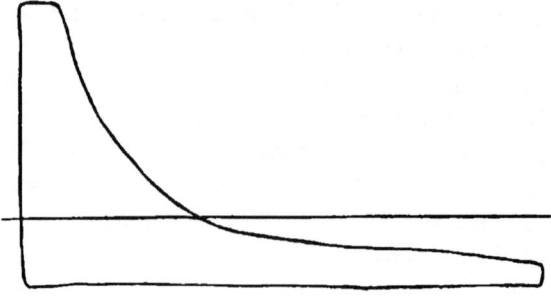

cut off at 13 in. of the 9 ft. stroke.   The maximum steam pressure in the diagram is 29¼ lb., and the maximum vacuum rather over 12 lb., whilst the average vacuum is 11 lb., and the average effective pressure on the piston throughout the stroke 13·6 lbs.   At a piston speed of 225 ft. per minute this gives an indicated horse-power of rather over 201 horses, the engines being each rated at 125 horse-power nominal. The vacuum would, no doubt, be higher if good water could be obtained for condensing; at present the condensing water is drawn from the river, at what, in warm weather, is a comparatively high temperature; but an artesian well is in course of being sunk, from which, it is hoped, that an abundant supply of suitable water will be obtained.   Of this well we shall speak presently.   We have by us another indicator diagram taken from the top of the cylinder of the "Alexandra" engine during a late trial; this trial lasted three and a half days, during which time a duty was obtained of 87,000,000 lb. raised 1 ft. high by the consumption of 1 cwt. of coal.   This diagram is almost exactly similar to the one of which we have given an illustration, the steam being cut off at the same point of the stroke; it is, however, a little fuller, the maximum pressure being 35¼ lb.   It was taken whilst the engine was working at 11 double strokes per minute, which is about the average speed.

To return, however, to our description of one of the engines :—the parallel motion, in addition to being coupled to the main beam, is also attached to another beam 16 ft. long between end centres, the other end of this beam being carried by a pair of vibrating links hung from the engine frames.   To the centre of this beam is coupled the air-pump rod, which therefore has a stroke of 4 ft. 6 in., the diameter of the pump barrel being 2 ft.   The rod of the cold-water pump is also connected to the same beam, the point of attachment being 4 ft. from the fulcrum.   The cold-water pump thus has a stroke of 2 ft. 3 in., whilst its diameter is 1 ft. 6 in.   The distances of the centres of the air-pump and cold-water pump barrels from the centre of the cylinder are 7 ft. 10 in. and 11 ft. 9¾ in. respectively.

The two main pump barrels are each 12 ft. in diameter, and are each fitted with four plungers. The plungers, of 4 ft. 6 in. in diameter, and their rods are coupled to the beam in pairs—two pairs on each side of the main centre. The distances from the main centre to the points of attachment of the plunger-rods are 5 ft. 0¾ in. and 10 ft. 1½ in. respectively, so that two pairs of the plungers have a stroke of 2 ft. 3 in., and two pairs a stroke of 4 ft 6 in. The plunger-rods are coupled to crossheads working in guides fixed above the pump-barrels, and any of them can be disconnected at pleasure, the plungers so detached being secured at the lowest point of their stroke by an arrangement provided for the purpose (see Fig. 8, Plate XVI.). The plungers are made of cast iron, the metal being 1½ in. thick, and they are each provided with a central rod, cottered into them, and coupled to the crossheads above mentioned. The pump barrels are also made of cast iron, and are formed in four rings; their total height is 25 ft., and they rest upon cast-iron girders, which are in their turn supported by stone blocks bedded upon concrete.

Around the lower part of the pump-barrels are formed openings, each 3 ft. high and 10 in. wide, for the admission of the sewage. The suction-valve gratings are fixed in the barrels at a height of 16 ft. above the bottoms, the valves being flap-valves (see Figs. 4 and 5, Plate XVI), formed of leather held between two ½ in. wrought-iron plates. The openings in the suction-valve gratings are, except where reduced to suit the curve of the pump-barrels, each 1 ft. 6 in. by 9 in. The delivery-valves (Fig. 6 and 7, Plate XV.) are also flap-valves, and are hung on a vertical grating fixed to a branch leading from the top of each pump-barrel. Each of these gratings has twenty-four openings, each 1 ft. 6 in. by 12 in. The engines are arranged in the engine-house in pairs, so that the fly-wheels are situated in the four corners of the house, and the pumps of each pair of adjoining engines discharge the sewage into an iron passage 10 ft. high by 11 ft. 6 in. wide, placed on the top of the wall dividing the two pump-chambers. From this iron passage two culverts, each 9 ft. high, and 4 ft. 9 in. wide, lead to the upper story of the triple culvert which we have already described. The *maximum* lift is 33 ft. 6 in., of which height the sewage is raised 12 ft. by suction.

As we have just mentioned, the four engines are placed in a single engine-house. This is a handsome building, standing back some distance from the river front of the works, and having its floor considerably elevated above the level of the surrounding ground. The interior is very tastefully decorated, and altogether we think that the whole forms the best specimen of what may be called " engine-house architecture " that we have yet seen.   At the back of the engine-house, and joined to it, is the boiler-house, in which are placed the twelve Cornish boilers which supply the engines with steam.   These boilers were made by Messrs. D. Adamson and Co., and are arranged below the ground level, in two rows, six in each row.   The firing space between the rows is 40 ft. wide, and it is traversed by rails laid to a 3 ft. gauge, on which run the wagons which bring the coal from the vaults.   It was originally intended to have made a raised platform down the centre of the firing space for the conveyance of the coal; but the arrangement which has been adopted is that of discharging the coal into vaults formed by the side of the boiler-house and bringing it thence to the boilers by means of the wagons above mentioned.   From the floor of the boiler-house, a small tunnel, provided with a tramway, is led to the outskirts of the works for the discharge of ashes.   The coals are brought to the works by water, and being unloaded at the river wall, are conveyed to the vaults by small wagons running on tramways laid to a 3 ft. gauge.

The boilers are of the single-flued Cornish class, 6 ft. in diameter and 30 ft. long, and are, as we have said, arranged in two rows, 40 ft. apart, each row consisting of 6 boilers, placed side by side at a distance of 9 ft. from centre to centre.   As the boilers are all similar, it will only be necessary that we should give the particulars of one of them, referring for this purpose to the figures on Plate XVII.

The flue is 3 ft. 3 in. in diameter for a length of 10 ft. from the front end plate, and is then decreased by means of a taper ring about 2 ft. long, to a diameter of 2 ft. 11 in.   In this latter portion of the flue are placed two vertical and six diagonal water-tubes, each 8 in. in diameter.   These tubes, which are introduced to facilitate the circulation of the water as well as to obtain more heating surface, are flanged over at the ends for attachment to the flue plates.   The centre line of the front part of the flue is 10 in. below the centre line of the boilers.   The flue plates, the thickness of which has not been supplied to us by the makers, are each formed by means of a welded longitudinal joint into a solid ring; the ends of these rings are then flanged over so as to form the patent seam, of which an enlarged section is given in our illustration above the longitudinal section of the boiler.   In this seam, which has been extensively used by Messrs. Adamson and Co., with excellent results, a stiffening ring is introduced between the flanges of the flue plates, as shown in the sketch.   All the rivet holes in these rings and flanges, as well as all those in the boiler shells, are drilled; the drilling

being performed after the plates are bent and put together, so that
perfectly fair holes are obtained.   The plates of the outer shells are
$\frac{3}{8}$ in. thick, and are united to the end plates by 3 in. angle iron rings.
At the front end the angle iron ring is placed outside, and at the back end
inside the boiler, as shown in Fig. 1.   The end plates are each strengthened by four gusset stays, extending about 2 ft. 8 in. along the boiler
shell, and arranged as shown on Figs. 2 and 4, and also by an angle
iron ring, and two longitudinal stays, placed as shown by the same
figures.   A dome, 2 ft. 3 in diameter, and 2 ft. 9 in. in total height, is
placed on the top of the boiler, the hole in the boiler shell by which the
dome is placed in communication with the barrel being 14 in. in
diameter, and strengthened by a ring riveted round it.   The boiler has
a manhole, 1 ft. 4 in. in diameter, formed in the top of it, about 9 ft.
6 in. from the front end.   The manhole cover and ring are of cast
iron, and a wrought-iron strengthening ring is interposed between the
cast-iron ring and the boiler shell.

The boiler is fitted with two 3 in. safety valves, one of the valves
being loaded by a spring and the other by a weighted lever.   The
valves are placed on the top of a short cast-iron column, 5 in. in
diameter inside.   The steam pipe leading from the top of the dome is
8 in. in diameter, and is furnished with a screw-down valve, from the
casing of which a similar pipe leads to a cast-iron pipe, 18 in., placed
over each row of boilers.   The boiler is furnished with two gauge
glasses, and a float connected with an alarm whistle is also supplied,
the whistle coming into action when the water level becomes too low.
The scum cock is connected with a perforated pipe, which extends round
the boiler near the water level, as shown by Figs. 1 and 4; and the
blow-off cock is connected with a similar pipe running along the bottom
of the boiler under the flue, as shown in the same figure.   Near the
front end of the boiler, the pipe last mentioned is bent down into a
casting 12 in. deep, 6 in. in diameter at the upper and 3 in. in diameter
at the lower end; from the bottom of this a pipe is led to the blow-off
cock, which is conveniently placed under the foot-plate, and from it a
pipe is led to a 12 in. collecting pipe, running along in front of the
row of boilers, as shown in Fig. 1.   A pipe is also led from the scum
cock to the same collecting pipe.   The feed water is supplied to the
boilers by means of a 6 in. pipe placed in front of each row of boilers,
as shown in Fig. 1, branch pipes furnished with cocks leading from this
pipe to the check feed valve of each boiler.   A pressure gauge is fixed
on the front of each boiler, as shown by Figs. 1 and 2.

The dead plate is 1 ft. 2 in. long, and placed 1 ft. 5$\frac{1}{4}$ in. above the
bottom of the flue.   The firegrate is 7 ft. long, thus having an area of

$22\frac{3}{4}$ square feet. The firebars are arranged in two lengths, and are carried by cast-iron bearers ; the bridge is also supported upon a casting, as shown in Fig. 1. The top of the bridge is 1 ft. 3 in. below the crown of the flue, and the area over it is therefore equal to about 2.8 square feet. The firedoor frame is furnished with two firedoors, each of which is fitted with an arrangement for the admission of air through it, as shown by Fig. 2. In front of the ashpit is placed a curved plate, fitted with ventilators for the admission of air, this plate being hinged at the bottom, so that it can be turned down when it is required to clean out the ashpit. The space enclosed by this plate is in communication with a flue leading to the sewage reservoirs, this flue being fitted with a damper, as shown by Fig. 1. By opening this damper and closing the ventilators in the plate in front of the ashpit, the air for the fire is drawn from the sewage reservoir, this arrangement being used when the reservoirs are being filled, or when it is required to free them from bad air.

The draught from the internal flue is first led along the bottom of the boiler and then split and returned along the sides; the form of the flues is shown by Figs. 4 and 3, the former being a transverse section through the boiler and flues, and the latter a section through the flues only beyond the inner end of the boiler. The bottom flue is 3 ft. wide between the side walls, and 1 ft. 6 in. deep below the bottom of the boiler ; its sectional area is thus slightly over 5 square feet. The distance between the outside walls of the side flues is 7 ft. 6 in., and the total height of the flues 3 ft. 8 in., the tops being 12 in. above the centre line of the boiler. The least distance between the boiler and the side walls of the flue is thus 9 in., and the sectional area of each flue is about $4\frac{1}{4}$ square feet, the corners being rounded. The flues are all lined with firebrick, and the side flues are provided with doors at the front end for the removal of soot and ashes ; these are shown in Fig. 2. The short vertical flue which connects the internal flue with that under the barrel of the boiler is 3 ft. 4 in. wide at the upper part, and 3 ft. wide at the bottom, the end wall being 2 ft. from the end of the boiler. Figs. 1 and 5 will show clearly the arrangement of the bottom and side flues ; and from these it will be seen that the former only reaches to within about 2 ft. 4 in. of the front end of the boiler, whilst the latter are carried nearly the whole length, the thickness of the front supporting wall being 14 in. The main part of the boiler is supported upon six cast iron brackets, of the shape shown in Fig. 4. These are placed three on the top of each side wall of the bottom flue, the positions of them being shown by Fig. 1. The boiler flues are connected with a chimney, of excellent architectural design, 159 ft. 9 in. high, and 8 ft.

3 in. in diameter inside.   The chimney is at a distance of 110 ft. from
the centre of the engine-house, and is connected with the boilers by a
semicircular topped flue, 9 ft. 9 in. high, and 5 ft. 6 in. wide inside.   In
conclusion, we may say that the boilers at Crossness are, both in their
construction and setting, excellent examples of the best modern boiler-
making practice.

The boilers at Crossness had been found to work extremely well ;
with good Welsh coal, 10 lb. of water have been evaporated in them
by a pound of fuel.   At present, Tanfield coal is being extensively used
at Crossness, and is found to answer well; the evaporative power being
little below that of the Welsh coals, whilst the price is considerably
less.   We believe that it is now being supplied at the works at 14s. 6d.
per ton.   Generally speaking, six boilers are in use at one time, these
supplying steam to the three engines which are usually worked.

In the cement testing-house at the Crossness works is situated Mr.
Grant's simple lever testing-machine.   Mr. Grant is the resident engineer of the South Drainage Works, and during the past seven years he
has tested samples taken from every lot of cement delivered for use.
During the last six years the strain, which a 1½ in. square bar of the
cement delivered is required to stand, has been 500 lbs., and upwards of
70,000 tons of cement have been received and used under this stipula-
tion.   At Crossness are stored away an immense number of samples all
duly ticketed, some of these being preserved in order to test the effect
of age.   All the mortar used about the works consists of equal parts,
by bulk, of cement and sand, whilst the concrete is formed of one part
of cement to eight of ballast.   In some places the proportion of cement
in the concrete has been increased to one-sixth.   A very large proportion of the cement has been supplied by the Burham Company.

The artesian well which is being sunk at Crossness is intended to draw
water from the green sand which crops out at Farnborough, about 400 ft.
above the level of the works at Crossness.   A depth of 709 ft. has already (June, 1866,) been reached, of which depth about 100 ft. consists
of a well lined with iron cylinders, a further length of about 400 ft. of a
bore containing 18 in. wrought-iron piping, and the remaining depth of
a 13 in. bore through the chalk.   The surface water has been carefully
excluded and, as yet, no other water has been obtained ; indeed, it is
not likely that it will be until the chalk is pierced, unless by accident a
fault is struck.   The well is being sunk by Mr. Clark, under a sub-con-
tract from Mr. Webster, who is the contractor for the whole works.
It is expected that the water when reached will rise to the surface, and
there certainly seems every probability that this will be the case.
Good water is much wanted at Crossness, as the river water at present

used, being brackish, is very bad for the boilers, whilst its temperature prevents a thoroughly good vacuum from being obtained in the condensers.

From the cement testing-house and well we proceeded to the river wall, and witnessed the discharge of the sewage (to which we have already alluded) from one of the high-level outlets. The river wall itself is a fine piece of work. It is founded on oval cylinders, each about 8 ft. by 13 ft., and placed about 18 ft. apart from centre to centre along the line of the wall. These cylinders were sunk down to the gravel and partly filled in with concrete; the upper parts were then removed and arches turned between them, and upon these the river wall was built. In concluding our description of the pumping station at Crossness we cannot help remarking upon the thoroughness with which the whole of the work has been carried out—a thoroughness which reflects the utmost credit upon both the engineer and the contractor.

THE CABIN JOHN BRIDGE.

The Washington Aqueduct—a work of which Quartermaster-General Montgomery C. Meigs is the chief engineer—was projected and constructed between the years 1852 and 1859, for the purpose of supplying to Georgetown and Washington water taken from the river Potomac at a point about eleven miles above the last-mentioned city. The aqueduct consists for the main part of its length of a masonry conduit 9 ft. in internal diameter, this conduit being carried, partly through tunnels, partly through excavations, and partly on embankments and bridges, a length of $11\frac{1}{28}$ miles from the source of supply to a receiving reservoir, situated near the Potomac river, on the boundary of Maryland and Columbia, and thence to a distributing reservoir near Georgetown. From the latter reservoir a large iron main leads to Georgetown and thence to the Capitol, the total length of the aqueduct, including these mains, being $16\frac{1}{8}$ miles. The fall of the masonry conduit averages 9 in. per mile, and the aqueduct is capable of supplying to the town reservoir 100,000,000 gallons per day.

It has been the object in carrying out the work to avoid unnecessary expenditure by constructing all parts in as simple a manner as possible without regard to external display. Thus the various water-gates and pipe-vaults have in most cases been arranged within the masonry embankments; and thus, whilst the fittings are out of the reach of frost, much of the expense which would have been incurred, by the erection of gate-houses, &c., above ground, has been saved. We shall not, however, now enter more minutely into the constructive details

M

of the Washington Aqueduct, but shall for the present confine our attention to one of the principal works on the line of the conduit from the source of the supply to the receiving reservoir; namely, the bridge over Cabin John Creek—a creek which joins the river Potomac about seven miles above Washington.

The Cabin John Bridge, of which we give engravings on Plates XVIII. and XIX., is a stone-arched bridge, of greater span than any other in existence, its clear span being 220 ft., or 20 ft. greater than that of the Grosvenor Bridge at Chester. The arch is an arc of a circle of 134.2852 ft. radius, and its rise is 57.2624 ft. The general appearance of the bridge will be seen from the perspective view on Plate XVIII., whilst on Plate XIX., Fig. 1, is a side elevation; Fig. 2, a longitudinal section; Fig. 3, a sectional plan; Fig. 4, a transverse section through the eastern abutment (or that on the right-hand side of the engraving), taken partly through the springing of the arch; Fig. 5, an enlarged section of the cornice; Fig. 6, a transverse section through the crown of the arch; Fig. 7, an elevation of the western end of the bridge; and Fig. 8, a transverse section through the third relieving arch of the western abutment.

The intrados of the arch is, as we have said, struck with a radius of 134.2852 ft., whilst the radius of the extrados is 143.2695 ft., the depth of the voussoirs being 6 ft. 2 in. at the springings, and 4 ft. 2 in. at the crown. Outside the voussoirs is another series of arch stones, which make up the total thickness of the arch at the springings to 20 ft., this thickness diminishing towards the crown, as shown in the figures. The width of the bridge on the face of the arch is 20 ft. 4 in. The abutments are formed by the solid rock on each side of the creek, the face of this rock being stepped down, as shown in Fig. 2, and the steps filled in with concrete on which the footings of the arch bed. The channel through which the water is conveyed consists of a conduit of circular section, 9 ft. in diameter inside and 2 in. thick, this conduit being embedded in the masonry of the bridge, as shown in the sections. The haunches and abutments of the bridge are lightened by relieving arches, these arches, of which there are five on the western and four on the eastern side, as shown in our engravings, extending through half the thickness of the bridge.

The centring on which the arch was constructed was supported from temporary piers formed in the bed of the creek, as shown in Fig. 2, the vertical timbers bearing upon these piers, and the bracing connecting them carrying a series of struts radiating to the lines of timbers beneath the lagging boards. The keystone was inserted in mid-winter, and the centres were not struck until some ten or twelve months later;

and it may be remarked that at times the rise of temperature lifted the arch off the centring. When the centring was struck, careful observations were made to discover if any settlement took place; but none was noticed.

The Cabin John Bridge is altogether a bold work, and it was designed by Quartermaster-General Montgomery C. Meigs, who is, as we have stated, the engineer-in-chief to the Washington Aqueduct, and to whom we are indebted for the drawings from which our illustrations have been prepared. The assistant engineer on that division of the aqueduct to which the bridge belongs was Mr. Alfred L. Rives.

WATER-PIPE BRIDGE, WASHINGTON AQUEDUCT.

We give, on Plate XX., an engraving showing the singular " pipe bridge," over Georgetown Creek, at Washington, U.S., and which carries the waters of the Washington Aqueduct into the American capital. Quartermaster-General Montgomery C. Meigs, the engineer of this work, has furnished us with a large number of photographs and original drawings, from which we have made our selection, and we shall describe the " pipe bridge " by extracting a portion of a paper read by Mr. Colburn, in May, 1863, at the Institution of Civil Engineers :

" In 1858, an aqueduct bridge was erected at Washington by Captain Meigs, of the United States Engineers, who used for this work two arched ribs formed of water-pipes, through which the water flows, the pipes being circular in section, as that form encloses the greatest quantity of water with the least amount of iron. The span of this bridge is 200 ft., the rise being 20 ft.; and the width of the bridge over all is 28 ft. The pipes are 4 ft. in diameter inside, and 1½ in. thick. They are lined with staves of resinous pine, 3 in. thick, to prevent the freezing of the water. The pipes are not cast to the curve of the arch, but are in straight lengths of about 12 ft., with flanged joints, faced in planes parallel to the corresponding radii of the arch. At the skewbacks, the ends of the pipes are faced to large conical bases admitting the water, and resting upon the masonry. There is no allowance for expansion or contraction. The roadway is of timber, supported on spandrils formed of rolled wrought-iron beams 9 in. deep, and weighing 90 lbs. per yard. The bridge was tested with the arched ribs filled with water, and with a load of 125 lb. per square foot upon the roadway. The weight of each arched rib, when filled with water, is about 160 tons ; that of the spandrils of each rib and of one-half of the roadway is about 30 tons ; while the test load was equal to about 160 tons on each half of the roadway, making the whole weight about

350 tons on each rib. The thrust of one-half of this weight upon each abutment would be about 470 tons, and as there are 238½ square inches of sectional area of iron in the pipes, this would correspond to a strain of about 2 tons per square inch. This strain, while it includes that due to the weight of the water in the pipes, is exclusive of that due to its pressure. The pipes were proved to a pressure of 300 lb. per square inch."

The pine lining of the pipes has since been removed, as it was found, that the water never froze, no matter how cold the weather, and the bridge was affected to a much greater extent by changes of temperature than when the water was allowed to flow in contact with the metal of the pipes.

THE ROQUEFAVOUR AQUEDUCT.

The Aqueduct at Roquefavour is situated on the line of a canal constructed for the purpose of conveying to Marseilles a supply of water derived from the river Durance. The Durance is a stream rising in the Alps and flowing into the Rhone, and is separated from Marseilles by three low mountain ranges, the numerous ramifications of which formed considerable obstacles to the construction of the canal. As long ago as the year 1507 it was proposed to supply Marseilles with water from the Durance, but it was not until more than three hundred years after that date that anything definite was done. In 1836 M. de Mont Richer was commissioned by the inhabitants of Marseilles to make the necessary surveys, and in 1838, the requisite sanction having been obtained, the execution of the work was entrusted to him.

The canal of Marseilles has a total length of 51 miles, and its construction involved the execution of many works of great magnitude, of which that forming the subject of the present notice is the principal. The Roquefavour Aqueduct, of which the figures on Plate XXI. represent an elevation and transverse section, is constructed across the valley of the Are, about five miles from Aix. It was described (principally from some particulars furnished by M. C. Nepveu) in a paper by Mr. George Rennie, read before the Institution of Civil Engineers in 1855, in the course of the discussion on which a communication from the engineer, M. de Mont Richer, containing a short account of its construction, was also brought forward.

The aqueduct is composed of three tiers, the first consisting of twelve arches, 49.21 ft. span, and 111.87 ft. high from the standard level of the river; the second of fifteen arches, 52.49 ft. span, and 123.36 ft. high; and the third tier of fifty-three arches, 16.4 ft. span, and 35.92 ft. high to the top of the parapet. The total height of the parapet above the level of the river is therefore about 272 ft.; but, measured from the lowest part of the foundation, it is about 305 ft., while its total length is about 393 metres, or nearly 1200 ft. The width of the lowest range of arches between faces is 16.07 ft., this width being diminished in the upper tier of arches to 14.76 ft. The piers of the first range are at their bases 18.04 ft. wide by 21.32 ft. thick in the line of the bridge, and they diminish upwards with a batter of 1 in 66, so that their thickness at the springing of the arches is 19.68 ft. The piers of the second tier of arches are 15.91 ft. in breadth by 17.38 ft. in thickness, and those of the third range 14.76 ft. by 6.56 ft. The piers of the two lowest ranges are, as shown on Plate XXI., furnished with counter-forts, these having, from the base line to the springing of the first arches, a batter of 1 in 12½. From that point to the springing of the second tier, the batter is 1 in 16⅔, and for the remainder of their height it is 1 in 25.

Above the haunches of the first row of arches a semicircular passage, 10.82 ft. span, has been left in order to lighten the structure, and a footway is formed over the first arcades, an opening, 3.28 ft. wide by 6.56 ft. high, being formed in each of the piers of the second range. The piers are all founded on the solid rock, the greatest depth to which it was necessary to excavate in order to reach this being 32.8 ft. below the low-water level of the river. The width of the aqueduct channel is 7.54 ft. at the top, and 6.56 ft. at the bottom, the average thickness of the face walls being 3.6 ft. The channel is laid with a fall of 1 in 250, and a cornice, furnished with a parapet, forms a passage on each side of it. Hard cut stone has been employed for the face walls of the aqueduct and piers, while the body of the arches and the backing of the haunches consist of rubble masonry. The total cost of the aqueduct was 148,000l., that of the whole canal being given by M. Pascal, the engineer to the port of Marseilles, as 800,000l. The aqueduct was commenced on the 6th of August, 1839, and completed on the 30th of June, 1846, the whole of the canal being finished in June, 1847. All the works connected with it were designed by M. de Mont Richer, and there is no doubt but that they will long remain to give evidence of his energy and skill.

THE END.

N

LONDON:
PRINTED BY C. WHITING, BEAUFORT HOUSE, STRAND.

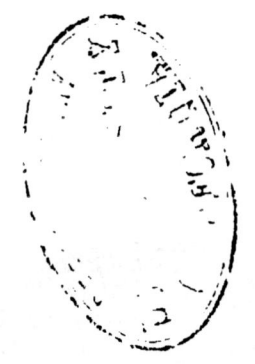

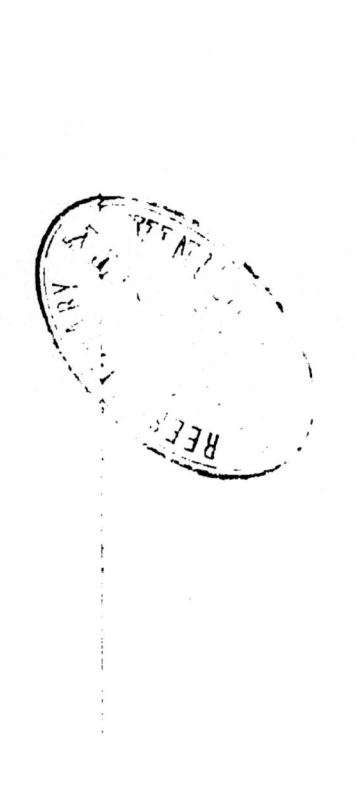

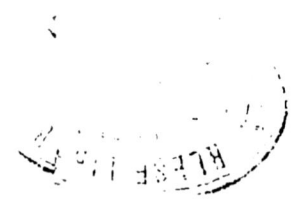

Lightning Source UK Ltd.
Milton Keynes UK
UKOW022101040412

190191UK00004B/47/P